SHAPING A NEW
ECONOMIC RELATIONSHIP

SHAPING A NEW ECONOMIC RELATIONSHIP

The Republic of Korea
and the United States

Edited by
JONGRYN MO and
RAMON H. MYERS

HOOVER INSTITUTION PRESS
Stanford University
Stanford, California

Hoover Institution Press Publication No. 417

Copyright © 1993 by the Board of Trustees of the
    Leland Stanford Junior University

First printing, 1993
99 98 97 96 95 94 93   9 8 7 6 5 4 3 2 1
Simultaneous first paperback printing, 1993
99 98 97 96 95 94 93   9 8 7 6 5 4 3 2 1

Manufactured in the United States of America

The paper used in this publication meets the minimum requirements
of American National Standard for Information Sciences—Permanence
of Paper for Printed Library Materials, ANSI Z39.48–1984. ⊗

Library of Congress Cataloging-in-Publication Data

  Shaping a new economic relationship : the Republic of Korea and the
United States / edited by Jongryn Mo and Ramon H. Myers.
        p.   cm. — (Hoover Institution Press publication ; 417)
  "The papers in this volume were presented at the U.S.-Korea
Economic Relations Conference, held at the Hoover Institution
December 5–7, 1991"—Ackn.
  Includes bibliographical references and index.
  ISBN 0-8179-9251-0. — ISBN 0-8179-9252-9 (pbk.)
  1. Korea (South)—Foreign economic relations—United States—
Congresses.   2. United States—Foreign economic relations—Korea
(South)—Congresses.   I. Mo, Jongryn, 1961– . II. Myers, Ramon
Hawley, 1929– . III. Series.
HF1602.5.Z4U67   1993
337.5195073—dc20   93-24019
                                                             CIP

Contents

Contributors

BYUNG-IL CHOI received his doctorate in economics from Yale University and is currently a senior fellow of the Korea Information Society Development Institute and a special adviser to the Republic of Korea's minister of communications. Since 1990 he has represented the ROK in several telecommunications trade negotiations.

J. MICHAEL FINGER, lead economist of the World Bank's trade policy program, earned his Ph.D. in economics from the University of North Carolina. Following service as senior economist with the United Nations Conference on Trade and Development, from 1974 to 1980 he was director of the U.S. Treasury Department's Office of Policy Research and deputy assistant secretary for research and policy planning. In spring 1990 he was a visiting professor of international economics at the Stockholm School of Economics.

JEFFREY A. FRANKEL is a professor of economics at the University of California at Berkeley (where he is also director of the Center for International and Development Economics Research), as well as a research associate and the associate director for international finance and macroeconomics of the National Bureau of Economic Research.

From 1983 to 1984 he served as senior staff economist on the U.S. President's Council of Economic Advisers, with responsibility for international economic policy. In 1988 and 1989 he was a visiting professor of public policy at the Kennedy School of Government at Harvard University. He has often been a visiting scholar at the Institute for International Economics, the International Monetary Fund, and the Federal Reserve Board; and has held visiting appointments at the Federal Reserve Bank of San Francisco, the World Bank, and Yale University.

IN-JUNE KIM, who received his Ph.D. in economics from Harvard University, has been a visiting associate professor in Dartmouth College's Department of Economics (1986–87) and a visiting research fellow of Japan's Foundation for Advanced Information and Research (1988). He is currently the editor of the *Korean Economic Journal*, a member of the Financial Development Deliberation Board of the Republic of Korea (ROK) Ministry of Finance, and a professor in the Department of International Economics at Seoul National University.

KIHWAN KIM earned his doctorate in economics from the University of California (UC) at Berkeley and has since then had wide experience in academia, government service, and business. He has taught economics at a number of American universities, including UC at Berkeley. He was president of the Korea Development Institute during 1982–1983 and has served as the ROK's vice-minister of trade and industry (1983–86) and secretary-general of its International Economic Policy Council (1984–86). He is currently the senior adviser at Kim & Chang, a leading legal and management consulting firm in Korea.

OKYU KWON was an economist in the Economics and Research Department of the World Bank from 1985 to 1987. He has held numerous leadership positions in the ROK's Economic Planning Board, of whose Bilateral Trade Division he is currently the director.

JONGRYN MO, a specialist in international political economics, is an assistant professor of government at the University of Texas at Austin and a research fellow of the Hoover Institution.

RAMON H. MYERS is a senior fellow of the Hoover Institution and curator-scholar of its East Asian Collection.

MARCUS NOLAND, who received his Ph.D. from Johns Hopkins University, is a research fellow of the Institute for International Economics in Washington, D.C., and a visiting assistant professor at Johns Hopkins University. From 1990 to 1992 he was an assistant professor in the Department of Economics of the University of Southern California, and he has been a visiting professor in Saitama University's Graduate School of Policy Science (1988–89) and a visiting research fellow of the Korea Development Institute (1991). He has received fellowships from the Japan Society for the Promotion of Science and the Council on Foreign Relations. In addition, he has served as a consultant to the World Bank, the New York Stock Exchange, and the Advisory Committee on Trade Policy and Negotiations.

HI-TAEK SHIN, who received his J.S.D. from Yale University in 1990, is a partner in Kim & Chang.

MARION SPINA, an attorney, was active in the American Chamber of Commerce in Korea; he now practices law at Bannerman and Spina, Washington, D.C.

YEN-KYUN WANG is a professor in the Department of Economics at Chung Ang University in Seoul and a visiting scholar in Stanford University's Department of Economics.

Acknowledgments

The papers in this volume were presented at the U.S.-Korea Economic Relations Conference, held at the Hoover Institution December 5–7, 1991. The conference was organized by Ramon Myers and Jongryn Mo as part of a Korean studies initiative at the Hoover Institution.

The Hoover Institution is indebted to the Posco Educational Foundation of the Pohang Iron & Steel Co., LTD. of Pohang, Korea, for significant financial support toward this conference and publishing this volume. The Korea Foundation, whose support was instrumental in establishing the Korean Studies Program at the Hoover Institution, also helped bring this volume to fruition.

The Korean initiative seeks to sponsor research and dialogue through conferences, scholar exchanges, and the publication of timely articles and books. We gratefully acknowledge the generosity of the Korea Foundation and its president, Son Chu-Whan, and the Posco Educational Foundation and its chairman, Myungsik Chung. Our thanks to Tim McGuire for his excellent work in preparing the manuscript and compiling the index. We also wish to thank Hoover Institution director John Raisian and Associate Director Thomas H. Henriksen for their administrative support, which helped see this project through to a successful conclusion.

Ramon H. Myers
Jongryn Mo

Glossary

AmCham	American Chamber of Commerce in Korea
APEC	Asia-Pacific Economic Cooperation Organization
ASEAN	Association of Southeast Asian Nations
COCOM	Coordinating Committee on Export Controls (NATO)
EAEG	East Asia Economic Group
EC	European Community
G-5	Group of Five: France, Germany, Great Britain, Japan, United States
HS	Harmonized system
IMF	International Monetary Fund
KIET	Korean Institute for Economics and Technology
NIE	Newly industrialized/industrializing economy
Numeraire	The currency in which a measurement is denominated
OECD	Organization for Economic Cooperation and Development
OSROK	Office of Supply, Republic of Korea
Plaza Accord	A 1985 agreement among the G-5 countries to coordinate the orderly depreciation of the dollar against other major currencies
SDR	Special drawing right
SEC	(U.S.) Securities and Exchange Commission
Section 301	of U.S. Trade Act of 1974
Super 301	U.S. legislative provisions mandating sanctions against countries that engage in unfair trade practices injurious to U.S. industries

USTR   U.S. trade representative

VER   Voluntary export restraint/restriction

SHAPING A NEW
ECONOMIC RELATIONSHIP

Introduction

Jongryn Mo and
Ramon H. Myers

The 1980s represented a major turning point in the economic relationship between the United States and the rapidly developing economies of East Asia, commonly referred to as the newly industrialized countries (NICs). In the previous two decades, the Republic of Korea, Hong Kong, the Republic of China, and Singapore had rapidly expanded their exports in a world economy that had been growing at rates of 8.5 percent in the 1960s and 5.9 percent in the 1970s, the most rapid period of world trade growth ever recorded.[1] These two decades of rapid, trade-led economic growth in East Asia made it possible for the NICs to expand their manufacturing industries; by 1982 these countries alone accounted for 10 percent of the world's total manufactured exports.[2] The United States was the largest recipient of their exports. Between 1980 and 1985, however, the United States began to run an unprecedentedly large trade imbalance with Japan, the Republic of Korea, and the Republic of China. This new development created political conflict between the United States and these three trading partners.

Before the late 1980s, the relationship between the Republic of Korea and the United States had its roots in a strong partnership dating from the invasion of South Korea by communist North Korea on June 24, 1950, when the United States led United Nations troops to save the Republic of Korea from certain defeat. That relationship began to change after 1985, when economic friction between the two partners increased, threatening to spill over into other areas of the partnership and thus imperil the peace and security of East Asia. Between 1985 and 1990, both countries' politicians and officials worked diligently to resolve their economic disputes, and by 1992 sufficient progress had been achieved to build a new foundation for better economic integration of the two countries in the future.

This volume of essays tries to understand the origins of economic friction between the United States and the Republic of Korea (ROK) and the way in which both partners resolved their trade differences. Understanding how the United States and the ROK improved their economic relations has relevance for the United States and other East Asian trading partners, particularly Japan. Even more important, the U.S.-ROK example illustrates how both countries might improve their economic relations in the future.

Origins of the Trade Crisis

Between 1981 and 1987, Korea's exports to the United States rapidly increased, reaching a peak around 1987–1988, when the United States absorbed nearly 39 percent of Korea's exports to account for almost 3 percent of the total imports into the United States (see table 1, panels a and b). At the same time, the overall trade deficit of the United States with its trading partners had rapidly deteriorated, growing from a modest $28.0 billion in 1981 to a whopping $159.5 billion in 1987.[3] It was not surprising that in 1987 the U.S. bilateral trade deficit with Korea had reached nearly $10 billion, compared with a surplus in favor of the United States of over $300 million in 1981.

In the 1980s Korea exported capital-intensive goods such as semiconductors, but most exports still were labor-intensive products such as consumer electronics, textiles, and footwear. U.S. exports to Korea remained the traditional resource-based products from agriculture and capital goods such as chemicals and machinery. This complementary trade relationship had worked well in previous decades but not in the 1980s because of unique macrodevelopments in the American economy: The U.S. government went into deep deficit and the U.S. dollar appreciated (see chapter 1 and chapter 2). Tax reform in the first administration of President Ronald Reagan and the failure of the U.S. Congress to cut spending pumped huge amounts of income to the private sector. At the same time, the strong American dollar permitted consumers and business firms alike to purchase imports on an unprecedented basis. U.S. imports stood at $265.1 billion in 1981 but then soared to $409.8 billion in 1987. U.S. exports actually declined, from $237.1 billion in 1981 to $223.4 billion in 1986, rising slowly to $250.1 billion in 1987.[4] This flood of imports, largely from East Asia, greatly benefited

Table 1.   U.S.-ROK Trade, 1975–1991 (in USmillions of dollars)

Year	PANEL A (BASED ON U.S. TRADE STATISTICS)			PANEL B (BASED ON KOREAN TRADE STATISTICS)		
	Exports to Korea	*Imports from Korea*	*Trade balance*	*Exports to Korea*	*Imports from Korea*	*Trade balance*
1975	$1,762	$1,586	$176	$1,536	$1,881	$ − 345
1976	2,015	2,646	− 631	2,498	1,963	535
1977	2,371	3,162	− 791	3,127	2,448	679
1978	3,160	4,087	− 927	4,076	3,044	1,032
1979	4,191	4,349	− 158	4,389	4,603	214
1980	4,685	4,433	252	4,624	4,890	− 266
1981	5,116	5,474	− 358	5,688	6,050	− 362
1982	5,529	6,011	− 482	6,286	5,957	329
1983	5,925	7,657	− 1,732	8,262	6,278	1,984
1984	5,983	10,027	− 4,044	10,528	6,877	3,651
1985	5,956	10,713	− 4,757	10,789	6,554	4,235
1986	6,355	13,497	− 7,142	13,920	6,548	7,372
1987	8,099	17,991	− 9,892	18,382	8,761	9,621
1988	11,257	21,164	− 9,907	21,478	12,706	8,772
1989	13,478	20,543	− 7,065	20,203	15,445	4,758
1990	14,399	19,287	− 4,888	19,446	16,946	2,500
1991	15,518	17,742	− 2,224	18,311	18,183	− 872

Data for both panels obtained from various issues of International Monetary Fund, *Directions of Trade Statistics Yearbook* (Washington, D.C.).

consumers and many American business firms. But this new trade trend was associated with a severe decline in many U.S. manufacturing firms, which struggled in the early 1980s to cope with high interest rates and the flood of low-priced, high-quality foreign imports.

It was not surprising that American businesspeople began besieging Washington, demanding that their government take forceful action to reduce the flood of foreign imports as well as give them greater access to foreign markets. The auto industry successfully lobbied Congress, which pressured the government to force Japan to adopt voluntary quotas on automobile exports to the United States. Representatives of the nonrubber footwear industry succeeded in getting Congress to demand that the U.S. government negotiate orderly marketing agreements with suppliers in Taiwan and Korea to limit their shipments to the United States.[5] Many firms filed antidumping and countervailing duty suits against their foreign competitors (see chapter 3). This rising tide of business complaints eventually compelled the American government to use Section 301 of the 1974 Trade Act to pry open foreign markets, and Korea became a notable victim of this development. Although imports from Korea into the United States in 1989 made up only 4.2 percent of the total, from 1975 to 1991 the Republic of Korea received 9 percent of Section 301 investigations (see chapter 3). In fact, most cases—six out of eight—went against Korea, and the threat of U.S. sanctions forced Korea to speed up trade liberalization to allow more U.S. imports to enter the country (see chapter 4).

Meanwhile, in September 1985, the United States organized the Plaza Accord with the major economic powers of the West (G-5, see Glossary) to intervene in foreign-exchange markets so as to lower the value of the U.S. dollar. As a result of these activities, the trade-weighted value of the U.S. dollar depreciated from an index of 131.9 in 1985 to 88.0 in 1988. By 1988, even this tactic had failed to reduce the trade deficit between the United States and Korea, which still stood at between $8 billion and $9 billion in favor of Korea. Meanwhile, the U.S. government insisted that Korean officials allow the Korean currency, the won, to appreciate rapidly (see chapter 2). By 1985, then, the U.S. government had begun using a three-pronged policy to reduce the trade deficit between Korea and the United States: (1) restrict Korea's access to U.S. markets; (2) pressure Korea to open its markets to American goods and services; and (3) compel Korea to appreciate its currency.

The perception of U.S. businesspeople, politicians, and bureaucrats had been that legally erected barriers in the Republic of Korea were chiefly responsible for the worsening trade deficit. This perception was misleading, as the essays in this volume confirm. Even before 1982, when barriers had been the highest on the Korean side, the largest trade surplus Korea had with the United States had been $1 billion in 1978 (based on Korean statistics, see table 1, panel b); in 1981 the trade balance had turned to favor the United States by $362 million. The huge trade surplus in favor of Korea, beginning in 1983 and lasting until 1990, was principally caused by macroeconomic changes in the United States economy (see chapters 1 and 5).

In 1991 the trade balance shifted in favor of the United States, to US$872 million, as the total trade volume between the two countries declined (see table 1, panel b). The slight decline in Korean exports to the United States (from US$19.4 billion to US$18.3 billion between 1990 and 1991) reflected rising costs to Korean producers and the appreciation of the won. Meanwhile, U.S. exports to Korea rose from US$11.2 billion to US$15.5 billion between 1988 and 1991 (see table 1, Panel a).

The outcry from American businesspeople of unfair trade practices toward Japan quickly spilled over to criticism of the Republic of Korea (see chapter 9). Mounting U.S. pressure against the Republic of Korea soon elicited a flood of anti-American rhetoric in the Korean press. What was the basis for these charges that trade barriers in Korea prevented greater integration of markets between the two countries?

Trade Barriers

As early as the 1960s the Korean government put into place formal barriers of tariffs and quotas to protect the country's infant industries. Despite these barriers, in the 1970s U.S. exports to Korea rose ninefold in value terms and Korean exports to the U.S. increased roughly tenfold. The trade balance was not excessively in imbalance for either side in these decades; only between 1982 and 1988 did Korea's exports to the United States surge.

Beginning in 1983, however, the Korean government began to reduce the average tariff rate on manufactured goods, from 22.6 percent to 9.7 percent in 1990 and an expected low of 6.2 percent by 1994, a level comparable to that of the European nations (see chapter 4). During the same decade, the average tariff rate for agricultural goods fell from 31.4 percent to 19.9 percent; by 1994 it will be 16.6 percent. Therefore, as Korean exports began entering the United States in greater volume, Korea already was lowering its tariff duties. That action, however, failed to reduce the growing trade imbalance between the two countries. The United States nearly eliminated its deficit with Korea in 1991, when the value of U.S. exports to Korea, around US$15.5 billion, was more than three times what it had been in 1980 (see table 1, panel a). According to Korean statistics, the United States ran a small surplus with Korea (see table 1, panel b). Korea had certainly responded to U.S. demands to dismantle its tariff system and allow greater imports from the United States, but that factor alone was not responsible for changing the trade balance between the two countries.

The critical factor that reduced the ballooning trade surplus of the 1980s was U.S. pressure on the ROK to appreciate its exchange rate, along with new manufacturing cost increases. In-June Kim compares the long-term equilibrium exchange rate that maintains price competitiveness for Korean goods in world markets with the actual exchange-rate changes in the 1980s (see chapter 6). This comparison shows that the won was undervalued during the years when Korea's exports to the United States surged. But after the foreign-exchange rate converged with the long-run equilibrium rate, the won became overvalued, which helped reduce the current account deficit by making imports cheaper during a period when real tariffs had rapidly declined. Yen-Kyun Wang's chapter provides a descriptive account of this story and also shows that real wages and other costs increased for manufacturing during the late 1980s (see chapter 7). These twin developments, when combined with falling tariffs, rapidly reduced the trade deficit between the United States and the ROK.

By the late 1980s, therefore, more and more American businesspeople were trying to sell their products in the Korean marketplace, and indeed many successfully did so. To that end, they were greatly assisted by the American Chamber of Commerce in Seoul, an organization that gathered information on business conditions in Korea for its members. In March 1991, the chamber published its annual reports, which listed the complaints of American businesspeople about trade barriers and unfair practices they claimed still restricted their entry into the Korean market:[6] restrictive licensing, high tariffs (especially in agriculture), means of limiting deferred payment, and the discretionary behavior of Korean officials and the press (see chapter 9). The chamber praised the Korean government for making progress to lower barriers in recent years but claimed that more had to be done. In Washington, this document fueled new protectionist demands as well as demands that the Korean government open its markets. The Korean press responded, as it had in the past, by accusing the Americans of being unfair to Korea and thus fanning the anti-Americanism that had been growing in recent years.

Just as the chamber served as a powerful instrument for U.S. businesspeople both in Korea and at home to pressure the U.S. government, so special interest groups appealed to Congress to demand that the government file complaints against Korean businesses for dumping their products in the American market. These complaints were successful. The U.S. government requested that the Korean government impose export quotas on Korean steel producers and force Korean producers of color television sets to adjust their prices upward when selling in the United States (see chapter 3). Thus after the bilateral trade surplus in Korea's favor had ballooned in the mid-1980s, American businesspeople pressed their officials to threaten trade sanctions against Seoul to lower trade barriers even at the cost of rising anti-Americanism among the Korean public.

But trade barriers did rapidly fall in the late 1980s; the Korean won appreciated; the ROK's financial markets were opened; and the trade surplus in Korea's favor finally ceased to be a problem in 1991. The Korean market indeed had become more open, partly because of Korean government efforts to liberalize the Korean market and partly because of U.S. efforts to force that liberalization process. In this complex way the trade relationship between the two countries improved but with painful effects on the Korean economy in the late 1980s, whereas the United States had experienced considerable economic distress in the early 1980s. Whenever the U.S. government threatened trade sanctions on the Korean government, those efforts politicized trade friction on an unprecedented basis.

The Politicization of Trade Friction

When business parties attempt to enforce contracts and carry out transactions in foreign markets, they often encounter difficulties that greatly raise their costs of doing business or even threaten their ability to survive in business. Under these circumstances, businesspeople sometimes ask the state to grant them the protection and assistance they believe necessary to their survival. When the state uses its power to negotiate with another state about trade and opening markets, a political process begins that may or may not produce favorable outcomes for all parties concerned.

In the 1930s, for example, the politicization of trade disputes led to states retaliating rather than negotiating: markets closed and trade volume fell. In the late 1980s, however, the politicization of trade disputes between the Republic of Korea and the United States contributed to opening up the Korean market and protecting special business groups within the United States. This outcome certainly favored the United States, yet the Republic of Korea still could export to its most preferred market, the United States, and make its economy more competitive. American businesspeople greatly expanded their exports to the Korean market, helping to integrate the two economies more closely than ever before. Why had trade friction become more politicized by the mid-1980s?

Unlike Japanese businesspersons, who adapt better in foreign markets and seek local remedies to solve their difficulties, American businesspersons sought assistance through political channels in Korea and the United States (see chapter 8), rather than finding local agents and using the Korean legal system to seek redress for their difficulties in conducting business in the Korean market. Nor did American businesspeople receive the assistance they expected from Korean bureaucrats. Korea is developing new legislation and regulations for dealing with problems likely to afflict foreign business, and these unfamiliar, often inhospitable, business conditions are slowly improving. Within a few years most American businesspeople can expect to incur lower transaction costs when doing business in Korea (see chapter 8, Hi-Taek Shin).

A major outcome of politicizing trade difficulties occurred in 1988 when the U.S. Congress and government enacted the Omnibus Trade and Competitiveness Act, which requires the U.S. Treasury to identify trading partners who manipulate their exchange rates to gain unfair competitive advantage in international trade and to negotiate with them to eliminate such practices.

In its published reports of October 1988 and April 1989, the Treasury charged that Korea's exchange rate was being manipulated; in March 1990, after responding to heavy U.S. government pressure, the Korean government introduced a flexible exchange-rate system instead of the fixed rate of the past. Since then, the U.S. Treasury has been satisfied that manipulation of the exchange rate in Korea no longer exists. Although it can be argued that small countries should have the freedom to maintain fixed, rather than flexible, exchange rates, it was U.S. government pressure that compelled Korea not to link its currency, the won, with the U.S. dollar after 1985, merely loosening the link between the won and the U.S. dollar and bringing the won closer to the Japanese yen. Another sign of the increased influence of the yen in Korea is the sudden increase in the yen share of Korea's external debt, rising from 16.6 percent in 1980 to 29.5 percent in 1988 (see chapter 5). This trend, however, is part of a pattern throughout the Asian region, according to Jeffrey Frankel, because the share of the yen in official reserve holdings rose from 13.9 percent in 1980 to 26.7 percent in 1988, although in 1989 it declined to 17.5 percent.

Conclusion

The resolution of trade friction between the United States and the ROK in the 1980s produced a remarkable opening up of the Korean market and a greater integration between the two economies. This achievement occurred because of the complex process discussed in this volume and the special relationship between the ROK and the United States.

First, the ROK began reducing tariffs in the early 1980s in an effort to open its economy in the world market. Second, by the mid-1980s the United States had developed a new managed trade policy based on the following elements: using its powerful Section 301 law, imposing antidumping regulations, requesting voluntary export restrictions, engaging in high-level governmental negotiations, working through the GATT to exert pressure upon Korea, and forcing currency appreciation against the U.S. dollar. These actions, along with Korea's liberalization of its market, greatly increased U.S. exports to the ROK and eliminated the large trade deficit in Korea's favor that had built up by the mid-1980s.

The complex process of trade adjustment and increased integration between the U.S. and the ROK economies also owed much to the special security relationship Korea had with the United States and the willingness of Korean officials to agree eventually to U.S. government demands. This achievement did not come without high costs: the Korea media bitterly criticized the United States, and anti-American feeling spread throughout

Korean society. By the early 1990s, however, that bitter feeling had eased somewhat, and the two governments continued to negotiate to find solutions to their economic disagreements. Both countries still face many unresolved issues related to specific industries and products such as the United States wanting to export rice to a Korean rice market that has yet to be opened.

There are a variety of means by which these short-term difficulties can be negotiated and possibly resolved. The final chapter, by Okyu Kwon, lists five broad measures, to be combined wherever possible, that focus on significant industry-opening measures to achieve greater bilateral market integration and enhance welfare in both societies (see chapter 10). These measures call for officials in both countries to use local remedies, develop major industry-opening initiatives, and engage in multilateral negotiations to resolve the short-term problems quickly and defuse the politicization of trade disputes. Even more important, several measures suggest great benefits for both sides if they can adopt a longer time horizon by which to integrate the two countries' markets.

To reduce the politicization of economic friction and ensure continued economic integration, the United States and Korea should establish a formal institution in which their representatives negotiate a long-term schedule of trade liberalization. That institution must have access to the executive and legislative bodies in both political systems so that negotiators can authorize economic relations leading to trade expansion.

Both trading partners took an important first step toward such a cooperative framework when Presidents George Bush and Roh Tae Woo launched the so-called Presidents' Economic Initiative (PEI) in January 1992 to remove barriers to bilateral trade and investment. The PEI negotiations clearly demonstrated the benefits of managing economic relations in a nonpoliticized, cooperative environment. Because the PEI was not initiated as a response to a particular complaint, negotiators were relatively insulated from media attention and interest-group pressure. The United States also offered to help with high-tech transfers in exchange for greater market openings in Korea, a gesture that greatly contributed to a cooperative atmosphere for negotiations.[7]

The editors suggest that the United States and Korea should not rule out negotiating a full-fledged free trade agreement (FTA) after laying the groundwork through the type of cooperative institutional framework just cited. As Kihwan Kim argues in chapter 2, an FTA has many advantages for both sides. From the Korean perspective, an FTA can minimize future economic friction with Korea's biggest trading partner. For those Korean policymakers who see trade liberalization as essential to enhancing the Korean economy's competitiveness, an FTA will protect and build on the gains made since the late 1980s. Although domestic opposition from protectionists will be formidable, it is important to remind them that a comprehensive program such as an FTA allows more actors and agents representing the economic sectors to bargain and reach agreement.

In his Agenda for American Renewal on September 10, 1992, President Bush declared that the United States was ready to enter into new FTAs. The criteria for the United States will be whether a particular country is prepared to open its markets to American goods, services, and capital.[8] Using this standard, the United States should consider the Republic of Korea as a prime candidate for an FTA in East Asia. The ROK has made great strides in trade liberalization since the early 1980s, in large part as a result of its successful negotiations with the United States in the mid and late 1980s.

Notes

1. World Bank, *Korea: Development in a Global Context* (Washington, D.C.: World Bank, 1984), p. 40.

2. Ibid., p. 41.

3. U.S. Council of Economic Advisers, *Economic Report of the President, Transmitted to the Congress January 1990* (Washington, D.C.: United States Government Printing Office, 1990), p. 412.

4. Ibid.

5. U.S. Council of Economic Advisers, *Economic Report of the President, Transmitted to the Congress February 1986* (Washington, D.C.: United States Government Printing Office, 1986), p. 113.

6. American Chamber of Commerce (AmCham) in Korea, *United States–Korean Trade Issues* (Seoul: AmCham, March 1991).

7. *Far Eastern Economic Review*, August 20, 1992, and October 22, 1992.

8. United States Information, U.S. Embassy, Seoul, Korea, *Moscow Outlines Free U.S. Trade Agreement Criteria*, October 23, 1992.

PART ONE

REPUBLIC OF KOREA AND UNITED STATES ECONOMIC FRICTION IN THE 1980s

1

The Origins of U.S.-Korea Trade Frictions

Marcus Noland

Introduction

The United States and the Republic of Korea (ROK) have maintained mutually beneficial economic relations since the founding of the ROK in 1948. For the first decade of the republic's existence, this relationship was largely one of the United States providing aid to Korea; by the late 1950s the United States was financing 80 percent of Korea's import bill. This policy was pursued as part of the broader political relationship and the United States policy of containing communism.

Economic reforms begun in the 1960s have transformed Korea from a poor dependent to an increasingly important customer and competitor for the United States. As Korea's largest trading partner, in 1990, the United States absorbed 32 percent of Korean exports and supplied 24 percent of Korean imports. Korea is the seventh-largest trading partner of the United States, its sixth-largest export market, and its third largest for agricultural products.

The pattern of trade is largely complementary specialization. Although capital-intensive engineering products such as semiconductors make up a growing share of the Korean export basket, the bulk of Korean exports are still in relatively labor-intensive products such as consumer electronics, textiles, and footwear. U.S. exports to Korea are in turn concentrated in natural resource–based products and capital goods such as agricultural products, chemicals, and machinery. The largest sectors of Korean net exports are electronics ($2.8 billion), footwear ($2.5 billion), and leather goods and clothing ($1.4 billion each). The sectors of largest net imports are raw leather ($0.9 billion), aircraft and cereals ($0.8 billion each), and fuels ($0.7 billion).

This beneficial relationship is not limited to trade. The United States is the second-largest investor and the second-largest source of technology transfer to Korea (following Japan in both cases), and Korea has begun investing in the United States.

Although this relationship is of great advantage to both countries, it has been accompanied by underlying tensions and periods of extreme rancor and distrust due to three forces: institutional differences in trade policy formation, the complementary trade structure (which implies that large and painful adjustment costs will accompany any significant expansion of trade), and, finally, the existence of macroeconomic imbalances that recently contributed to the politicization of trade conflicts.

Trade Policy

Trade policy is used to raise and maintain the relative incomes of protected factors, typically those that are scarce in international trade terms. In the case of the United States and Korea, two countries with very different factor endowments, their respective trade policies will likely run directly counter to their partners' area of comparative advantage. Moreover, to the extent Korea follows Japan, Korea may encounter disproportionate barriers to its exports in foreign markets.

As a developing country, Korea has historically maintained far more extensive barriers to trade than has the United States. In 1978 Korea initiated a unilateral and gradual, though uneven, trade liberalization. In 1980, the average tariff was 24.9 percent, and nearly one-third of imported products were under some sort of quantitative restriction. By 1990 the average tariff had been lowered to 11.4 percent, and less than 5.0 percent of imported products were subject to quantitative restrictions (Kwon 1991, table 2). Further scheduled reductions would reduce the average tariff to 7.9 percent in 1993, comparable with that of some developed countries.[1]

Beyond these relatively low levels of protection, high tariffs on some individual products are of concern to the United States.[2] An example is that of almonds (35 percent); the U.S. industry believes that elimination of this tariff could quintuple U.S. exports, from $5 million to $25 million annually. Other sectors where exports are blocked by high tariffs include paper products (again, a potential quintupling of exports, from $5 million to $25 million), raisins ($10 million to $15 million), cling peaches ($5 million to $10 million), kiwifruit ($1 million to $5 million), and avocados ($2 million to $3 million).[3]

Korea implements quantitative restrictions through an import licensing system. More than 95 percent of goods receive automatic approval; the remainder (mostly agricultural and fishery products) are subject to quotas. Although Korea was the United States third-largest agricultural export market, a vast majority (86 percent) of these exports are accounted for by bulk commodities. The United States remains concerned that the agricultural quotas effectively exclude U.S. producers from Korean markets for high value-added or processed agricultural products. Items of particular interest include fruits (e.g., frozen peaches), vegetables (e.g., rice and barley), beef, paper, and solid wood products.[4] Indeed, calculations reported in Hayes (1991, table 3) indicate that the tariff equivalents of these nontariff barriers can be as much as thirty times the nominal tariff rates.

The United States has also expressed concern over certain Korean customs practices. These include arbitrary delays, inability to obtain customs classifications, arbitrary reclassifications, and unduly cumbersome inspection procedures (e.g., inspecting every container of imported chocolates or cherries). Delays can take up to a month. These practices are more than a nuisance because the products are not refrigerated during inspections and can consequently spoil or have a reduced retail shelf life.

Standards, testing, labeling, and certification requirements imposed by Korea on U.S. imports are another subject of contention. Many of these problems relate to agricultural imports. Exporters report unduly restrictive and arbitrary phytosanitary requirements. In many cases importers are denied requests for scientific data on which imported food shipments have been rejected. Korea issues new standards without notifying the General Agreement on Tariffs and Trade (GATT), and frequently these standards are vague and do not provide basic information or documentary requirements.

Although Korea has traditionally maintained a variety of practices to encourage domestic firms in government procurement, in 1990 it submitted a formal offer to join the GATT Government Procurement Code. If Korea does indeed successfully accede to the code, this would presumably eliminate a number of the practices that have been a source of contention between itself and the United States, depending on the entity and product coverage of its commitments.

In 1988 the United States placed Korea on its priority watch list under the Section 337, special 301, intellectual property provisions of the 1988 Trade Act. Because of subsequent progress in bilateral negotiations, in 1989 Korea was downgraded from the priority watch list to the watch list, where it remains. The major areas of U.S. concern have been pirating and counterfeiting, lack of pharmaceutical patent protection, and lack of protection for semiconductor designs. Korea passed a law on video piracy in 1991, and a law protecting semiconductor designs is under consideration. Enforcement of laws against counterfeiting has been strengthened.

The recent antidumping case brought against U.S. (and Japanese) makers of polyacetal resin has caused consternation in the United States. Korea's sole polyacetal resin maker, Korea Engineering Plastic (KEP), filed charges of dumping against DuPont, Hoechst Celanese of the United States, and Asahi Chemical in May 1990. The Korean Trade Commission ruled that KEP had been injured by dumping, and the Office of Customs Administration estimated dumping margins of 58.2–92.2 percent for DuPont, 20.6–43.5 percent for Hoechst, and 31.0–107.6 for Asahi Chemical. In July 1991 the Customs Deliberation Committee affirmed the dumping ruling but imposed far lower margins, apparently questioning the extent of injury in light of the fact that KEP's market share had grown from nil to 60 percent in two years, that it had doubled capacity, and that it was earning a high rate of return on capital. Bilateral consultations have begun under the auspices of the GATT.

Korea currently restricts foreign access to its service markets through a negative list, which restricts foreign investment through equity participation or other requirements. Progress has been made in financial services and advertising, though the 1990 *National Treatment Study* of the U.S. Treasury indicated that "significant denials of national treatment continue" in the banking and securities sectors. Areas of continuing U.S. interest include maritime, trucking, and rail freight services, insurance, and wholesale and retail distribution. The distribution sector is of considerable concern. Vertical integration in the retail sector (especially in automobiles and electronics), illegal under U.S. antitrust law, acts as a significant barrier to trade and keeps prices of imported products uncompetitively high. The Korean government has announced a partial relaxation of restrictions; that relaxation would permit restricted foreign investment in the wholesale and retail distribution system and fully liberalize the sector for 1995.

Restrictions on investment in other sectors have been gradually relaxed. In 1980, less than 50 percent of five-digit Korean Standard Industrial Classification (see Glossary) sectors were unconditionally open to foreign direct investment (FDI); since 1989, 79 percent of these sectors were open to FDI, 16 percent were conditionally open, and 5 percent were closed. Openness is highest in manufacturing (98 percent), lowest for agriculture (20 percent), and in-between in services (62 percent). However, even in open sectors, investment approval has not been automatic, and investors have encountered considerable delays and nontransparency in the implementation of existing regulations. Moreover, certain individual laws permit the government to impose restrictions on investments in particular sectors. In response to U.S. complaints about these difficulties, the government of Korea has streamlined its investment regulations to provide for a more rapid and less discretionary approval process. It has also agreed to phase out most existing local equity requirements on an expeditious basis; a new set of less restrictive procedures are to take effect in 1993.

Beyond these systemic problems, the United States and Korea have been embroiled in conflicts over Korean policies in several sectors. One major area of dispute has been telecommunications. U.S. firms estimate that access restrictions in the Korean market cost them $25 million to $50 million in foregone sales annually. In response Korea has undertaken a variety of reforms, including accelerating its scheduled tariff reductions on telecommunications and formally submitting an application to the GATT Government Procurement Code. U.S. policymakers appear satisfied with the pace of reform.

In shipbuilding, the United States has sought to gain Korean adherence to Organization on Economic Cooperation and Development (OECD) restrictions on subsidies. It has sought and obtained Korean agreement to restrict drift-net fishing. The United States also has sought and obtained relaxed restrictions on the sales of foreign wine, cigarettes, and motion pictures.

Although the U.S. economy is relatively open, Korea, too, has complaints about trade practices it encounters in its partner's market. These center on the implementation of Section 301, Section 337, and contingent protection rules; restrictions on Korea's textile, apparel, and steel exports; customs practices; and standards, testing, and certification requirements. Data on Korean exports under nontariff restrictions are shown in table 1. These data indicate that the share of Korean exports to the U.S. subject to some kind of nontariff trade barrier has fallen from more than half in 1981, to just over a fifth in 1989. Of these, around three-quarters are textile and apparel exports restricted by multifiber arrangement (MFA) quotas, while another fifth are steel exports subject to a so-called voluntary export restriction (VER). (The steel VER is scheduled to lapse in March 1992.)

Section 301 of the Trade Act of 1974 authorizes the president to retaliate against "unfair trade practices" in foreign countries that U.S. negotiators have been unable to remove. Proportional to its trade with the United States, Korea has been heavily targeted by Section 301, especially during the period 1985–1989.

The 1988 Trade Act greatly enlarged the scope of Section 301. In 1989

Table 1.   Share of Korean Exports under U.S. Nontariff Restrictions
                (in percent)

Year	Total	Antidumping
1976	37.5	na
1981	50.5	1.4
1982	45.1	1.8
1983	42.5	3.6
1984	44.5	4.9
1985	43.3	1.8
1986	33.3	2.7
1987	26.5	1.0
1988	20.3	1.5
1989	20.1	1.7

SOURCE: Bark 1991a, tables 2 and 6.

the United States and Korea entered into negotiations over agricultural trade barriers and foreign investment restrictions before the United States trade representative's naming of priority countries and practices under super 301 (see Glossary) provisions. Although Korea was able to avoid being designated as a priority country under super 301, many Koreans viewed this episode as an example of unilateral bullying on the part of the United States.

Section 337 involves intellectual property protection. Korean products have been cited under Section 337 in ten cases. Eight cases were resolved through negotiation, but in two cases (semiconductors and plastic bags) no mutually agreeable solutions were found; in 1987 the U.S. International Trade Commission issued import bans. In 1989, a GATT panel ruled that certain provisions of Section 337 were GATT-inconsistent.

Thirty-one cases of dumping have been initiated in the United States against Korean producers. Twelve cases have been charged with definitive duty, and four are under investigation. Of the twelve cases charged with duty, six have been terminated; the other six remain under restriction (Bark 1991a).[5] Even in the cases where no duty is levied, direct costs of defending against the charges and uncertainty about market access can significantly impede exporters. Indeed, Bark reports that despite the nine-and-one-half-month investigation stipulated in U.S. law, actual periods of investigation ran up to fourteen months. Moreover, the periods of restriction were long, averaging two to three years, and there "was a wide disparity in the determination of dumping margins between the preliminary and final verdicts and a wide variation in the margin rates imposed on the different firms. In addition, there was a large discrepancy between the final dumping margins derived by the Department of Commerce and the Court of International Trade. This seemingly arbitrary nature of determining dumping margins causes great uncertainty for Korean firms facing anti-dumping charges" (Bark 1991a, 55).

Of greater quantitative impact than the dumping cases are restrictions imposed by the MFA and the steel VER, although research by Tarr (1987) suggests that the steel VER has actually helped Korean steel makers through the transfer of large economic rents. Rents, however, are unlikely to exceed profits from exports foregone in the textile and apparel sector. Research by Trela and Whalley (1988) indicates that eliminating the multilateral quotas alone would result in a 185 percent increase in Korean textile and apparel export revenue. Complete freeing of the textile and apparel markets would lead to a 241 percent increase. Moreover, the internal mechanism for allocating quota rights imposes efficiency costs on the Korean economy. Trela and Whalley (1991) estimate that when these domestic inefficiencies are taken into account, Korea would experience a 525 percent increase in export revenue, along with a freeing of world textile and apparel trade. Although these figures are derived from a model calibrated on 1986 data, and Korean competitiveness in these sectors has certainly declined, they nonetheless give an indication of the restrictiveness of the MFA.

Like the United States, Korea has complaints about its trade partner's customs practices. Hong (1991) includes a litany of horror stories: arbitrary reclassifications to increase duty, different duties charged by different customs offices, excessive delays, arbitrary alterations in origin labeling, discrimination depending on whether the customs broker is an American or Korean firm. Hong also details the discriminatory phytosanitary requirements, including U.S. Food and Drug Administration quarantines of more than one month for Korean pears and instant noodles and more than three months for seaweed.

These bilateral trade conflicts are intensified by differences in policy formation and institutions. The United States is an immigrant society whose political culture emphasizes procedural justice as manifested in U.S. concerns over fairness in trade. The institutions of trade policy formation are relatively open and adversarial, reflecting U.S. political and legal culture. In contrast, Korean policy formation has historically been more closed, with bureaucrats wielding considerable discretionary authority. Each system has its strengths and weaknesses, with the U.S. system being more transparent and the Korean less prone to rent seeking. These differences in style have tended to exacerbate tensions.

U.S. concerns about a lack of transparency in Korean policy formation were highlighted in the Korean "austerity" or "anti-import" campaign begun in the spring of 1990, when imported products were removed from store shelves, limitations were placed on promotional activities in response to government administrative guidance, and purchasers of imported automobiles were threatened with tax audits. Korean officials maintained that the campaign was against ostentatious and excessive consumption, not imports per se, but a number of examples suggest that this was not the case.[6] Perhaps the most infamous example was a comic book distributed by the National Agricultural Cooperative Federation (a quasi-governmental group) to around half a million school children suggesting that imported food was poisonous and recommending that the children stop their mothers from buying imported food.[7] Evaluating the austerity campaign, the American Chamber of Commerce in Korea concluded that "it has become increasingly clear that, at times, liberalization in Korea can mean absolutely nothing." In February 1991 the Korean government established guidelines to prevent discrimination against imports by trade and commerce officials.

Examples such as these feed negative U.S. perceptions of Korean trade policy. Korean restrictions on foreign automobile imports were featured in television commercials run by Representative Richard Gephardt during his unsuccessful 1988 campaign for the Democratic party presidential nomination. Major U.S. newspapers have given prominent coverage to informal Korean bureaucratic obstruction of the trade agreements. An incident in which Korean trade negotiators allowed Korean firms' legal representatives secretly to monitor and tape bilateral trade negotiations made the front page of the business pages in the United States. All these incidents contribute to a popular perception that Korea is insincere about its trade commitments.

If Americans believe that Korea is two-faced in its trade dealings, Koreans might understandably characterize the U.S. posture as sanctimonious. Although Americans are concerned about maintaining procedural justice domestically, this concern does not appear to extend to international organizations (just ask the Nicaraguans). The United States, in fact, has a poor record in conforming to negative GATT rulings, including some, such as Section 337, that are of direct interest to Korea. (When this track record is infrequently discussed in the United States, the United States is sometimes characterized as an idealistic patsy needing protection against unprincipled foreign countries such as Korea, giving rise to the image of duplicitous Koreans squaring-off against bullying Americans.) Such posturing, however, is not constant. Despite the ample potential for discordant trade tensions, these conflicts flare and recede. The macroeconomic policies of each country are the key to understanding this pattern of intermittent conflict.

Macroeconomic Policies

As one Korean policymaker observed, "Korea-U.S. trade frictions became serious in the second half of the 1980s as the U.S. twin deficits (trade and budget) expanded concurrently with Korea's widening surplus with the U.S." (Kwon 1991, p. 12). The U.S.-Korea trade balance remained within $1.5 billion of balance until 1982, when the Reaganomics package of fiscal profligacy was combined with tight monetary policy and currency appreciation (see figure 1). The deterioration of the U.S. trade position vis-à-vis Korea paralleled the growth in the United States' global trade deficit, which peaked at nearly $160 billion in 1987. At the same time the reverse was occurring in Korea: the trade balance went into surplus for the first time in 1986, eventually reaching $11.4 billion in 1988.

The growing bilateral trade deficit with Korea (see figure 1) prompted U.S. officials to examine Korean macroeconomic policy with a focus on exchange-rate policy, the putative source of the rapidly increasing Korean surplus. The U.S. Treasury, in implementing Section 3004 of the 1988 Trade Act, investigates whether the United States' trade partners are "manipulating their exchange rates for purposes of preventing balance of payments adjustment or gaining unfair competitive advantage in international trade." Korea was accused of being an "exchange rate manipulator" in the first three Treasury reports but was removed from that list in the fourth report in April 1990.[8] The Treasury, however, does not discriminate between nominal and real exchange rates (or between bilateral and effective exchange rates), and it confuses the *means* of exchange-rate determination with the *goal* of maintaining the correct exchange rate for macroeconomic balance. Indeed, it is unclear what in practice distinguishes exchange-rate management (what the United States and the other Group of Seven countries do) from exchange-rate manipulation (what the Treasury accuses Korea of doing).

Historically the won has been pegged to the basket of currencies that constitute the special drawing right (i.e., the currencies of the Group of Five major industrialized nations; the weight of these currencies in the basket are undisclosed) plus a "policy adjustment" factor. In reality, the policy adjustment factor has predominated, as the won depreciated against all five currencies in the basket between 1984 and April 1987 (Balassa and Williamson 1990). In March 1990 a new exchange-rate system, the market-average exchange-rate (MAR) system, was introduced under which the midband won-dollar rate is calculated as an average of the previous day's transactions

Figure 1.   U.S.-Korea Trade Balance

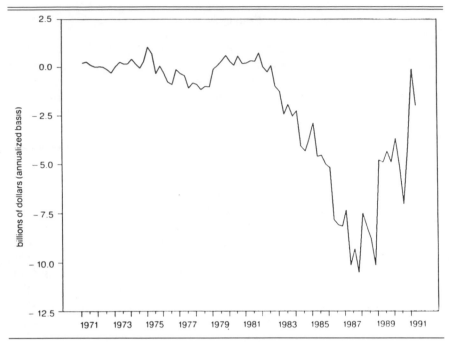

and then is allowed to float within officially proscribed margins around this rate. Thus the exchange rate floats on a limited basis and moves day to day according to market pressures. In September 1991 the government widened the intradaily band.

To investigate the macroeconomic determinants of the bilateral trade balance, a small macroeconomic model was estimated (see the technical details in the Appendix). That model was used to investigate causality relationships between U.S. and Korean macroeconomic variables.

The results indicate that, in time-series econometric terms, the real exchange rate and the U.S. macrovariables caused the Korean macrovariables, which in turn caused the bilateral balance. This suggests that the U.S. policy on Korean exchange rates might not have been misplaced. Nonetheless, both the far greater size of the United States and the causally prior character of U.S. macropolicies imply that changes in U.S. macropolicies would have a more substantial impact on the bilateral balance than would policy changes in Korea.

Prospects for the Future

The macroeconomic determinants of the trade balance are subject to policy-instigated shocks and are difficult to predict except over relatively short time horizons. The underlying pattern of trade specialization evolves in a reasonably systematic manner, however. Noland (1990a) reports projections of the Korean pattern of trade for forty-six industries encompassing the trade goods sector. These were derived from an econometrically estimated multicountry model in which a country's commodity composition of trade is a function of national income, technology, and relative factor endowments. (See Noland [1990b appendix] for details of the model and its estimation.)

According to this model, Korea will likely continue its shift into manufactured exports of increasing capital intensity and sophistication. Iron and steel are projected to emerge as the largest export sector in the year 2000, followed by electronics and fabricated metal products. The largest export increases would be in iron, steel, and basic chemicals. The largest export share declines would be in textiles and apparel, but this is conditional on MFA-scale trade restrictions continuing in those sectors. The largest import categories are oil, textile fibers, basic chemicals, and machinery.[9] Comparing and contrasting these projections with Korean Ministry of Trade and Industry medium-run projections to 1996, the largest Korean export sectors appear to be electronics, textiles, machinery, and steel, with machinery, electronics, and chemicals experiencing the fastest growth.[10]

According to the trade projections, Korea's export similarity index (Noland 1991a) in 2000 would have the highest pairings with Spain, Austria, and Taiwan, indicating that Korea would be a developed country (at least in international trade terms) by that time. The index also compares export patterns across time, showing that for Korea's projected export pattern in 2000, the pairing with Japan's actual export pattern in 1968 yields the highest value of any combination. Korea may be thus following Japan's development path, lagging behind Japan by around a generation.[11]

To analyze the implications for the United States of the prospective changes in Korean trade specialization, Noland (1990a) reports calculations of bilateral trade in 2000 with the U.S. market share of Korean exports and imports of each product category remaining unchanged from its 1987 value. Thus Korea is modeled as a small country and the United States as absorbing or supplying a constant share of the Korean trade mix. These figures should not be regarded as forecasts but rather as indicators of how trade composition might change if constant market shares were maintained.

Under these assumptions the share of exports to Korea in traded goods output would rise to 1.5 percent in 2000, while imports from Korea would account for 2.2 percent of traded goods consumption. Apart from the aberrant leather products sector, the export share of output would be highest in basic chemicals (5.2 percent), aircraft (4.0 percent), and nonfuel primary products (3.4 percent). Imports of Korean goods would account for nearly 33.3 percent of domestic consumption in footwear, 30.3 percent of motor-cycles and bicycles, 22.6 percent of leather products, and 12.3 percent of iron and steel, assuming that the steel VER is in fact allowed to lapse.

The employment impact of these trade changes was calculated using a projected input-output table supplied by the Bureau of Labor Statistics. Exports to Korea in 2000 would generate 381,500 jobs.[12] Sectors with the largest export-related employment would be nonfuel primary products (178,500) and aircraft (38,000). Imports from Korea would represent 781,300 foregone jobs in apparel (123,400), footwear (99,500), electronics (98,100), and fabricated metal products (85,000). The net employment loss between 1987 and 2000 due to trade changes would be 307,200 potential jobs. The largest trade-related employment gains would occur in nonfuel primary products (162,400) and aircraft (38,100). The biggest potential net losses would occur in apparel (87,300), fabricated metal products (82,400), and footwear (73,900).[13]

A similar set of projections have been made for Korea; unfortunately, owing to a lack of data, they cover only the manufacturing sector. These calculations indicate that total employment associated with trade in manu-factured goods with the United States is 363,400 jobs. The sectors that generate the most employment from trade with the United States are apparel (134,200), footwear (56,000), and electronics (52,400). According to the projections, the net employment gains from trade with the United States in 2000 would be highest in apparel (218,500) and fabricated metal products (199,400).[14] Net potential employment losses would be highest in aircraft (54,300) and professional goods (25,400).

It should be reiterated that these calculations are not predictions but computations of what would occur if the U.S. market share in the exports and imports of Korea remains unchanged. This convenient assumption does not say that these outcomes will in fact occur. There are cases in which the constant market share assumption is unlikely to be fulfilled,[15] and how these adjustments will play out will depend on the international policy environment. The key issue is the outcome of the Uruguay Round (UR) of multilateral trade talks under the auspices of the GATT. Both the United States and Korea have enormous interests at stake in the round.

The agenda of the UR reflects the legacy of its predecessor, the Tokyo Round.[16] Although Tokyo Round negotiators made considerable strides in the areas of tariff reduction and the development of codes of conduct on nontariff measures, a variety of important issues were left unresolved: Agriculture and textiles were essentially exempted, safeguards negotiations broke down, and developing countries were left only loosely obligated to adhere to GATT strictures. Moreover, despite the ground-breaking nontariff barrier codes, many issues relating to nontariff barriers were left vague or unresolved.

The agenda of the UR negotiations focuses on extending the GATT regime to areas previously not under the GATT (e.g., intellectual property rights, investment, and services), strengthening the GATT regime in traditional areas such as textiles and agriculture, and increasing adherence to GATT discipline by strengthening the dispute settlement mechanism and narrowing the opportunity for developing countries to evade GATT obligations. Progress has been uneven. The talks, which nearly collapsed in December 1990, were brought to a head a year later when GATT director General Arthur Dunkel proposed a compromise text. Agriculture is arguably the key to UR success. Not only is agriculture important in economic terms, but without a major breakthrough in agriculture a large number of countries (including the United States) may be unwilling to accept significant liberalization or new obligations in other areas under discussion.

At the outset of negotiations in 1986, the United States demanded a phased removal of all subsidies, receiving support from the Cairns Group of self-identified nonsubsidizing agricultural exporters. This demand was moderated in 1990 to a 75 percent cut in domestic support programs and a 90 percent cut in export subsidies. In response, the European Community (EC) offered to reduce total support 10–15 percent from 1989 levels, apparently believing, along with Japan and Korea, that with sufficient intransigence agriculture would be taken off the agenda as it had been in previous rounds. The impasse was broken only when it became apparent that the United States and others were prepared to walk out if there were no agreement in agriculture. A compromise proposal by Swedish agriculture minister Mats Hellstrom—the basis of General Dunkel's text on agriculture—calls for a five-year phased cut of 30 percent in 1990 levels of export subsidies, border measures, and domestic supports. For its part, Korea has accepted the basic framework of the aggregate measure of support, tariffication (except some sensitive commodities including rice), and the reduction of export subsidies. Korea, however, wants to receive special and differential treatment in agriculture and to have nontrade concerns provisions included in the agriculture agreement (Choe and Choi 1991).

Unfortunately, progress toward an agreement on textiles and clothing, another area of major concern for the United States and Korea, has been equally problematic. The shared objective of the United States and Korea has been to reform the MFA to bring textiles and apparel trade back under the GATT. Under the Dunkel compromise countries would agree to eliminate a specified number of quotas at fixed intervals over a period of ten years and to expand the remaining quotas each year during the transition period. The fear is that, under this proposal, countries would eliminate quotas in inverse order of restrictiveness. Moreover, quota expansion during the transition period is likely to be low, so that these quotas could actually become more restrictive and actual liberalization would be highly back-loaded. The obvious fear is that, facing rapid deprotection at the end of the transition period, countries would either exploit safeguards provisions to avoid liberalization (or to induce "voluntary" export restraints) or renege on their commitments altogether.

In other areas the Dunkel text strengthens intellectual property protection, tightens dumping definitions and anticircumvention rules, and strengthens the dispute settlement mechanism and establishes the framework for a multilateral trade organization. At this juncture, it appears that there are two scenarios for completing the UR. If an agreement had been reached in agriculture, the round could have been brought to a successful conclusion as early as spring 1992. Without an early agreement in agriculture, two outcomes are possible: negotiations could drag on until the deadline for U.S. fast-track consideration in March 1993, or negotiators could pursue the Aiken option: forget agriculture, reach agreement on a smaller package of issues, declare victory, and come home.[17] Unfortunately, either outcome will be widely viewed as a failure and foreshadow a shift away from a GATT-centered international trade regime.

The key event in determining the character of the future trade regime will be the success or failure of the UR. A successful UR would strengthen the multilateral trade system and provide a policy anchor for traditional trade negotiations. This is particularly important for Korea, for it would be among the major losers in any move away from a rules-based international trade system.

Beyond the UR, countries will increasingly seek to harmonize what have traditionally been considered domestic policies such as tax policy, competition policy, and so forth. By harmonize I mean the extent to which domestic business environments are characterized by similar sets of rules and institutions; observed international flows of products and factors are the outcome of market exchanges emerging from this common environment. Interstate trade within the United States might be thought of as arising from a completely harmonized environment. The polar opposite case would be management in which there is no attempt to create a common business environment and in which observed international product and factor flows are simply the outcome of cross-border negotiations by government officials. Trade among centrally planned economies might be thought of as an extreme form of management; recent proposals for "managed trade," a more moderate variant.

The current GATT system—in which restrictions are placed on the use of border measures but there is little restriction on more traditional "domestic" policies—might be viewed as an intermediate solution. In Lawrence's (1991a) terminology the GATT would be a regime of "shallow integration" while the interstate trade regime within the United States would be "deep integration." Even a successful UR, however, would be unable to achieve deep harmonization or integration because the membership of the GATT is simply too large and too diverse to take on the deep harmonization issues. Consequently, efforts in this direction will be pursued either bilaterally (as in the U.S.-Japan Structural Impediments Initiative [SII] talks) or multilaterally through regional groupings (such as EC '92) or through clubs of like-minded members (such as the proposal for an OECD [see Glossary] free trade and investment area).

The SII negotiations are instructive in this regard. The talks were proposed by the Bush administration in July 1989 both to address a real lacuna in the economic negotiations between the two increasingly interdependent countries and to undercut growing illiberal economic sentiment at home. In some sense the model was the yen-dollar talks on financial liberalization begun during the first Reagan administration: a relatively technocratic set of negotiations with a rolling agenda of topics not traditionally subject to international economic diplomacy. The Japanese government accepted the invitation to participate in the talks, similarly regarding them as an opportunity to forestall potentially more damaging political developments in the United States, as well as an opportunity to further desirable, though politically difficult, reforms at home.[18]

The history of SII points toward the types of issues raised in these deep harmonization efforts: competition policy, tax policy, investment policy, and so forth. The United States is likely to continue efforts in this regard either on a bilateral, regional, or like-minded group basis. Indeed, a U.S.-Korea SII-type negotiation could be in the offing.

In contrast to the scenario outlined above, failure of the UR would further erode the rule-based trade regime and increase the tendency toward government mandated managed trade market-sharing arrangements. As in the case of the MFA, Korea would be a major loser. In addition, failure of the UR would increase momentum toward non-GATT initiatives, particularly regional trade blocs.

Interest has centered on three potential blocs: the EC, a North American free trade area (NAFTA) comprising the United States, Canada, and Mexico and a more vaguely defined East Asian bloc. From an Asian standpoint,

European integration would appear to have the biggest impact on Japan, mainly through restrictions on automobile trade. Other Asian countries could be affected as well, however. Research by Alizadeh and Griffith-Jones (1991) indicates that the inclusion of the European free trade area (EFTA) countries, as well as Poland, Hungary, and the Czech and Slovak Federated republics, in some sort of broad European economic space could result in considerable trade diversion from Asia, especially from Taiwan and Korea.

Korean interests appear to be less affected by the potential NAFTA agreement. In some ways NAFTA is less an economic agreement than the political cement for Mexican economic reform. Much of North American trade is effectively free already; the sole significant possibility of trade diversion would be if there were a major reallocation of MFA quotas from Asia to Mexico. In the long run, investment diversion, owing to rules of origin included in the pact, may be a more significant issue for Korea.

The situation with regard to a potential trade bloc in Asia is more uncertain. Trade among Japan, Hong Kong, Singapore, Taiwan, South Korea, Malaysia, Thailand, the Philippines, Indonesia, and China is certainly growing: in 1970, intraregional trade accounted for 30 percent of the total trade of these countries; in 1980 the figure stood at 34 percent, and by 1990 it had risen to 40 percent. Recent studies indicate, however, that there has been no movement toward intra-Asian trade independent of conventional growth forces.[19] To this conclusion one is tempted to add the caveat: as long as Japanese foreign direct investment (FDI) into the region does not continue at its late 1980s pace. That enormous surge of Japanese FDI in the region in the late 1980s appears to be tapering off (it fell 14 percent between 1989 and 1990), which suggests that the huge FDI flows were the result of unusual circumstances in the Japanese economy (a 50 percent exchange-rate appreciation, virtually costless capital) that are unlikely to be repeated. If, however, the growth of Japanese FDI returns to its late 1980s rates, this could fundamentally alter the pattern of trade flows within Asia.

There is evidence of growing Japanese influence in finance. The yen is increasingly used to invoice trade flows and as a reserve currency. Moreover, analysis of interest- and exchange-rate movements in Asia by Frankel (1991) indicates that Japanese capital markets are exerting an increasing influence on interest and exchange rates in Asia (though no more than U.S. capital markets).

Thus far this does not establish any prima facie case for policy action. Within Asia, however, rising bilateral deficits with Japan have been a growing concern, especially in Korea and Taiwan. Both countries have undertaken policies explicitly aimed at diverting trade from Japan, and Japan has, in fact, threatened to take Korea to the GATT over its "import diversification" program.[20]

Outside Asia, some argue that the result of these market-driven forces will be the creation of a "nontreaty bloc." Although the current trends toward regional orientation do not involve any formal preferences, much of the actual integration is being carried out by Japanese *keiretsu*, which are inherently preferential. The result, it is argued, will ultimately be a private nontreaty bloc in which non-*keiretsu* firms would be excluded.

Beyond this possibility, there are two proposals to formally extend economic integration in the region. The better known of the two is the organization of Asia Pacific Economic Cooperation (APEC); the second is the East Asian Economic Group (EAEG). Originally proposed by Australian prime minister Bob Hawke, APEC was launched in November 1989. Its membership initially included, in addition to the ten East Asian countries, the United States, Canada, Australia, and New Zealand. APEC has not been viewed as a free trade area but rather as an organization in which members could pursue policy objectives of mutual interest. These could include promoting multilateral trade liberalization and strengthening the GATT; harmonization of economic policies not covered under the GATT; liberalizing trade and investment flows on a regional basis beyond multilateral commitments; providing a neutral forum for discussing issues of multilateral interest currently conducted on a bilateral basis (e.g., exchange-rate policies, GSP issues); and developing common approaches to the evolving security concerns in the region. Until recently, however, APEC has been hung up on the "three Chinas" issue (which has been resolved with separate representation for Hong Kong, Taiwan, and China). With this procedural matter resolved, APEC is now confronted with the task of showing demonstrable accomplishments or facing the dustbin of history.[21]

What, then, are the likely outcomes in the trade arena? If the UR succeeds, the multilateral system would be reinvigorated and there would be a slowing in the movement toward blocs. Deep harmonization efforts would continue either bilaterally or multilaterally.

If the UR fails, however, there would be, in addition to the deep harmonization efforts, a movement toward managed trade deals and greater pressure toward blocs. Japan would have a difficult time forming a bloc along the lines of EAEG; instead, Japan would probably attempt to turn APEC into a free trade area. This would link APEC and NAFTA into a U.S.-centered trans-Pacific bloc consisting of APEC, NAFTA, and probably more-liberal Latin American countries such as Chile. The end result would be a world dominated by two blocs, the EC and the trans-Pacific group, with an unorganized periphery of largely poor, unaffiliated countries.

In comparison, the two-bloc world is a decidedly second-best option. It would limit access to markets outside the bloc, force sensitive political issues to the fore, and probably not preserve some of the procedural protection Korea currently secures through the GATT.

Conclusions

U.S. and Korean trade patterns are largely complementary. Korean exports to the United States an increasingly diverse basket of manufactures, while the United States supplies Korea with primary products and high-tech goods. In such a situation, trade expansion causes economic dislocation in the import-competing sectors of each country. This is usually accompanied by demands for protection and international political friction, a pattern likely to continue in U.S.-Korea trade for the foreseeable future. Korean imports will exert a depressing effect on incomes, output, and employment in a wide range of U.S. manufacturing industries. Conversely, imports from the United States will remain a threat to Korean agriculture and emerging industries such as aircraft and professional goods.

Under these circumstances policymakers will be under considerable pressure to use trade and industrial policy interventions to ameliorate the condition of import-competing sectors. That problem is exacerbated by some special conditions in the U.S.-Korea case. Korea, whose development path has followed that of Japan, is widely viewed as a "second Japan" in a pejorative sense and has consequently faced disproportionate trade barriers in U.S. markets made sensitive by Japanese import penetration. Thus it is unfortunate but likely that Korean producers will continue to encounter significant problems with antidumping and Section 301 policies in the United States. Similarly, the United States will continue to face barriers to trade in agriculture and will probably encounter problems associated with Korean development programs in emerging manufacturing sectors. The dispute over fighter aircraft and the polyacetal resin dumping case are probably harbingers of the future.

Trade frictions have at times been worsened by large emerging trade imbalances. These imbalances were mainly the result of U.S. macroeconomic policies. Although U.S. authorities were correct in principle (though not in specifics) in pushing for exchange-rate policy reform in Korea, the main responsibility for the bilateral imbalances of the late 1980s lies with U.S. macropolicy.

In light of the fundamental difficulty of adjustment, differences in trade policy institutions and practices, and the periodic emergence of macroimbalances, the vitality of the GATT system is crucial to the future of U.S.-Korea trade. A successful Uruguay Round would provide a framework for resolving the bilateral trade tensions previously identified. Even a successful

UR, however, would not be able to further the deep integration or harmonization of the two economies, and thus bilateral or multilateral SII-type negotiations involving Korea and the United States are likely.

An unsuccessful UR would increase momentum toward regional trade blocs. Two blocs already exist; it is probably not in anyone's interest for a bloc to form in East Asia. Japan is the key; if the UR fails, Japan will most likely try to turn APEC into a free trade area. This would effectively create a two-bloc world, in which the EC or European Economic Space and the trans-Pacific APEC-NAFTA bloc would dominate a periphery of largely poor, unaffiliated countries. This would be a decidedly second-best result from a U.S., Korean, or global perspective.

Notes

1. Yoo (1991) has analyzed the determinants of Korean protection. Although the results varied somewhat depending on econometric specification, he found that in general the degree of protection depended on factors affecting the "demand for protection," the "supply of protection," and the government's own bureaucratic objectives. In particular, protection was positively associated with demand factors such as the number of workers in an industry and the industry concentration ratio. Protection was positively related to share of output exported and negatively related to share of output purchased by consumers, both reflecting domestic opposition to protection. The extent of protection was also related to the government's own agenda, with the agriculture, infant industries, and sectors with high import penetration ratios all receiving protection.

2. Much material in this section is drawn from the United States trade representative (1991), pp. 139–49.

3. In 1989 Korea announced temporary tariff reductions of between 5 and 15 percent on eighty-six products. Items of particular interest to U.S. exporters included almonds (tariffs reduced from 40 to 35 percent), pistachios (40 to 35 percent), avocados (40 to 35 percent), raisins (40 to 35 percent), and wine (50 to 35 percent, with an additional 25 percent in 1991).

4. In 1989 Korea agreed to a phased removal of 243 restrictions on agricultural and fishery products. Items of particular interest to the United States included soybean oil, alfalfa, avocados, poultry parts, and bourbon. Imports of several products (e.g., pecans, strawberries) were subsequently restricted by phytosanitary barriers. In the case of beef, a GATT panel ruled in 1989, in response to a complaint initiated by the United States, that Korea's beef quota was inconsistent with the GATT balance-of-payments exception. The following year the United States and Korea agreed to a phased opening of the Korean market involving a relaxation of the quota and the establishment of a buy/sell system linking certain large buyers directly with producers.

5. The most infamous of these cases was the antidumping ruling against Korea producers of photograph albums. The photo album market in Korea is one virtually

perfect competition among small producers, and it is difficult to believe that these producers could exercise any price discrimination. Nonetheless, U.S. producers filed a complaint in January 1985, and in March the U.S. International Trade Commission made a determination of injury. In June, the Department of Commerce made a preliminary estimation of a 4.04 percent dumping margin; the complainants did not accept this finding and refiled the dumping charge. Commerce then accepted, without investigation, the complainants' charge and in October imposed a 64.81 percent dumping duty uniformly across all sixty-four Korean producers. Korean exports to the United States of photo albums fell from $26.6 million in 1985 to $0.3 million in 1986. The case came up for administrative review in 1989, but Commerce sustained the 64.81 percent dumping margin (Hong 1991). Although it is difficult to comprehend how these atomized producers could maintain price discrimination, it is not hard to understand the sense of outrage felt in Korea.

6. For example, purchasers of new cars are required to purchase subway bonds; when the amounts were increased in May 1990, the increase for buyers of imported cars was far higher than that assessed on the buyers of domestic models. Some boutiques selling foreign-made clothing were closed in department stores, while boutiques selling similarly priced domestically produced clothing remained open. Indeed, the definition of *luxury good* appears to be so elastic as to include even the simplest of foreign products, Tupperware.

7. In response to the comic book the Korea Foreign Trade Association (KFTA) published its own comic book extolling the virtues of liberal trade policies. Unfortunately, the KFTA comic book does not appear to have received anything close to the circulation or attention of the NACF comic book, and the NACF would have to be judged the winner in the comic book war.

8. It should be noted, however, that the United States initially attempted to resolve its dissatisfaction with Korean exchange-rate policy through the International Monetary Fund (IMF) and was unsuccessful. Indeed, in 1985 the IMF was counseling greater currency *depreciation* than the Korean authorities felt was desirable.

9. In assessing these projections two important caveats must be kept in mind. First, the projections implicitly assume that there are no dramatic changes in sectoral trade policies, either in Korea or in the rest of the world. If there were significant liberalization in textiles and apparel or increased restrictions in steel, for example, trade patterns would change in ways not captured by the model. Second, the data are expressed in 1980 relative prices. If there are significant shifts in relative prices, such as a large change in the price of oil, the current price composition of trade could look considerably different than the projected values. However, with the possible exception of the textile and apparel industries, where export growth is inhibited by the MFA, changes in Korean trade are not expected to affect world prices.

10. It should be noted that the two set of figures are not directly comparable. The Noland figures are in constant 1980 prices, while the MTI figures are in nominal dollars.

11. A similar result, that Korea appears to be "following" Japan, was obtained by Pearson (1989, 18–19) who compared the countries export similarity and correlation indexes over the period 1962–1986.

12. These figures refer to the direct effects. Total (direct plus indirect) figures were not calculated because some significant differences in the trade and input/output industry definitions could have propagated large errors throughout the calculation.

13. The figures refer to losses of *potential* jobs and as such do not imply that any particular workers would lose their current jobs. Indeed, as U.S. imports are far more labor-intensive than U.S. exports, even balanced trade growth implies a loss of potential jobs. In fact, given the incremental increases in domestic consumption, exports, and normal turnover and attrition rates, it is possible that increases in import penetration on this scale would not generate significant involuntary unemployment.

14. Unlike the U.S. figures, the employment projections for Korea do not take into account likely increases in the average product of labor. Consequently, the Korea figures should be regarded as upper-bound estimates.

15. The bilateral pattern of trade could change because of changes in third-country markets, for example, because of differences in the growth rates of third-country markets. The relative competitiveness of U.S. and Korean producers both relative to each other and relative to third-country suppliers could change.

16. This discussion draws heavily (though not exclusively) on Schott (1991).

17. This stratagem is named for Senator George Aiken, who suggested it early in the Vietnam War.

18. The United States and Japan issued a report in June 1990 elaborating a long list of specific actions that each country committed to under the SII agreement. Since then, a number of reforms have been undertaken in Japan under the SII banner. The Fair Trade Commission has been strengthened and is more vigorously enforcing antitrust policies. Attempts at land policy reform have been made, and Japan has set off on a ten-year program of expanded public investment. In the United States, preoccupation with the gulf war and then events in the Soviet Union has diverted political attention from the commitments undertaken in the SII negotiations, with a few exceptions such as relaxation of COCOM (see Glossary) export controls (Noland 1991, 5–9).

19. Over the last thirty years, these countries have approximately tripled their share of world trade and income. In other words, the Asian countries have been growing very rapidly relative to the rest of the world. It would not be surprising, then, to observe the share of intraregional trade rising precisely because they would be one anothers' most rapidly growing markets. Indeed, Lawrence (1991b, 16–17) made a "constant market share" calculation and found that this differential growth-rate effect completely explained the increase in intraregional trade. More-sophisticated econometric models have yielded the same conclusion. If anything, these economies are becoming more *globally* oriented and the degree of intraregional pull is declining (Petri 1991, 8–11).

20. As part of its strategies of placating the United States and reducing import dependence on Japan, Korea since 1987 has sent special buying missions to the United States. Total purchases from these missions was $4.7 billion in 1987–1988, $3.3 billion in 1989, and $4.6 billion in 1990 (Ministry of Trade and Industry 1991). It is unknown how much of these purchases represent additional purchases from the

United States that would not have occurred in the absence of the trade mission or genuine trade diversion from Japan, however.

21. An alternative proposal made by Prime Minister Mohamed Mahathir of Malaysia is for an East Asia Economic Group (EAEG), essentially APEC without North America and Oceania. His proposal appears to be largely for domestic consumption, though he has appealed to the resentment felt around the region in response to bilateral pressure from the United States. However emotionally appealing EAEG might be, it appears to make little economic sense. It excludes the United States, the region's largest market and its second-largest investor, and would be dominated by Japan, arguably the group's least trusted member. Not surprisingly, the proposal has been received rather coolly elsewhere in Asia.

References

Alizadeh, Parvin, and Griffith-Jones, Stephanie. 1991. "European Integration and Its Implications for the LDCs." Paper presented at the Seminar on the Dynamics of International Markets and Trade Policy, El Escorial, Spain, July 8–12.

Balassa, Bela, and Williamson, John. 1990. *Adjusting to Success: Balance of Payments Policies in the East Asian NICs.* Rev. ed. Policy Analyses in International Economics Series 17. Washington, D.C.: Institute for International Economics.

Bark, Taeho. 1991a. "Anti-Dumping Restrictions against Korean Exports: Major Focus On Consumer Electronic Products." KIEP Working Paper no. 91-02. Seoul, May.

———. 1991b. "The Uruguay Round Negotiations and the Korean Economy." Paper prepared for Second U.S.-Korea Academic Symposium: U.S.-Korea Economic Relations, Bloomington, Indiana, September 27–28.

Department of the Treasury. 1990. *National Treatment Study Report to Congress on Foreign Treatment of U.S. Financial Institutions.* Washington, D.C.

Dickey, D. A., and Fuller, W. A. 1979. "Distribution of the Estimators for Autoregressive Time Series with a Unit Root." *Journal of the American Statistical Society* 74.

Frankel, Jeffrey A. 1991. "Is Japan Creating a Yen Bloc in East Asia and the Pacific?" Unpublished paper, University of California at Berkeley.

Granger, C. W. J., and Engle, Robert F. 1987. "Co-Integration and Error Correction: Representation, Estimation, and Testing." *Econometrica* 55, no. 2:251–76.

Hayes, Dermot J. 1991. "Recent Developments and Analysis of U.S.-South Korean Agricultural Trade." Paper presented at the Second U.S.-Korean Academic Symposium on U.S.-Korean Economic Relations, Bloomington, Indiana, September 27–28.

Hong, Wontack. 1991. "Bilateral Trade Relations: The U.S. Trade Policies Toward Korea." Paper presented to the Symposium on Korea-U.S. Economic Issues, Bloomington, Indiana, September 27–28.

Kwon, Okyu. 1991. "An Assessment of Korean Trade Policies and Trade Prospects with the U.S." Paper presented to the Second U.S.-Korea Academic Symposium on U.S.-Korea Economic Relations, Bloomington, Indiana, September 27–28.

Lawrence, Robert Z. 1991a. "Developing Countries and Global Trading Arrangements." Paper presented at the Seminar on Dynamics of International Markets and Trade Policy, El Escorial, Spain, July 8–12.

———. 1991b. "An Analysis of Japanese Trade with Developing Countries." Brookings Discussion Papers no. 87. Washington, D.C.: Brookings Institution.

Ministry of Trade and Industry. 1991. "United States–Korea Trade Relations."

Nelson, Charles R. and Plosser, Charles I. 1982. "Trends and Random Walks in Macroeconomic Time Series." *Journal of Monetary Economics* 10:139–62.

Noland, Marcus. 1990a. "Prospective Changes in the Commodity Composition of U.S.-Korea Trade." In Korean Economic Institute, *Impact of Recent Economic Developments on U.S.-Korea Relations and the Pacific Basin*. Washington, D.C.: Academic Studies Series, Joint Korea-U.S. Academic Symposium. Vol. 1.

———. 1990b. *Pacific Basin Developing Countries: Prospects for the Future*. Washington, D.C.: Institute for International Economics.

———. 1991. "SII At Nine Months: Notes on the Structural Impediments Initiative." Paper presented at the U.S.-Japan Core Group Meeting, Tokyo, April 23–24.

Pearson, Charles K. 1989. "The Asian Export Ladder." Paper presented at the Seminar on Manufactured Export Expansion of Industrializing Economies in East Asia, Hong Kong, June 7–9.

Petri, Peter A. 1991. "One Bloc, Two Blocs, or None? Political-Economic Factors in Pacific Trade Policy." Brandeis University Department of Economics no. 297. Waltham, Mass.: Brandeis University.

Schott, Jeffrey J. 1991. "U.S. Policies in the Uruguay Round." Paper presented at the Second Annual Korea-U.S. Academic Symposium, Bloomington, Indiana, September 27–28.

Sims, Christopher A., Stock, James H., and Watson, Mark W. 1990. "Inference in Linear Time Series Models with Some Unit Roots." *Econometrica* 58, no. 1:161–82.

Stock, James H., and Watson, Mark W. 1989. "Interpreting the Evidence on Money-Income Causality." *Journal of Econometrics* 40, no. 1:161–82.

Tarr, G. David. 1987. "Effects of Restraining Steel Exports from the Republic of Korea and Other Countries to the United States and the European Community." *World Bank Economic Review* 1, no. 3:397–418.

Trela, Irene, and Whalley, John. 1988. "Do Developing Countries Lose From the MFA?" NBER Working Paper no. 2618, National Bureau of Economic Research, Cambridge, Mass.

———. 1991. "Internal Quota Allocation Schemes and the Costs of the AAMFA." NBER Working Paper no. 3627, National Bureau of Economic Research, Cambridge, Mass.

United States Trade Representative. 1991. *National Trade Estimates*. Washington, D.C.: U.S. Government Printing Office.

Yoo, Jung-ho. 1991. "Political Economy of the Structure of Protection in Korea."

Paper prepared for the Second Annual East Asian Seminar in Economics, Taipei, June 19–21.

Appendix

Considerable recent econometric research has focused on the specification and analysis of multivariate models in which some or all of the variables may be integrated or possess unit roots. Particular interest has centered on the possibility of cointegration explored by Granger and Engle (1987), where some linear combination of variables exhibit reduced orders of integration. More generally, Sims, Stock, and Watson (1990) have shown that the asymptotic distributions of neutrality and causality tests are sensitive to unit roots and time trends in the series. This has underscored the importance of examining the time-series properties of the data series prior to model specification and estimation.

Frequently used diagnostic tests include the Stock-Watson (SW) and Dickey-Fuller (DF) tests for a unit root (i.e., for a unit root in the series), against the alternative that the series is stationary around a linear time trend (Dickey and Fuller 1979; Stock and Watson 1989); the modified Stock-Watson test (MSW) for a single unit root when there might be a quadratic time trend; and the augmented, or higher-order, Stock-Watson (ASW) and Dickey-Fuller (ADF) tests for a second unit root (i.e., for a unit root in the first difference of the series), against the alternative that the series is stationary in first differences around a linear time trend.

These diagnostic tests were applied to six series: the bilateral trade balance (USKOTB), the bilateral exchange rate (REER), the U.S. gross national product (USGNP), the Korean gross national product (KOGNP), the U.S. fiscal deficit (USDEF), and the Korean fiscal deficit (KODEF). Together they represent domestic output in each country, policy-instigated domestic demand, the relative price of output between the two economies, and the bilateral pattern of excess demand, the bilateral trade deficit. Such a set of variables could be derived from a variety of simple exchange models. All variables are in real terms and, with one exception, were expressed in logs. (USKOTB could not be expressed in logs because the series took both positive and negative values for the sample.) In most cases the data showed no signs of seasonality, the exceptions being KOGNP and KODEF, which were then seasonally differenced. Examination of autocorrelation and partial autocorrelation functions indicated that, with one exception, all the series could be represented as AR2 functions; consequently, all the diagnostic tests were calculated with this correction. (The exception was KODEF, which was AR1.) The sample period was from 1972:1 to 1990:4.

According to the results in appendix table 1, the existence of two unit roots can be rejected for all the series. The existence of a single unit root can be rejected in favor of the alternative: that the series is stationary around a linear time trend for two series—KOGNP and KODEF—but recall that these two series were seasonally differenced.

To ascertain the order of the polynomial in time, the first differences of each series were regressed against a constant, time, and four of its own lags. The t-statistics of these deterministic regressors are reported in the final two columns of appendix table 1. According to these results, none of the variables exhibit time trends in first differences. However, when the time trend is omitted from the regression, the constant term on USGNP is significant, indicating the presence of a stochastic trend, or drift. This is consistent with the characterization of national income variables by previous researchers (e.g., Nelson and Plosser 1982). To summarize, the Korean macrovariables were highly seasonal, seasonally differenced, and did not exhibit unit roots. The other variables had single unit roots, with drift in the case of USGNP.

Having established the univariate properties of the data, the next step was to investigate the possibilities of cointegrating relationships among the series. No evidence of cointegration was found using the Stock-Watson test. In the absence of cointegration, simple vector autoregressions (VARs) are appropriate. Chi-square tests indicated that four lags were the cutoff point for rejecting the hypothesis that all greater lags were equal to zero.

The results for this model are summarized in appendix table 2. The reported statistics include the F-tests on the block exogeneity of each variable, the adjusted coefficient of determination (RBAR**2), and the adjusted Box-Ljung Q statistic for serial correlation. The results are appealing in that the adjusted coefficients of determination are high and the Q statistics are low, indicating the absence of serial correlated errors. Taken at face value the F statistics imply that USGNP, USDEF, and REER form a three-variable system of feedback. USGNP and REER are causally prior to KODEF, which in turn is causally prior to KOGNP. (It is difficult to understand how the real exchange rate and U.S. macrovariables could affect the Korean deficit except through the level of economic activity. Just think of the three-variable feedback system as being causally prior to the Korean macrovariables jointly.) The hypothesis that USKOTB is exogenous to the system could not be rejected. Again, it is probably better to think of the bilateral balance as simply being an outcome of the interaction of the other five macrovariables.

All of this suggests that the real exchange rate and the U.S. macrovariables cause the Korean macrovariables, which in turn cause the bilateral balance

Appendix Table 1. Tests for Integration and Time Trends

| | | | TEST | | | | t-statistic on 1st diff | |
VARIABLE	MSW	ASW	ADF	SW	DF		Time	Constant
USKOTB	-5.56	-88.65^a	-6.26^a	-5.90	-1.05		0.78	0.08
REER	-4.92	-38.61^a	-4.27^a	-6.13	-2.29		1.15	-0.50
USGNP	-12.31	-46.97^a	-4.09^a	-11.33	-2.83		0.27	2.41^b
KOGNP	-26.54^c	-92.40^a	-5.11^a	-25.74^b	-3.34^c		-0.31	0.06
USDEF	-13.59	-81.90^a	-5.11^a	-12.26	-2.32		0.18	-0.47
KODEF	-82.17^a	-110.71^a	-7.75^a	-80.49^a	-4.15^a		1.21	0.48

NOTE: The superscripts a, b, and c indicate statistical significance at the 1 percent level, the 5 percent level, and the 10 percent level, respectively.

Appendix Table 2. VAR Summary Results

| LHS VARIABLES | RHS VARIABLES | | | | | | | |
	USKOTB	REER	USGNP	KOGNP	USDEF	KODEF	RBAR**2	Q
USKOTB	11.68^a	0.88	0.71	1.25	1.87	0.98	0.94	15.62
REER	1.03	33.20^a	2.37^a	1.10	3.30^b	0.46	0.96	28.64
USGNP	1.40	2.77^b	23.48^a	0.65	2.63^b	0.55	0.99	27.90
KOGNP	1.40	0.54	1.36	15.51^a	0.47	2.20^c	0.99	24.06
USDEF	1.52	2.86^b	2.57^c	1.29	2.52^c	0.31	0.86	16.63
KODEF	1.88	3.43^b	3.32^b	2.55^c	1.66	10.13^a	0.85	24.31

NOTE: Superscripts indicate the level of statistical significance of the null hypothesis that all lagged coefficients of the RHS variable are jointly equal to zero; a, b, and c indicate that the null hypothesis can be rejected at the 1, 5, and 10 percent levels, respectively.

in the sense of Granger-Sims. Thus the U.S. negotiating emphasis on Korean exchange-rate policy might not have been misplaced. At the same time, both the far greater size of the United States and the causally prior character of U.S. macropolicies would imply that changes in U.S. macropolicies would have a more substantial impact on the bilateral balance than policy changes in Korea.

2

The Political Economy of U.S.-Korea Trade Friction in the 1980s: A Korean Perspective

Kihwan Kim

Future historians will no doubt record the 1980s as a decade in which relations between the United States and Korea became highly strained due to a sharp rise in trade disputes. That decade witnessed not only a conspicuous increase in the usual disputes over alleged unfair trade practices by Korean firms but also the emergence of new areas of conflict as the United States tried to open Korea's markets for its goods and services and decrease its trade deficit through a realignment in the dollar-won exchange rate. Trade friction between the United States and Korea is by no means over.

Even now, the U.S. government is pressuring the Korean government to stop austerity campaigns that the United States believes could reduce imports from the United States. The U.S. government is also requesting that Korean government extend full national treatment to U.S. banks and other financial institutions doing business in Korea.

Observers on both sides of the Pacific have expressed concern that the tension over trade, if it continues unabated, could undermine the traditionally strong and friendly ties between the United States and Korea. Maintaining these strong ties is vital not only for the economic well-being of the two nations but for their long-term security interests as well.

Given the above situation, this chapter asks four questions: First, why did so much trade friction arise between the United States and Korea in the 1980s? Second, what were the main issues and disputes, and how were they resolved? Third, how have strained trade relations affected Korea's economy, polity and its relationship with the United States overall? Finally, are there better ways to deal with trade problems between the two nations in the future?

Underlying Causes of Trade Friction

The sharp increase in trade friction between Korea and the United States in the 1980s stemmed from a combination of economic, political, and cultural factors. One factor lies in the nature of the macroeconomic policies pursued by the two countries.

The major thrust of the economic policies of the Reagan administration was to increase defense spending and cut taxes. When taxes were reduced, the administration hoped that high growth, achieved through an increase in savings and investment stimulated by tax reduction, would eventually increase tax revenue sufficient to offset the initial budgetary deficit due to tax reduction. This hope failed to materialize. Rather than decreasing America's already substantial deficit, that deficit ballooned, exerting inflationary pressures on the economy. To finance the budgetary deficit and reduce inflation, U.S. interest rates had to be raised. The dollar became overvalued as a result, hurting U.S. export competitiveness across the board. From 1980 to 1986 the U.S. trade deficit grew from $25.5 billion to $145.0 billion. The burgeoning trade deficit led to a great upsurge in protectionist sentiment in the United States.

While the United States was pursuing a set of macroeconomic policies that became known as "Reaganomics," Korea, too, was implementing a set of economic policies that could be characterized as a form of Reaganomics. But Reaganomics in Korea had a different origin and content and consequently bore different results.

In 1980, Korea faced an economic crisis of major proportions. For the first time in more than twenty years Korea experienced negative growth— minus 3.7 percent. The immediate causes were the oil shock of 1979, a poor agricultural harvest, a worldwide recession, and political uncertainty in Korea following the death of President Park Chung Hee. The deeper cause, however, lay elsewhere. In the 1970s, Korea pursued a policy that was designed to accelerate the development of heavy and chemical industries, which included iron and steel, petrochemicals, machinery, automobiles, communications equipment, and electronics. To promote these so-called strategic industries, the government extended cheap loans and preferential tax treatment. These policies fueled inflation and severely distorted Korea's industrial structure.[1]

To deal with these problems, the new government that came into power in 1980 adopted a rigorous deflationary policy and at the same time undertook wide-ranging institutional reforms. The reforms were designed in large measure to bring about small government with a balanced budget and a greater reliance on the market mechanism to both allocate resources more efficiently and improve income distribution.

In time, these reforms had their desired results. Government budgetary deficits were eliminated. Inflation was brought under control and income distribution improved. With a decline in inflation, Korea's export competitiveness strengthened and overall economic growth resumed.[2]

Ironically, the juxtaposition of the two Reaganomic policies created a wind tunnel, as it were, across the Pacific that sucked Korean products into the U.S. market. Without the benefit of this wind tunnel, Korea would not have succeeded in turning its long-standing trade deficit with the United States into a surplus in such a short time. In 1980, Korea's trade deficit with the United States was $280.0 million, but by 1985 this deficit had become a surplus of $4.3 billion. For about two years following the Plaza Accord in 1985, this wind tunnel effect was reinforced by the movement of the won-dollar exchange. During this period most major currencies were rising against the U.S. dollar but not the Korean won. As a result, Korea's surplus with the United States had ballooned to $9.6 billion by 1987.[3] As Korea's trade surplus with the United States grew, however, Korea increasingly became a target of U.S. trade actions.

Another factor contributing to the sharp increase in trade disputes between the United States and Korea was the legacy of the industrial policy Korea pursued in the 1970s. That policy, which promoted heavy and chemical industries, had many elements of import substitution, particularly in the incentive schemes it used. Besides cheap credit and preferential tax treatment, import protection was given to "strategic" industries. In the early 1980s, as part of the reform, the Korean government did its best to phase out these incentive schemes. However, enough remained on the books to annoy U.S. government officials and convince them that Korea still adhered to import substitution.[4]

The industrial policy of the 1970s contributed to trade friction between the two countries in yet another way. In the early 1980s, those "strategic" industries were suffering from excess capacity and cash flow problems. The cash flow problem was particularly serious owing to the rigorous stabilization policy that was in effect. As a result, these industries were driven to seek overseas markets aggressively. In the United States, this caused import surges from Korea. Because the import surges occurred in more or less the same industrial sectors where U.S. industry had had running battles with the Japanese, it was concluded that Korea was a second Japan.[5]

That widely shared perception—that Korea was a second Japan—was itself a major cause of tension between the United States and Korea. The U.S.

experience in negotiating with Japan to open markets had been one of continuous frustration. Even after more than twenty years of continuous efforts beginning in the early 1960s, the United States felt that the market opening it had achieved in Japan was at best limited. Indeed, many U.S. negotiators often compared the process of opening Japan's market with peeling an onion. Furthermore, as one high-level U.S. official put it, Japan's market opening always came "too late and too little"[6] to be of any use in counteracting rising protectionism in the United States, particularly in Congress. For its part, U.S. industry had been badly hurt by Japanese competition. As a result, when American consumers eagerly bought Korean-made color televisions, microwave ovens, refrigerators, telephones, personal computers, and automobiles, U.S. industry saw in Korea a contender for "the mantle of the export superstar" worn by the Japanese.[7]

The United States was also dissatisfied with the pace of market opening in Korea. The Korean government announced an import liberalization initiative in 1978 but failed to make much headway with that policy. Soon after the announcement was made, Korea was hit by the second oil shock, which led to an alarming deterioration in Korea's balance of payments. With the inauguration of the new government, however, in 1981 Korea reaffirmed its commitment to import liberalization.[8] That commitment was incorporated in the Fifth Social and Economic Development Plan (1982–86). That plan indicated that by 1986 Korea would achieve a degree of import liberalization comparable to that of OECD countries, meaning that the percentage of imports eligible for automatic approval over total imports would rise from less than 75 percent in 1981 to more than 92 percent by 1986.

In carrying through its market-opening reforms, the Korean government overcame many political and cultural obstacles. One such obstacle —resistance from sectors with vested interests in import protection—is common to any country trying to lower trade barriers, but another hurdle was unique to Korea. Before adopting an outward-looking strategy in the early 1960s, Korea had looked inward for more than five hundred years. Since the founding of the Yi dynasty in 1392, Korea had kept its door closed to the outside world. As a result, as late as the last half of the nineteenth century, Korea was literally a "hermit kingdom," refusing to trade with any country. The hardships under Japanese rule (1909–45) did little to change Korea's inward-looking tradition. Although fighting side by side with U.N. forces during the Korean War (1950–53) gave Koreans, at least those in the south, an opportunity to appreciate the benefits of working with foreign countries, this newfound appreciation did not extend to trade. Strapped by the chronic shortages of foreign exchange, the Korean government constantly exhorted citizens to save more and spend less, particularly on foreign goods. Thus, the presumed virtues of high savings and loyalty to domestic products were instilled in Koreans from an early age. The message was reinforced as recently as the second oil shock (1979–1980).[9]

Given such deeply ingrained prejudices against foreign products, it was remarkable that by early 1984 the Korean government had managed to work out a preannounced import liberalization schedule covering 92 percent of Korea's imports. The schedule not only identified individual commodities to be liberalized but assigned the timing of liberalization for each product. Although this import liberalization schedule was considered radical by many in Korea, it failed to satisfy expectations of Korea's trading partners, particularly the United States,[10] because it failed to adequately cover the two areas of special interest to the United States: agricultural products and services. In addition, the schedule did not give explicit attention to such new issues as the protection of intellectual property rights.[11]

Key Issues and Disputes

The major trade disputes between the United States and Korea in the 1980s occurred in three areas. First, disagreements arose over U.S. industry attempts to restrict the access of Korean products to the U.S. market by resorting to various provisions of U.S. trade laws or arranging so-called voluntary export restraints (VERs) with select Korean industries. Second, the United States pressured Korea to open its market to U.S. goods and services. The U.S. administration saw in such market-opening efforts not only a way to increase U.S. exports to Korea but also a way to lessen protectionist sentiment, particularly in Congress. The most blunt form of pressure was applied by invoking Section 301 of the Trade Act of 1974, as amended. Finally, as the U.S. trade deficit failed to shrink even after the Plaza Accord in September 1985, the U.S. government asked several East Asian newly industrialized economies (NIEs), including Korea, to allow their currencies to appreciate. I shall discuss major issues and disputes in these three areas in turn.

Restricting Korea's Access to the U.S. Market

During the 1980s, U.S. industry filed an unprecedented number of trade actions against Korean producers. From 1980 to 1988, no fewer than fifty-seven trade law cases were initiated against Korean firms, not counting several Section 301 cases initiated by the U.S. government and private industry. Although some petitioners genuinely sought the temporary import relief they were entitled to under law, substantial evidence suggests that many others were motivated by purely protectionist considerations.

Of the fifty-seven trade law cases, twenty-two were antidumping actions.[12] This number was more than three times the number of antidumping cases recorded during the 1970s. Nearly one-half the antidumping charges were brought against Korea's steel and steel products manufacturers, who, by the early 1980s, were considered the most efficient in the world. The electric and electronics industries were the second-largest target for antidumping actions. The actions against electric and electronics producers for the most part involved color televisions. Of the twenty-two antidumping actions initiated against Korean firms, ten resulted in affirmative findings.

From 1980 to 1988, eight countervailing duty actions were initiated against Korean producers. In this case, however, the number was comparable with nine cases initiated in the 1970s. It is worth noting that all but one of these countervailing duty cases were initiated against steel and steel related industries. Out of eight actions initiated, four were given affirmative findings. With respect to safeguard actions (Section 201 of the Trade Act of 1974, as amended), a total of eleven cases were initiated against Korean firms from 1980 to 1988. Again, the main targets were electric and electronic products and steel and steel products manufacturers. Out of eight cases filed, only two were given affirmative findings.

From 1980 to 1988, thirteen unfair practice actions were filed against Korean firms under Section 337 of the Tariff Act of 1930. This was more than three times the number of actions filed during the 1970s. Most of the charges alleged infringement of U.S. patent rights. Six cases were filed against electric and electronics producers, two against steel products manufacturers, two against chemical companies, and one against a textile manufacturer. The predominance of electric and electronics producers likely reflects the concern of some U.S. electronics giants that Korean firms might catch up technologically by infringing on their patents. Eight of the thirteen unfair practice cases filed resulted in affirmative findings.

From 1980 to 1988, three charges were initiated against Korean firms on the national security clause of Section 232 of the Trade Expansion Act of 1962. One charge was leveled against steel product manufacturers and two against machinery manufacturers. None of the charges, however, resulted in an affirmative determination. This was significant for two reasons: (1) even with the upsurge in American protectionist sentiment, any attempt to exclude foreign products on the grounds of national security was legally very difficult, and (2) the particular cases involving Korea were weak.

As already noted, the total number of non-Section 301 cases filed against Korean firms from 1980 to 1988 was fifty-seven. Of these, twenty-four cases resulted in affirmative findings. Given the fact that fewer than half the cases resulted in affirmative findings, it may be fair to conclude that at least some of the petitioners sought to use U.S. trade law to harass Korean competitors, fix alternative marketing arrangements, or enter into licensing agreements, joint ventures, or second-sourcing agreements.[13] This seems to have been the case particularly with steel and steel products.[14]

Schott (1989) has observed that VERs have been the villain of U.S. trade policy.[15] This observation is clearly applicable to Korea. During the 1984–1988 period, about 32 percent of Korea's exports to the United States were carried out under various restrictions, and nearly three-quarters of exports under restrictions were accounted for by two important VERs: one on textiles and clothing and the other on steel and steel products. The two VERs were negotiated at the government level, indicating that there was nothing voluntary about them.[16]

The VER on textiles and clothing between the United States and Korea was worked out under the multifiber arrangement (MFA). The stated aim of the MFA is to expand world trade in textiles and clothing by reducing trade barriers and at the same time preventing undue disruptions in individual markets. But each time the MFA was renewed, more product categories came under its coverage. The number of product categories subject to the MFA rose from twenty-seven in the MFA II period (1978–81) to seventy-five in the MFA IV period (1987–91). As a result, the percentage of Korea's textiles and clothing exports to the United States restricted under the MFA rose from 73 percent in the 1978–1981 period to more than 97 percent in the 1987–1991 period.[17] It is worth noting that Korea accepted these severe restrictions in large part to avoid even more protectionist legislation,[18] such as the 1985 Thurmond Bill, which President Reagan vetoed.

In 1984, Korea acceded to a VER on steel. This move was preceded by numerous antidumping and countervailing duty actions, as already noted. The stated purpose of the VER was to control "unfairly traded" steel. The Korean steel industry did not receive any government subsidy, nor did it enjoy any cross-border protection against foreign imports. As a result, it was widely acknowledged that Korea was not only the most efficient producer of steel but also a fair trader in steel. Yet Korea had no choice but to accede to the 1984 VER. The 1984 agreement limited Korea's steel exports to less than 1.9 percent of U.S. domestic steel consumption for a five-year period ending September 30, 1989. When the 1984 agreement expired, the U.S. government extended the steel VER for another two and a half years but allowed Korea to increase its share of the U.S. market up to 2.45 percent during the October 1, 1989–December 31, 1990, period and to 2.65 percent during the January 1, 1991–March 31, 1992, period.

U.S. Pressures to Open Korea's Market

Before 1985, U.S. presidents made only sparing use of Section 301, except in a few narrowly defined cases, for fear of setting precedents that would expand the scope of the provision.[19] But after 1985, the U.S. government made aggressive use of Section 301 and an augmented version known as "super 301." Of about fifteen Section 301 cases initiated by the government since 1985, two targeted Korea. One of them sought greater access to the Korean insurance market.

Before September 1985, U.S. insurance firms in Korea had for the most part been limited to serving U.S. citizens. Two U.S. firms had been allowed in fire insurance, but their business was nearly nil as they were excluded from participating in the "pool," a cartel-like arrangement for sharing business among indigenous firms. Thus, what the United States sought was access to Korea's market for all types of insurance as well as the dissolution of the pool.

After several months of intense negotiations, the first of three agreements was reached in July 1986. It allowed a specified number of U.S. firms to enter the Korean life and nonlife insurance markets on a staggered timetable. U.S. firms were also permitted to participate in the fire insurance pool until the pool was dissolved. The subsequent agreements removed the limitation on the number of U.S. insurance companies that could do business in Korea. In addition, the two governments agreed on a set of standards for determining the eligibility of U.S. firms wishing to do business in Korea.

The other government-initiated Section 301 case against Korea, which complained of inadequate protection of intellectual property rights, took the two governments much longer to settle because the issues involved were far more complex. For one thing, the United States wanted protection for product patents; Korean law protected only process patents. The U.S. government also sought full copyright protection for all copyrighted publications under the Universal Copyrights Convention; Korean law provided copyright protection only to those books first published in Korea. The United States also wanted computer software protected by copyright law or special legislation rather than patent law. In addition, the two governments disagreed over the use of trademarks and the protection of sound recordings.

Negotiations to resolve these issues proved difficult. Two issues were particularly thorny. The United States sought protection for those product patents granted in the United States during the ten-year period preceding the time when the new Korean product protection law would take effect.[20] The United States also wanted Korea to treat those U.S. applications for process patents pending at the time when the new law would take effect as if they had been applications for product patents. Initially, the Korean government refused to grant either request on grounds that doing so would amount to "retroactive" legislation. Owing to its inferior bargaining strength, however, the Korean government had no choice but to accept the U.S. position on both issues.

At least two aspects of this settlement became highly controversial. Some Korean legislators and others contended that the retroactive protection was unconstitutional. Furthermore, retroactive protection was granted only to U.S. patents. The European Community and Japan lodged a vigorous protest with the Korean government, claiming that the differential treatment amounted to a violation of the most-favored-nation principle of GATT. In October 1991, the Korean government agreed to extend similar retroactive patent protection to the European Community. But to date it has not done so to Japan.

On at least one occasion, U.S. industry used the threat of a Section 301 investigation to gain market access. Shortly after the U.S. government initiated the two Section 301 cases discussed above, the U.S. movie industry threatened to file a petition for Section 301 action with the U.S. trade representative (USTR) unless the Korean government agreed to discuss possible changes to laws and regulations that prohibited foreign movie companies from directly selling and showing films in Korea. The threat worked. Because the Korean government already had the two U.S. government-initiated 301 cases on its hands, it did not care to have yet another. It thus readily agreed to discuss the issues, which were resolved more or less to mutual satisfaction before the end of the year.[21]

Other Section 301 cases initiated by U.S. industry did not fare as well. A case in point is the petition for 301 action filed by the U.S. tobacco industry. In September 1986, the Korean government took the first step toward liberalizing imports for U.S. cigarettes. The U.S. share of the market for the first year was to be limited to 1 percent of domestic sales. Given the strong general sentiment against the import of foreign cigarettes, the government wanted to increase the U.S. share of the market gradually over several years before it completely liberalized the imports.[22] Not satisfied with the pace of Korea's initiative, however, the U.S. tobacco industry kept pressure on the U.S. government to accelerate the process. The result was that in 1987 alone, four rounds of negotiations were carried out between the two governments on cigarette issues to no avail. In January 1988, the U.S. Cigarette Export Association filed a petition for section 301 action with the USTR. After still another round of unsuccessful negotiations, an agreement was finally arrived at in May 1988. Under that agreement, Korea replaced its Tobacco Monopoly Act with the Tobacco Business Act, which not only removed the ban on the sale of foreign cigarettes in Korea but also permitted foreign producers to make direct sales.

In July 1985, the United States requested Korea to open the market for

U.S. wine. In April 1987, the Korean government announced a schedule for phased liberalization of wine imports. In this case again, however, the U.S. industry was not satisfied with the pace of the Korean initiative and filed a petition for 301 action. After three rounds of heavy negotiations, an agreement was reached in January 1989 that provided not only a reduction in tariff but also the abolishment of import quotas by 1990.

In 1982, the Korean government launched a misconceived policy of encouraging domestic production of beef. This resulted in a tremendous increase in the number of cattle being bred in Korea, which in turn led to the collapse of the price of cattle, making farmers extremely unhappy. Frightened by strong protests across several regions, in 1985 the government placed a ban on the import of all kinds of beef including the high-grade beef served at tourist hotels. The American beef industry, which supplied most of the high-grade beef, hoped that, at least, the ban would be modified to allow the import of high-grade beef in time for the 1988 Seoul Summer Olympics. When it seemed that this hope would not materialize, the U.S. beef industry decided in February 1988 to file a 301 petition with the USTR. After several unsuccessful bilateral negotiations, the United States together with Australia took the matter to the GATT. Two separate GATT panels were formed to deliberate on the U.S. and Australian complaints. The U.S.-Korea panel issued a report favorable to the United States; however, Korea did not agree to the adoption of the report by the GATT Council. The USTR then announced that unless substantial improvement toward a resolution were made soon, a proposed retaliation list would be published. In November 1989, Korea finally allowed the GATT report, which found Korea's claim for banning imports of beef on balance-of-payments grounds to be invalid, to be adopted. In line with this judgment, the United States and Korea reached an agreement in March 1990. The agreement provided a gradual increase in beef import quotas over a three-year period.

In late 1988, there was every indication that the United States would name Korea as a priority foreign country (PFC) under the so-called super 301 provision of the newly enacted Omnibus Trade and Competitiveness Act. The Korean government concluded that, given growing anti-American sentiment in Korea, it would be extremely damaging politically for Korea to be named a PFC and, therefore, offered to discuss issues of special interest to the United States. The United States responded by proposing to discuss its concerns in three areas: (1) market barriers to U.S. agricultural products, (2) restrictions on foreign investment, and (3) Korea's various policy measures aiming at import substitution. In the spring of 1989, four rounds of intense negotiations were carried out, which resulted in an agreement in May. Among other things, the agreement liberalized imports of some eleven U.S. agricultural products, including pecans and alfalfa, one year ahead of the time schedule previously announced.[23] In addition, Korea agreed to increase import quotas on whisky. In the area of foreign investment, Korea agreed not to impose such restrictions as the domestic content and export performance requirements on foreign-invested firms. Furthermore, Korea agreed to open travel services to U.S. investment. On the policy of import substitution, the Korean government agreed to remove all import restrictions designed to encourage domestic production and to revise technical standards and testing procedures impeding imports. Thanks to these agreements, Korea avoided a PFC designation but failed to prevent the United States from naming Korea's policy and practice in the field of telecommunications a "priority foreign practice."[24]

There were times when U.S. efforts to open Korea's market took more subtle forms. In the spring of 1983, President Reagan paid a visit to Korea the main purpose of which was to reassure the Korean government of the U.S. commitment to Korea's security; U.S. government officials, however, could not pass up the valuable opportunity to press for trade interests. During the visit, the Korean government received a list of some thirty commodities of special interest to the United States. Because the Korean government was in the early stages of preparing preannounced schedules for import liberalization, it was able to accommodate the United States without difficulty.

However, subsequent lists of commodities for which the United States requested liberalization could not be accommodated as easily. First, it was more difficult to incorporate U.S. requests into preannounced liberalization schedules at a later stage of preparation. Second, the lists contained many items for which the Korean government could not justify early liberalization. Cigarettes, beef, and wine were cases in point. Third, priorities indicated by the United States were not always consistent from list to list. It seemed to Korean officials that the lists were either prepared without much thought or compiled by simply putting together the wishlists of powerful members of Congress.[25] Nevertheless, the Korean government did its best to accommodate U.S. requests. Unfortunately, by so doing, the preannounced schedule approach to import liberalization lost much of its credibility with domestic industry.

In addition to its efforts to remove many nontariff barriers, the United States put pressure on Korea to reduce tariffs on U.S. products. Between 1983 and 1987, the United States requested tariff reductions on 433 products as defined by the eight-digit CCCN classification. As a result, the average tariff rate on these products fell from 39.9 percent in 1983 to 27.8 percent in 1988. Not satisfied, in 1988, the United States pressed Korea for further tariff reductions on 1,572 products as defined by the ten-digit harmonized system (HS) classification. Partly in response to this request, the Korean government announced a five-year tariff reduction plan covering the 1989–

1993 period. By so doing, Korea was able to accommodate nearly 94 percent of the industrial products and 58 percent of the agricultural products included in the U.S. request.

Exchange Rate and Other Policy Adjustments

In September 1985, the United States reached the Plaza Accord with the G-5 (see Glossary) countries. The accord led to effective coordination of economic policy among the G-5 countries, which resulted in weakening the dollar. The United States hoped to reduce its trade deficit by keeping the dollar weak. However, when the trade deficit continued to worsen, the United States blamed the exchange-rate policies of the East Asian NIEs such as Korea and Taiwan.

Starting in mid-1986, the United States began pressuring Korea to appreciate its currency, the won. The pressure became particularly strong in early 1987; Korea resisted as much as possible, making only minimal adjustments to the exchange rate. Korea, then anticipating a presidential election before the end of the year and a general election shortly thereafter, feared that undue appreciation of the won would slow down the economic boom then in progress, a consequence that could only hurt the party in power. In the later part of the year, however, when it was no longer possible to resist U.S. pressure, the Korean government took steps not only to accelerate appreciation of the won but also to sustain domestic demand at a high level.[26]

Negotiation Styles: The United States and Korea

The process of raising trade issues and settling disputes between the United States and Korea has been highly politicized, due in no small measure to the way trade policy is made and implemented in the United States. Under the U.S. Constitution, Congress has the final say on trade policy and negotiations. Unlike other policy areas, Congress has shown little inclination to delegate its authority on trade matters to the executive branch. The result is that U.S. trade policy is made, in effect, by a committee of 535 legislators,[27] each of whom tends to represent the interests of his or her constituency and typically operates within a short time horizon.

Trade negotiations with the United States are also made difficult by the conflicting institutional pressures on the Office of the U.S. Trade Representative (USTR), which is responsible for trade negotiations with foreign governments. Although the USTR organizationally belongs to the executive office of the president, it functions more like an agency of Congress for a variety of reasons.[28] For one thing, the USTR owes its birth in 1963 to the dissatisfaction of Congress with the executive branch over its conduct of trade negotiations with foreign governments.[29] For another, the USTR is required by law not only to report regularly to Congress but also to consult closely with members of Congress even in its day-to-day operations. In addition, it is required by law to consult representatives of the private sector through various formal and informal networks before it enters into any significant negotiations with a foreign government. Because of its confusing institutional mandate, the USTR often appears to suffer from a severe case of schizophrenia, being incapable of ordering its priorities in a consistent manner. Furthermore, it is highly limited in flexibility in negotiations and, most of the time, like individual members of Congress, has a very short time horizon.

Few foreign governments appreciate these organizational peculiarities of the USTR. As a result, they often take the inconsistency, inflexibility, and impatience of the USTR simply as a manifestation of American arrogance acquired in the days of U.S. hegemonic leadership. This certainly has happened many times in negotiations between Korea and the United States.

For its part, Korea does not have an organizational counterpart to the USTR. However, this does not make Korean trade policy any less politicized. Nor, for that matter, does it make Koreans any easier to negotiate with. When trade problems involve the United States, no political leader in Korea can afford to delegate too much authority. To this day, Korea depends heavily on the United States for its security. Furthermore, given that to many Korean governments Washington has served as the provider of legitimacy, no Korean policymaker can ignore the political consequences that serious trade disputes with the United States may bring domestically. By the same token, all trade problems, big or small, tend to be exploited by opposition political groups for partisan purposes.

Korea also lacks an adequate administrative channel for making consistent trade policy. For one thing, jurisdictions on trade matters are scattered among several ministries. As far as manufactured imports are concerned, the Ministry of Trade and Industry usually has the final word. With regard to trade in agricultural products, the Ministry of Agriculture and Fishery enjoys unchallenged authority. On financial services, it is the Ministry of Finance that has exclusive jurisdiction. On intellectual property rights, responsibilities are shared between the Ministry of Culture being responsible for matters relating to copyrights and the Office of Patents being responsible for patents and trademarks. On computer software, the Ministry of Science and Technology has exclusive jurisdiction. When it comes to the question of actual negotiation, the Ministry of Foreign Affairs insists on a major role, although it does not often possess the requisite competence or expertise. To minimize interministerial conflict on external economic policy-making in general and trade policy-making in particular, an International Economic Policy Council (IEPC) was established in 1983 under the chairmanship of the deputy prime minister, who is the top economic policymaker in the government. The council, whose membership is composed of several ministers who jealously guard their respective jurisdictions and prerogatives, is supported by a secretariat. In the beginning, both the council and the secretariat functioned effectively, but they soon lost their effectiveness owing to intense interministerial rivalry. In 1986, both the IEPC and the secretariat underwent a major reorganization, which resulted in a serious loss of power.[30] Korea's trade policy has not been known for either farsightedness or consistency since.

It has been aptly observed that when a Korean sits at the bargaining table, he does so with a chip on his shoulder. His Confucian upbringing has taught him not to compromise on anything he believes to be right. What's more, the Korean public treats compromise as a sign of moral weakness or betrayal of the national interest or both. Thus, Koreans tend to dig in their heels when it comes to negotiating.[31]

Apart from these considerations, there was another constraint operating on Korean negotiators in that the Korean public strongly believed that the United States was treating Korea unfairly. Koreans felt that their country was singled out as a scapegoat for the declining competitiveness of U.S. industry, that the emergence of a trade surplus with the United States was a result of their hard work, and that there was nothing in Korea's economic performance to be ashamed of.[32] Finally, Koreans resented being called a "second Japan."

The Effects of Trade Frictions

The question is how have U.S.-Korea trade disputes affected Korea's economy, polity, and overall relations with the United States? Let us first examine the effects of disputes in each area and then assess the overall effects.

Effects of Restricting Access to the U.S. Market

The amount of Korean exports to the United States affected by various U.S. trade actions has been substantial, about 9 percent of Korea's total exports to the United States for the 1980–1988 period. In dollar terms, on the average, they amounted to $1.2 billion a year, but more important were the associated political costs. The antidumping actions and countervailing duty cases caused enormous ill will among Koreans.[33] A case in point is the public reaction to the 1985 antidumping charge against Korean photo album producers. When the Korean public learned about the album producers' financial plight, many sympathetic housewives and angry students in Seoul and other large cities volunteered to purchase extra albums on the streets to help rescue the producers.[34] This campaign was followed by a group of radical students' forcefully occupying the American Chamber of Commerce office in Seoul to protest not only the U.S. handling of trade law cases but also its efforts to open the Korean market for U.S. products, particularly agricultural products.

Another point is worth noting. Once charges are filed against a Korean firm, the firm has no choice but to hire expensive American lawyers to deal with them. Owing to the time and expense involved, some Korean firms have given up the battle without a fight while others have voluntarily reduced exports.[35] In either situation, their decisions often have nothing to do with the merits of the cases against them.

There is little question that VERs on textiles and steel have limited Korean exports of these products to the United States, particularly the VER on steel. A conspicuous decline in Korea's steel exports was evident after the 1984 agreement. That year, the value of Korea's total steel exports to the United States was $975 million, which fell to $869 million in 1985 and $731 million in 1986, and the trend continued until 1989. Some argue that the declining trend had more to do with a rapid rise in Korean domestic consumption of steel, and although domestic consumption did rise, thanks to the economic boom of the 1986–1988 period, this argument overlooks the investment-deterring effect the VERs had on the steel industry in Korea.[36] In addition, one should also note that despite the investment-deterring effect, the amount of steel and steel products exported to the United States markedly increased after the 1989 VER allowed larger quotas.[37] It has also been argued that the VER on steel greatly benefited Korean producers by raising the price of steel.[38] However, despite the presumed rise in price of steel, the dollar value of the export declined noticeably after the 1984 VER had been arranged. This being the case, the amount of rent per unit of steel exported might have risen, but the total profit from the export of steel clearly did not.

As for the VER on textiles, despite growing product coverage, Korea's total exports of textiles and clothing grew from $1.1 billion in 1981 to nearly $4 billion in 1988. Much of this was due to product diversification and quality improvement.[39] One cannot conclude, however, that the VER on textiles and clothing has not harmed Korea unless one shows that such diversification and improvement would not have occurred but for the VER. Furthermore, it is not at all clear what costs Korea incurred to achieve such growth.

Section 301 actions and other efforts to force open the Korean market have also done enormous damage to Korea as well as to U.S.-Korea relations. To be sure, but for these actions, the Korean markets for certain U.S. products or services might not have opened as early as they did. One should bear in mind, however, the various other costs Korea and the United States have borne. For one thing, the forceful manner in which markets were opened convinced many Koreans that market liberalization is, after all, for the benefit of foreign powers, not for the benefit of Koreans. Other victims of the "crowbar"[40] approach to market opening have been liberal reformers in Korea. When the insurance market was opened and the issues on intellectual property rights were settled under what was seen by the Korean public as duress, those liberal reformers involved in the negotiations were seen as traitors to the national interest. Furthermore, public sentiment in favor of liberalization in Korea visibly evaporated shortly after the two Section 301 cases were settled. By bringing about such consequences, the crowbar approach has greatly harmed Korea's own initiative to liberalize imports. In addition, for the United States, a vicious circle has been created: once the United States resorted to the crowbar approach, it had few options but to use the approach with even greater force to achieve any new market opening in Korea.

American efforts to open the Korean market would have been more justifiable if the United States had not tried to restrict Korea's access to its own markets, to which the Korean response was, "Why should we open our markets when Americans are closing theirs?" Such experience with U.S. trade policy has led many Koreans to conclude that, for Korea to maintain its economic growth, it should make greater use of the domestic market or explore new markets in areas such as the Soviet Union, Eastern Europe, and China. This explains not only the recent inward orientation of Korea's economic policy but also the aggressive efforts Korean industries have made in recent years to explore markets in these areas, despite the great risks involved.

To reduce its bilateral surplus with the United States, Korea has stepped up efforts to divert its imports away from Japan to the United States. Although this may have improved the U.S.-Korea bilateral trade imbalance in the short run, Korea's long-run economic efficiency will no doubt suffer. What is more, by diverting imports away from Japan through administrative measures, Korea has violated the nondiscriminatory principle of the GATT. In fact, on various occasions, Japan has threatened to take this issue to the GATT.

Much damage was done by the United States to its relationship with Korea in forcing a showdown over cigarettes. First, the symbolism involved was unfortunate; to many Koreans, U.S. efforts to sell more cigarettes in Korea brought back painful memories of the Korean War, when American cigarettes were used as a means of payment for distasteful transactions involving women. Second, Koreans had difficulty understanding why the U.S. government was promoting cigarette sales in Korea while it was progressively banning smoking domestically.[41] Accusing the United States of hypocrisy, some Koreans likened the U.S. "cigarette war" to the Opium War Great Britain waged in the nineteenth century.

Effects of the Exchange Rate and Other Policy Adjustments

As a result of U.S. pressure, the Korean won appreciated about 30 percent in nominal terms against the U.S. dollar from the end of 1986 to the first quarter of 1989. Because Korea was experiencing a resurgence of inflation and a rapid increase in wages, particularly after 1987, the appreciation of the won was much greater in real terms and Korea's export competitiveness suffered. In 1989, Korea's overall exports in real terms registered negative growth—minus 4.6 percent—for the first time since 1979. In 1990, the exports recovered just enough to regain the loss suffered the previous year.

Korea's exports to the United States, however, did not recover as easily. In 1989, exports to the United States declined 3.6 percent; in 1990 and 1991 they further declined, 6.2 percent and 4.1 percent, respectively. Such a decline in exports coupled with a rise in imports from the United States brought about a dramatic decline in Korea's trade surplus with the United States. Korea's trade surplus fell from $8.6 billion in 1988 to $4.7 billion in 1989 and $2.4 billion in 1990. In 1991, the surplus became a deficit of $353 million.

What is important here is that the decrease in Korea's trade surplus with the United States appears to have been achieved at the cost of a growth in total trade between the two countries. The total volume of two-way trade fell from $34.0 billion in 1989 to $33.6 billion in 1990. In 1991, this decline was arrested, but the 1991 increase was barely 3 percent over the previous year. Needless to say, this stagnation in total trade volume is hardly an outcome that either Korea or the United States welcomes.

Furthermore, there is little question that the combination of a sharp rise in the number of trade law cases, Section 301 actions, and exchange-rate adjustments has pushed Korea to rely on domestic demand for growth. For the past 3 years little growth has stemmed from exports, and their role as a source of growth has been negative or at best negligible. If this trend leads Korea into becoming less dependent on trade, it will be difficult for Korea to become an important market for U.S. goods and services.

Better Alternatives for the Future?

From the foregoing discussion, we can draw several lessons as to how trade friction between Korea and the United States may be better handled in the future. First, the United States must put its macroeconomic house in order. The primary cause of protectionism and subsequent trade friction has been the shortage of savings relative to investment in the United States. Rather than face this basic problem, U.S. policymakers have chosen to blame the deficits on unfair trade practices by U.S. trading partners, including Korea. As many studies have shown, trade practices by U.S. trading partners have not been the primary cause of the U.S. trade deficit. One simply needs to recall that the United States had its current account more or less balanced during the 1970s, a decade when the markets of the East Asian NIEs, including Korea, were even less open than during the 1980s.[42]

Second, while attributing U.S. trade deficits to foreign trade policies might be acceptable in the United States, this practice has never carried much credibility abroad and certainly not in Korea. Many Koreans, as well as Japanese, refuse to take the blame. This does not mean, however, that efforts should cease to open those markets.

Third, in negotiating a market opening in Korea, the United States needs a more balanced and nuanced approach that takes into account the political constraints facing the Korean government. By pressing Korea to liberalize imports of such products as wine, beef, and cigarettes as top priority, the United States in effect has sidetracked the initiative and efforts of the trade reformists in Korea. This has not been in the interest of the United States or Korea.

Fourth, rather than asking Korea to liberalize only certain particular commodities at a given time, the United States should ask Korea to negotiate a program whereby the two countries would open their respective markets for all products within an overall time frame. This approach would have several advantages. For one thing, compared with a unilateral request for market opening for particular products at a certain time, a reciprocal request for comprehensive market opening is more consistent with the principles of free markets and free trade. As such, it would bring about a more efficient integration of the two economies, based on comparative advantage rather than political advantage. This would result in greater output and enhance the welfare of both countries. In addition, a comprehensive market opening with an overall time frame would allow the government of the importing country the time to undertake structural adjustment assistance programs in advance of market opening for those sectors of the economy such as agriculture and finance where automatic and speedy structural adjustments in response to market opening cannot be taken for granted. What is more, the political cost of comprehensive market opening would be less than the political cost of market opening for particular products at a given time. If it is made clear that all imports are going to be liberalized within a given time period, say ten years, then no industry would be motivated to lobby the government for an exemption. In other words, if all imports are to be liberalized within ten years, the producer of an import-competing product would, at most, ask that liberalization of his product be delayed as much as possible within the ten-year time frame rather than lobby for permanent protection. That would make the task of working out a liberalization schedule much easier. Finally, one should bear in mind that if certain imports are liberalized under duress from external pressure in a piecemeal fashion with little or no indication of the future scope or the pace of liberalization, tremendous political resistance builds before each round of liberalization and strong resentment against the government persists afterward. Korea has lost many able trade negotiators this way, and it cannot continue to offer them up as sacrificial lambs at the altar of public opinion after each round of liberalization.

The suggestion made here of course amounts to a proposal for a full-fledged U.S.-Korea free trade agreement. Apart from the great contribution it would make to the welfare of the two nations, such an agreement has inestimable value for the world as a whole. At the moment, the world trading system is in danger of sliding into tripartite regionalism with one axis in Europe, another in North America, and a third in the Asia-Pacific region. If the world economy is in fact divided up into three major blocs, we will see the recurrence of the unstable regime that prevailed before World War II. To minimize the possibility of such a development, an urgent need exists to form a powerful free trade alliance in the Asia-Pacific region that could effectively counteract the regional orientation of Europe in particular. A U.S.-Korea free trade area would be the most effective first step toward forming such an alliance. If Korea and the United States formed a free trade area, other dynamic Asian economies, such as Taiwan, could not afford to not partici-pate. If both Korea and Taiwan became parties to free trade with the United States, Japan could not and would not choose to stay out of the arrangement. In the end, all the major economies in the Asia-Pacific region and North America would form one free trade area. Such a free trade area would not only serve as an effective countervailing force to Europe but eventually become powerful enough to absorb Europe. Then, the entire world would in effect become one large free trade area, which, after all, is what the GATT is all about. In short, for their own interests as well as the interests of the world, it is high time for both the United States and Korea to give up the particular-istic approach to liberalization; instead, both should work together for a comprehensive market opening aimed at liberalizing all products and services within a reasonable time frame.[43]

Notes

1. For a fuller discussion on the heavy and chemical industry drive of the 1970s and its consequences, see Kim (1990), particularly pp. 2–6.

2. For a more detailed discussion of the content as well as the consequences of the reform, see Kim (1990), especially pp. 8–16.

3. Needless to say, this effect of the currency misalignment between the U.S. dollar and the Korean won in the period following the Plaza Accord should be separated from the effect of Korea's "Reaganomic" policy reforms of the early 1980s.

4. For an example, see the statement of Michael B. Smith, "Korea as a U.S. Trading Partner," in Bayard and Young (1989), particularly p. 79. For another, see "Statement of Peter A. Algeir, Assistant U.S. Trade Representative for Asia and Pacific," in U.S. House of Representatives, Committee on Ways and Means, *Managing United States-Korean Trade Conflict,* 100th Congress, 1st Session, September 21, 1987 (Washington: U.S. Government Printing Office, 1987).

5. Schott (1989), p. 101.

6. Remarks made by William Brock, former United States trade representative, in a conversation with the author in 1985.

7. Schott (1989), p. 101.

8. In 1981, import liberalization efforts were stepped up. The import liberalization ratio rose from 68.6 percent in 1980 to 74.4 percent in 1981. Some reformers in the Korean government held the view that the weak balance-of-payments position was an argument in favor of rather than against import liberalization.

9. Young (1989), p. 133.

10. Ibid.

11. One further consideration here relates to the existence of many special laws, which had the effect of reducing the significance of the import liberalization ratio. These laws permitted individual ministries to designate certain commodities as requiring government approval for import. See Young (1989), p. 135, for a brief discussion on this point.

12. The following discussion on non–Section 301 trade law cases relies heavily on Nam (1990), especially pp. 24–38.

13. For an excellent discussion on the ways U.S. industries have made use of U.S. trade laws to achieve their protectionist aims, see Schott (1989), particularly pp. 87–94.

14. It is instructive in this regard to recall that in 1986 Pohang Steel Corporation entered a joint venture with one of U.S. Steel's subsidiaries in Pittsburg, California.

15. Schott (1989), p. 95.

16. Nam (1990), p. 26.

17. Nam (1989), p. 28.

18. It is sometimes said that Korea did not strongly object to the continuation of

the MFA because, as an early participant in the market restricting arrangement, Korea was a beneficiary of larger export quotas and derived much rent as a result.

19. Schott (1989), pp. 90–91.

20. The rationale offered by the United States was that patents granted in recent years were not yet embodied in commercial products. As a result, there were dangers of patent infringement through reverse engineering when products embodying the patents would come to the market unless such "retroactive" protection was given.

21. This, however, did not mean an end to the dispute. Many problems later occurred in implementing the agreement.

22. One particular institutional factor made it extremely difficult for the Korean government to rapidly liberalize the cigarette market. Following the Japanese colonial period, the manufacturing and distribution of tobacco products were government monopolies. Furthermore, the employees manufacturing these products were bona fide civil servants whose status could not readily be changed without new legislation.

23. The schedule referred to here was announced in March 1989. The schedule specified the liberalization of 265 agricultural products over the 1989–1991 period. The announcement of the schedule was motivated in large measure to avoid the PFC designation. This being the case, the announcement should be considered part of the policy package offered to the United States in the negotiation.

24. The key issue raised by this action centered on the question of whether U.S. firms would be allowed to participate in telecommunications valued-added network business in Korea. After ten rounds of negotiations an agreement was reached in February 1992.

25. For another elaboration on this point, see Kim (1988).

26. It is interesting to note that at about this time the Korean government had its version of the Maekawa Report issued, signaling its intention henceforth to emphasize domestic rather than external demand in its macroeconomic policy.

27. A similar point is made in Schott (1989), p. 84.

28. This probably explains why no U.S. president since John Kennedy has been happy with the USTR as an institution and why several have attempted to abolish or reorganize it.

29. From the congressional point of view, the greatest fault of the executive branch, especially the State Department, was that it tended to give too much emphasis to national security considerations and too little to commercial interests.

30. The 1986 reorganization was basically due to long-standing interministerial rivalry. However, a case can be made that the proximal cause was the two U.S. government-initiated 301 actions. When the actions were initiated, several ministries jointly blamed the IEPC secretariat rather than themselves for not preventing the actions beforehand. After the disputes were settled, the same ministries blamed the secretariat for what they considered excessive concessions to the United States.

31. For these points, see Stokes (1986), pp. 814–19.

32. Ibid.

33. There is no question that some antidumping actions, especially those against the Korean producers of color televisions, benefited Korean consumers by lowering

the prices of television sets in Korea. But this was appreciated more by the economists than the general public.

34. One important reason why the Korean public was so exercised about this case was that the U.S. Department of Commerce announced a dumping margin of 4.04 percent in its preliminary finding but a dumping margin of 64.8 percent in its final finding. The Korean public also had difficulty understanding why the final margin was based not on actual cost accounting data but on what the department calls "constructed value."

35. The examples of unilateral VERs include those on shoes, photo albums, videocassette recorders, microwave ovens and color televisions.

36. Nam (1990), p. 40.

37. The total export of steel and steel products rose from 1.1 million metric tons in 1989 to 1.6 million metric tons in 1990.

38. G. David Tarr, "Effects of Restraining Steel Exports from the Republic of Korea and Other Countries to the United States and European Community," *World Bank Economic Review* 1, no. 3 (May 1987).

39. Nam (1990), p. 28.

40. The term was used by Carla Hills to describe her job as USTR.

41. Fallows (1988), p. 29.

42. For a similar view, see Frankel (1991), p. 3.

43. During President Bush's visit to Seoul in January 1992, the U.S. and Korean governments agreed to reactivate bilateral working-level trade groups to deal with individual trade problems. Unfortunately, this agreement does not represent an innovative departure from the particularistic approach the two governments have pursued all these years despite its basic limitations. As such, the agreement does not obviate the need to consider seriously the free trade agreement being proposed. For another exposition on the problems associated with the particularistic approach, see Kim (1988).

References

Baldwin, Robert E. 1990. "U.S. Trade Policy, 1945–1988." In Charles S. Pearson and James Riedel, eds., *The Direction of Trade Policy: Papers in Honor of Isaiah Frank*. Cambridge, Mass.: Basil Blackwell.

Bayard, Thomas O., and Young, Soo-Gil, eds. 1989. *Economic Relations Between the United States and Korea: Conflict or Cooperation?* Special Report 8, Washington, D.C.: Institute of International Economics.

Choi, Y. H. 1988. "Korean Attitude toward Korea-U.S. Trade Friction: Content Analysis of Two Daily Newspapers," *Korean Observer* 29 (Autumn): 324-41.

Fallows, James. 1988. "Korea Is Not Japan," *Atlantic*, October.

Frankel, Jeffrey A. 1991. "Liberalization of Korea's Foreign-Exchange Markets and the Role of Trade Relations with the United States." Chapter 5 in this volume.

Ilhae Institute. 1987. *Korea-U.S. Economic Relations: Current Issues and Future*

Possibilities. Presentations at the Ilhae-Brookings Joint Seminar, the Ilhae Institute, Seoul, March 15–20, 1987.

Kim, Kihwan. 1990. "Deregulating the Domestic Economy: Korea's Experience in the 1980s." Paper presented at Senior Policy Seminar Sponsored by Economic Development Institute and Institudo de Estudios Superiores de Administracion, Caracas, Venezuela July 19–22, 1990 (to be published by the World Bank).

———. 1988. "Maintaining Korea's Competitiveness in a Changing Domestic and Global Environment," *FYI*, June 24, 1988, Korea Economic Institute of America, Washington, D.C.

Kim, Youn-Suk. 1990. "Korea-U.S. Trade Friction and Japan Factor." *Asian Profile* 18, no. 1 (February).

Korea Foreign Trade Association. 1991. *Hanmi Tongsang Machal Sa* [The History of Korea-U.S. Trade Friction] (in Korean). International Trade Report Series, 91-12, Seoul: October.

Kuznets, Paul W. 1989. "Trade, Policy and Korea–United States Relations." *Journal of Northeast Asian Studies* 8 (Winter): 24–42.

Nam, Chong-Hyun. 1990. "U.S. Trade Policy and Its Effects on Korean Exports." KDI Working Paper no. 9018. Seoul: Korea Development Institute.

Pearson, Charles S. 1987. "Free Trade, Fair Trade? The Reagan Record." In Robert M. Stern, ed. *U.S. Trade Policies in a Changing World Economy*, Cambridge, Mass.: MIT Press.

———, and Riedel, James, eds. 1990. *The Direction of Trade Policy: Papers in Honor of Isaiah Frank*, Cambridge, Mass.: Basil Blackwell.

Schott, Jeffrey J. 1989. "U.S. Trade Policy: Implications for U.S.-Korean Relations." In Thomas A. Bayard and Soo-Gil Young, eds., *Economic Relations between The United States and Korea: Conflict or Cooperation?* Special Report 8. Washington, D.C.: Institute for International Economics.

Stern, Robert M., ed. 1987. *U.S. Trade Policies in a Changing World Economy.* Cambridge, Mass.: MIT Press.

Stokes, Bruce. 1986. "Korea: Relations Worsen." *National Journal* 18 (April 5): 814–19.

———. 1987. "New Rivals in Asia." *National Journal* 19 (May 9): 1116–19.

Republic of Korea, International Economic Policy Council. 1985. *Korea's Economic Policy Reform: Progress to Date and Implications for U.S.-Korea Relations.* Seoul: March.

U.S. Congress, House of Representatives, Committee on Ways and Means. 1987. *Managing United States–Korea Trade Conflict.* 100th Congress, 1st Session. Washington, D.C.: U.S. Government Printing Office.

U.S. Congress, Senate. 1989. *Currency Manipulation*, Hearings Before the Subcommittee on International Trade of Committee on Finance, 101st Congress, 1st Session. Washington, D.C.: Government Printing Office, May.

Young, Soo-Gil. 1989. "Korean Trade Policy: Implications for Korea-U.S. Cooperation." In Thomas Bayard and Soo-Gil Young, eds., *Economic Relations between The United States and Korea: Conflict or Cooperation?* Special Report 8. Washington, D.C.: Institute for International Economics.

PART TWO

OVERCOMING
TRADE BARRIERS

3

A Rock and a Hard Place: The Two Faces of U.S. Trade Policy toward Korea

J. Michael Finger

U.S. trade policy since the early 1980s has differed from policy in the first two or three decades after World War II. Until the late 1970s, U.S. trade policy nurtured an economic world order that had been shaped by international agreements during and after World War II. For the past ten or fifteen years, however, trade policy has responded to the demands of various domestic constituents for greater access to foreign markets or for reducing foreign access to the U.S. market.

When concern for the world economic order was dominant, this concern helped temper actions the U.S. government might use to advance the interest of a particular constituent. But now these constituent-supporting actions *are* U.S. trade policy. In other words, the current objective of U.S. trade policy is to respond to each constituent's plea to apply this or that regulatory instrument (antidumping, 301, etc.) in a way that will win that constituent's vote. *Policy*, now, is no more than a generic label for the accumulations of these responses.

This chapter examines U.S. trade actions in the 1980s and pays particular attention to actions against Korea. Its underlying theme is that these actions have no unifying discipline, other than to respond in a politically acceptable way to constituent pressures. U.S. trade actions are responses to the politics and economics of each specific situation, not the automatic or hands-off extension of nondiscriminatory standards the still-popular rhetoric of a rules-based system would suggest.

The Changed Thrust of U.S. Trade Policy

The world trading system that U.S. leadership helped to create at the end of World War II—the GATT system—had two principal characteristics: (1) It would be a liberal, or open system, though not a laissez-faire system. (2) Government intervention in international trade would be predictable, that is, only in previously stated circumstances, and nondiscriminatory.

The system's objectives would be advanced through two related mechanisms. There would be successive rounds of multilateral bargaining to reduce each member country's import restrictions and to bind them against unilateral revision. In this way the openness of the system would be created. This openness would be preserved and the stability and even-handedness of the system would be provided through a system of multilateral rules—GATT rules—that would minimize new government interventions in international trade and would limit those interventions to previously stated circumstances. In line with this, some GATT rules specify policies that member countries may not use, such as assigning artificial customs values so as to inflate tariff charges. Other GATT rules specify circumstances in which a national government may restrict international trade, but the intent is always to limit intervention to the specified circumstances. Article 12, for example, states that

> any contracting party, in order to safeguard its external financial position and its balance of payments, may restrict the quantity or value of merchandise permitted to be imported, *subject to the provisions of the following paragraphs of this Article* (emphasis added).

Antidumping, antisubsidy, and several other sorts of import restrictions are similarly provided for.

For the first thirty-five or so years after the GATT was agreed, U.S. trade policy—and that of many other developed countries—was approximately what would be expected of a good GATT citizen. Trade policy was a part of *foreign* policy; a viable and equitable international trading system was a key part of the postwar foreign policy plan for world peace and stability. Participation in the GATT rounds did reduce trade restrictions on most manufactured goods practically to zero. Sectoral pressures for new protection did arise, but on the whole the apparent subjection of the instruments of protection to international rules helped the government parry many of these pressures. The net result was the liberal and stable trading system that GATT's founders, including American leadership, had envisaged.

But over the past decade the orientation of U.S. trade policy has changed. As Congress has reasserted its authority over trade policy, it has taken a less presidential, more congressional, orientation. Although foreign policy has been the favored political arena of recent presidents, constituent service is the lifeblood of congressional politics. Thus trade policy has become more constituent-oriented, and this shift has brought with it several important changes in the *mechanics* of U.S. trade policy. The most consequential change has been the *reversal* of the function of the "rules" part of the policy system.

Consider, first, the GATT rules such as those on antidumping and countervailing duties—those that allow import restrictions but attempt to limit those restrictions to a few circumstances. To a firm or industry losing sales to import competition, the crux of these rules is not what they say about when a national government cannot restrict imports; the crux is what they say about when a national government can restrict imports. To an import-competing interest these "trade remedies" specify when that constituent has a *right* to call on his government to impose a trade restriction—and these rights have the international sanction of the GATT. As a constituent views the GATT rules, so does the Congress, and import-competing interests understand the value of being vocal constituents. Over time, these constituents have pressed Congress and the government to fit their needs to the trade remedies' scope and to change the trade remedies' scope to fit their needs.

They have been quite successful, so successful that the GATT rules are now an expression of the domestic politics of trade policy, not a limit on it. As the policy-making system now works, the sequence of causation is as follows:

1. Concerns of domestic enterprises to have protection from import competition

2. Expansion of national administrative practice to accommodate

3. Revision of national laws and regulations to validate the expanded administrative practice

4. Agreement at the multilateral trade negotiations to expand the relevant international code to provide international sanction for the expanded national practice[1]

The fourth step is little more than gilding—maintaining the facade of the old GATT system. The essence of the new system is that it gives any enterprise or industry inhibited by import competition the right to call on his government to restrict imports.

The creation of Section 301 was a second notable change in the mechanics of U.S. trade policy. With 301, U.S. exporters no longer need trade negotiations to advance their interests. Section 301 uses the threat of tit-for-tat retaliation to force foreign governments to remove policies that impede U.S. exports, or to take other actions that favor U.S. exports. (The results of 301 cases will be discussed below.)

The menace of 301 is less that it serves the interests of U.S. exporters than that it unchains them from the necessity to oppose U.S. import-competing interests. Before 301, access to foreign markets for U.S. exporters was obtained in exchange for giving foreigners similar access to the U.S. market. For the president to negotiate such an exchange he had to be empowered with the authority to reduce U.S. restrictions. To pass a law to authorize such reductions or to schedule and then execute fast-track implementation, U.S. exporters had to provide the government with political support to overcome the opposition that import-competing firms would raise. If the potential "winners" from a trade negotiations package can get what they want with 301, there is no one to press the Congress to impose such a package on the losers. Before 301, a GATT round put the focus on export politics and away from import politics. With 301, the U.S. government can simultaneously serve import-competing and exporting constituents.

In historical perspective, this shift to a constituent-oriented trade policy system signals a return to the traditional way of making trade policy in the United States. Once the federal income tax freed the tariff from its revenue function, U.S. trade politics soon came to be dominated by the "scientific tariff" conception—that tariff rates should be tailored to provide each U.S. industry a margin of protection equal to the difference between foreign and domestic costs. This was the economic philosophy that underlay the Smoot-Hawley tariff. In Smoot-Hawley days, calculation of the cost differences always showed that nature favored the foreigner, so that a positive tariff margin was needed to even things up. Today's calculations measure not the unfairness of nature in creating advantages for foreigners but the unfairness of the foreigners themselves. The following sections report the results of some of those calculations.

United States Import Restrictions

After many rounds of GATT negotiations, the tariff is no longer a major barrier: In 1990, though only one-third of U.S. imports entered duty free, the U.S. tariff averaged only 3.3 percent ad valorem. (On imports from Korea, it was higher, just above 6 percent ad valorem.) Table 1 provides a summary of the extent of major nontariff barriers that restrict foreign access

Table 1.   United States Imports, 1990: Percentage on Which
                the United States Imposes Nontariff Barriers

	Voluntary export restraints[a]	Restrictions on textile imports[b]	Antidumping and countervailing duty actions[c]
All merchandise			
Imports from all countries	7	5	6
Imports from Korea	9	15	5
Manufactured goods			
Imports from all countries	6	7	9
Imports from Korea	7	16	5

SOURCE: World Bank staff tabulation of information from the UNCTAD Trade Control Measures System.
[a] Includes voluntary price minimums and voluntary quantity maximums.
[b] Includes those under the multifiber arrangement (MFA) and those not under MFA.
[c] Includes antidumping and countervailing duty orders in place, agreed undertakings in place, and cases initiated in calendar year 1990.

into the U.S. market.[2] Note that the measure used in the table is not a measure of the *height* of nontariff barriers but of their *extent*—the proportion of imports to which nontariff barriers are applied. Something less than one-fifth of U.S. imports are subject to nontariff barriers of the types that have been tabulated (see table 1). On imports from Korea, the figure is higher—more than one-fourth of U.S. imports from Korea are regulated by a voluntary export restraint (VER), a similar restraint under the multifiber arrangement on textiles and clothing or an antidumping or countervailing duty action.

The more extensive application of nontariff barriers (NTBs) on imports from Korea is mainly a matter of the relative concentration of textiles and clothing imports from Korea: 21 percent of U.S. imports from Korea versus 7 percent of imports from other countries. About 70 percent of U.S. imports of textiles and clothing are subject to quantitative limits, the figure being about the same for imports from Korea as from other countries.

Particularly for established exporters like Korea, restrictions on textiles exports are not news; they have been around from the 1960s. The cutting edges of U.S. trade policy in the 1980s were 301 and the extensive use of antidumping and countervailing duty procedures to restrict imports. The remainder of this chapter will focus on these mechanisms and on the restrictions that have stemmed from their use.

Section 301

Section 301 (of the Trade Act of 1974) is an important part of the U.S. Congress's response to U.S. exporters' complaints about foreign practices and policies that reduce these exporters' access to foreign markets. As a weapon against foreign practices, the section ultimately authorizes the U.S. trade representative[3] to selectively reduce foreign access to the U.S. market. The section, as amended in 1979, 1984, and 1988, explicitly covers not only merchandise trade but services, investment, and intellectual property as well. Cross-retaliation is allowed; for example, the trade representative may retaliate by restricting imports of merchandise from a country in which U.S. *investment* or sales of *services* has been compromised.

Section 301 deals with three categories of practices that burden or restrict U.S. commerce: those that are unjustifiable, unreasonable, or discriminatory. *Unjustifiable* is defined as any act, policy, or practice that violates the international legal rights of the United States—including (but not limited to) those under a trade agreement such as the GATT, a bilateral voluntary export restraint agreement, or an agreement that settled a previous 301 case. When the agreement in question has its own dispute settlement process (as the GATT does), the trade representative is required to submit the matter to that dispute settlement process simultaneous with his investigation under 301. However, the schedule and the terms of the 301 investigation are dominant.

If the U.S. trade representative finds a foreign violation that is unjustifiable, she or he must retaliate.[4] But the section also allows the president to waive retaliation if the GATT dispute settlement process decides against the United States, if the foreign government takes action to remove or offset the violation, or if retaliation would backfire and significantly harm U.S. commercial interests or U.S. national security.

Section 301 defines *unreasonable* as an act, policy, or practice that is unfair and inequitable, though not necessarily a violation of explicit U.S. legal rights. Specific actions are listed as unreasonable, including denial of workers' rights, export targeting, denial of fair and equitable market opportunities, and government toleration of systematic anticompetitive activities.[5] *Discriminatory* means any act, policy, or practice that denies national or most-favored-nation treatment to U.S. goods, services, or investment. Retaliatory action in these cases is discretionary.

Besides tightening "regular" 301, the 1988 trade act added two major provisions, "super 301" and "special 301." Super 301 mandated that the trade representative, in May 1989 and April 1990, submit to Congress a list

Figure 1.   Initiations and Completion of 301 Cases, by Year

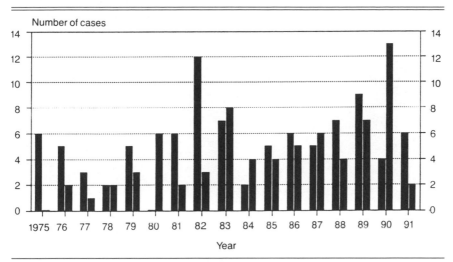

of "priority countries" and "priority practices" that pose significant barriers to U.S. exports. The act also requires the U.S. trade representative (USTR) to initiate investigations concerning each priority practice of each priority country. Special 301 provides similar requirements to identify and investigate priority countries that maintain barriers against U.S. exports of telecommunication products and services.

Let us now turn to a discussion of the case history of regular 301 and the impact of super 301 and special 301.

Industry-Country Incidence of Cases

Since 301 was created in the 1974 trade bill, the USTR has opened a total of eighty-six investigations, seventy-two of which had been completed[6]— as of August 15, 1991 (see figure 1). Of the twelve pending cases, six were suspended when the target country agreed to take up the matter in a multilateral negotiation.[7] Each of the other six is a recently initiated investigation that has not come to its mandatory completion date.

Section 301 can be criticized over many dimensions, but my tabulation of investigations and outcomes indicates that its primary function has not been to provide the U.S. government with an excuse to restrict imports. The

Table 2.   United States 301 Cases Completed through August 15, 1991, by Outcome and Country Group

Target country, by group	Total	Negative determination	TARGET COUNTRY LIBERALIZATION			U.S. retaliation	Other restrictive outcomes[a]
			Multilateral	Bilateral	Total		
All countries[b]							
Number of cases	74	11	35	12	47	10	5
(% of total number)	(100)	(15)	(47)	(16)	(64)	(14)	(7)
Developed countries[b]							
Number of cases	47	7	17	9	26	8	5
(% of total number)	(100)	(15)	(36)	(19)	(55)	(17)	(11)
Developing countries							
Number of cases	26	3	18	3	21	2	2
(% of total number)	(100)	(12)	(69)	(12)	(81)	(8)	(8)
Developing excl. Korea							
Number of cases	18	3	13	1	14	1	0
(% of total number)	(100)	(17)	(72)	(6)	(78)	(6)	(0)
Korea							
Number of cases	8	0	5	2	7	1	0
(% of total number)	(100)	(0)	(63)	(25)	(88)	(13)	(0)

Source: Tabulated from Office of the U.S. Trade Representative, "Section 301 Table of Cases," Washington, D.C., USTR, August 15, 1991, photocopied.
[a] In three of these, on the U.S. government's recommendation the petitioner withdrew his 301 petition and petitioned instead for an import-restricting action—an antidumping or a safeguards action. One of the others was the Canadian softwood lumber case, in which Canada imposed an export tax. The fifth was the Japanese semiconductor case, in which Japan agreed to import more U.S. semiconductors and to observe a minimum price on Japanese sales in third markets.

[b] In 1979 a U.S. firm complained about the Swiss customs service's testing of the gold content of eyeglass frames. The USTR's investigation revealed that U.S. standards for testing and making gold content were different from those used by many other countries. The U.S. industry agreed to shift to the more common standards and markings, which the Swiss customs service would accept without further testing. This action is classified as "liberalization by the United States" and does not fit into any of the categories listed in this table.

most frequent outcome is for the target country to liberalize the policy that the 301 case attacked (see table 2).

To understand the numbers in the table, the reader should be aware of several facets of 301 outcomes. For one, before a net liberalization was reached, several cases went through intermediate stages of retaliation by the United States and counterretaliation by the target country. For example, the National Pasta Association filed a petition on October 16, 1981, alleging European Community (EC) violation of GATT Article 26 and the GATT Subsidies Code in using pasta export subsidies that resulted in increased imports into the United States. The USTR initiated an investigation and consulted several times with the EC. The USTR also refereed the matter to the GATT Subsidies Code for conciliation. In 1982, a dispute settlement panel was established; consideration of its findings extended into 1985. In 1985 the United States increased its customs duties on pasta imports— technically in retaliation for the EC's discriminatory citrus tariffs. The EC counterretaliated on lemons and walnuts.

In August 1986 the United States and the EC agreed to end their retaliatory and counterretaliatory duties and to negotiate in good faith toward a settlement of the pasta dispute. In August 1987 the United States and the EC reached a tentative agreement whereby the EC would eliminate export subsidies on half the pasta exported to the United States. The U.S. Customs Service is now monitoring that agreement.

The pasta case also illustrates that it is difficult to say what is the final outcome of a case. In this example, the petitioner (the National Pasta Association) might, in the future, come to suspect that the EC has not reduced its subsidy as agreed. If so, he might file another 301 petition, and he will have the additional grounds that the EC is in violation of the agreement reached to end the previous pasta investigation.

Induced Liberalizations

Foreign liberalizations are in two categories, multilateral or bilateral (see table 2). The pasta case ended with an EC action that would benefit only U.S. producers. Another case that ended with a bilateral liberalization began with a petition in 1976 of the United Egg Producers complaining of a Canadian import quota on U.S. eggs. Eventually, Canada agreed to double the U.S. quota. In a more recent case that ended with a bilateral concession, the Amtech Corporation (a U.S. company) complained that Norway denied U.S. rights under the GATT government procurement code and in so doing adversely affected U.S. (i.e., Amtech's) sales of highway toll electronic identification equipment. In the end the Norwegian government agreed to several actions to offset the impact of their procurement practices on the petitioner.

Table 3. Subjects of U.S. 301 Cases, July 1975–July 1991 (number of cases)

	Merchandise Trade		Services trade	Intellectual property	Government procedures[a]	Investment regulations	Several subjects	Total
	Agriculture	Manufactures						
All countries								
Number of cases	40	24	11	7	2	1	1	86
(% of total number)	(47)	(28)	(13)	(8)	(2)	(1)	(1)	(100)
Developed countries								
Number of cases	30	19	3	0	0	0	0	52
(% of total number)	(58)	(37)	(6)	(0)	(0)	(0)	(0)	(100)
Developing countries								
Number of cases	10	5	7	7	2	1	1	33
(% of total number)	(30)	(15)	(21)	(21)	(6)	(3)	(3)	(100)
Developing excl. Korea								
Number of cases	7	5	5	6	2	1	1	25
(% of total number)	(28)	(20)	(20)	(24)	(8)	(4)	(4)	(100)
Korea								
Number of cases	3	2	2	1	0	0	0	8
(% of total number)	(38)	(25)	(25)	(13)	(0)	(0)	(0)	(100)

Source: Tabulated from Office of the U.S. Trade Representative, "Section 301 Table of Cases," Washington, D.C., USTR, August 15, 1991, photocopied.
[a]Customs valuation and import licensing procedures.

One of these was to clarify that the Amtech system met the requirements of the Oslo Toll Ring project; another was to provide a statement that the Amtech system had been proven to be reliable, competitive, and type approved by the Norwegian office of Post, Telephone, and Telegraph (PTT).

Although a number of countries found responses that benefited only the United States, almost three times as often the liberalization was a multilateral action—something that would benefit all exporters, not just the United States (see table 2). In 1979, in response to an investigation stemming from a petition by the National Canners Association, the EC agreed to discontinue a minimum import price system that had been applied to imports of canned fruits, canned juices, and canned vegetables. In another multilateral action pressed for by a 301 case, Taiwan in 1986 abolished a schedule for assigning customs duties that departed from the principle of basing such duties on invoice values. And a 301 case filed by Florida Citrus Mutual was part of the buildup to an agreement with Japan to eliminate quotas on imports of fresh oranges and orange juice. An intermediate stage, involving enlargement of import quotas, was perhaps skewed toward the United States.

Of course, the pressure of 301 was not the only impetus for many of the policy actions that terminated the cases and may even have slowed the target country's implementation of a reform it had already decided, but, qualifications aside, the pattern of these policy actions should be noted. Counting the one case that ended with a liberalizing action by the United States (see the footnote to table 2), two-thirds of the completed cases ended with a liberalizing action. Eleven petitions were dismissed as not justifying any action, leaving three times as many liberalizing outcomes as restrictive outcomes.

By far the biggest lump of cases (twenty-nine of the eighty-six) were about EC agricultural policies. (See tables 3 and 4 for information on the distributions of 301 cases across countries and across subject matter.) Subsidies were the subject of many of them, though there were other issues, such as the displacement of U.S. exports when Spain and Portugal joined the EC.

Almost half the cases that targeted a developing country were on subjects that the Uruguay Round labels *new issues*: services, intellectual property, and investment regulations that affect trade. In contrast, disputes with developed countries were almost all over *traditional issues*: restrictions that limited access of U.S. merchandise exports to foreign markets (see table 3).

Comparing the distribution of 301 cases with the distribution of antidumping plus countervailing duty cases in the United States across broad country groups (developed, developing, etc.), they are much the same (see table 4). Using the share of U.S. imports they supply as the norm, the EC and Brazil are relatively hard hit by 301 cases, Japan and Canada relatively lightly hit. The same is true for the incidence of antidumping plus countervailing duty cases. But while Korea suffers just about its share of antidumping plus

Table 4.   Countries That Are the Object of U.S. Antidumping and
                Countervailing Cases and of 301 Cases: Comparison
                (antidumping and countervailing duty cases, 1980–1988;
                301 cases, July 1975–July 1991)

Country or group of countries	CASES AGAINST THIS COUNTRY OR GROUP AS A % OF TOTAL AGAINST ALL COUNTRIES		Percentage of 1989 U.S. merchandise imports that originate in this country or group
	Antidumping and countervailing duty cases	301 cases	
All countries	100	100	100
Developed countries	58	61	63
Developing countries	37	38	36
Eastern European countries	5	1	0.5
European Community	40	34	18
Brazil	7	6	1.8
South Africa	2.6	0	0.3
Korea	4.7	9	4.2
Mexico	4.5	0	5.7
Taiwan, China	3.7	6	5.1
Hong Kong	0.1	0	2.1
Singapore	0.8	0	1.9
Canada	5	8	19
Japan	6	14	20
Argentina	1.4	6	0.3

SOURCE: Tabulated from Office of the U.S. Trade Representative, "Section 301 Table of Cases," Washington, D.C., USTR, August 15, 1991, photocopied.

countervailing duty cases, it has been the object of a relatively large number of 301 cases. The targets and the outcomes of these cases are discussed below.

Cases against Korea

Cases against Korea have covered the spectrum of 301's scope: merchandise, intellectual property, and services. (The eight cases against Korea are summarized in the Appendix.) One case ended with Korea significantly updating its intellectual property laws; four ended with Korea making significant *nondiscriminatory* reductions of barriers on imports of footwear, cigarettes, beef, and wine—ordinary products exported by many countries. The insurance cases—there were, in sequence, two cases leading to one outcome—led to the government of Korea admitting U.S. firms into several parts of the Korean market. This outcome was thus coded "liberalization-bilateral"; the best it does for third-country vendors is to spur them to negotiate for treatment similar to that extended to U.S. firms. The eighth case on the list concerned a complaint about production subsidies and import restrictions on wire rope and cable. But the U.S. steel industry was at that time filing many unfair trade petitions in an attempt to force the U.S. government to negotiate comprehensive import limits on steel. The industry succeeded in this objective, and though the petitioner eventually withdrew the petition before the 301 process reached a decision, I have classified the outcome as "retaliation" by the United States. It is an example of what many feared 301 would be—a means by which the United States would justify more trade restrictions of its own. But, as the previous section has shown, there have been few such outcomes. The profile of outcomes in cases against Korea—six liberalizations, only two bilateral, versus one restriction imposed by the United States—is close to the profile of the entire sample of cases.

Antidumping and Countervailing Duty Cases

The other side of contemporary U.S. trade policy is the use of antidumping and countervailing duty cases to regulate U.S. imports. As 301 is designed to provided a service for particular constituents who want better access to foreign markets, antidumping and countervailing duty regulations have been tailored over the past two decades to provide a service for particular U.S. constituents who are hurt by import competition. For these interests, unfair trade cases are where the action is. According to two of Washington's top trade lawyers (Horlick and Oliver 1988, 5), they "have become the usual first choice for industries seeking protection from imports into the United States." There have been many cases. From 1975 to 1979, the U.S. government processed 245 antidumping and countervailing duty cases, a pace of some 50 cases a year. In the 1980s, the case load rose even higher, to 774 cases between 1980 and 1988, or 86 cases a year. By comparison, there have been only four escape clause cases a year, cases in which an industry sought protection from import competition without accusing the foreign seller of employing or benefiting from unfair practices.[8]

Pattern of cases and outcomes.   For a summary of the country incidence of antidumping and countervailing duty cases, see table 5. In another paper, Tracy Murray and I have described at some length the pattern of these cases; here I will limit myself to noting several features that stand out in that pattern.

Table 5.   Countervailing Duty and Antidumping Outcomes Compared, 1980–89

Country or group	ANTIDUMPING AS A PERCENTAGE OF TOTAL NUMBER	RESTRICTIVE OUTCOMES AS A PERCENTAGE OF TOTAL CASES			NEGOTIATED EXPORT RESTRAINTS AS PERCENTAGE OF RESTRICTIVE OUTCOMES		
		Anti-dumping	*Counter-vailing*	*Both*	*Anti-dumping*	*Counter-vailing*	*Both*
All countries	50	72	67	70	63	66	64
Developed countries	49	69	61	65	65	82	74
Developing countries	46	73	77	75	55	46	49
Korea	54	77	100	86	82	86	84
Eastern European countries	87	91	60	87	77	100	78

SOURCE: Finger and Murray 1990, table 4, p. 45.

- For developed and developing countries, the proportion of cases is about the same as the proportion of U.S. imports that originate in each group. There are large differences within groups, however. Japan and the EC each supply about 20 percent of U.S. imports, but the EC has been the object of 40 percent of U.S. antidumping and countervailing duty cases, Japan of only 6 percent. Among developing countries, imports from Brazil generate a disproportionately high number of cases, and imports from Taiwan, Hong Kong, and Singapore, disproportionately low numbers. Korea's experience is representative of the central tendency (see table 4): Korea supplies 4.2 percent of U.S. imports and was hit by 4.7 percent of U.S. cases.

- Almost half the cases (348 of 774) have been superseded by negotiated export restraints. Thus virtually all of the import restrictions the United States has put in place are GATT-legal or better—better in the sense that the exporter preferred the negotiated restraint to the by-the-books action that was just around the administrative corner. Negotiated restraints have superseded nearly three-fourths of the cases against Korea.

- Cases against developing countries more often come to restrictive outcomes than cases against developed countries—three-fourths versus two-thirds. Against Korea, thirty-one of thirty-six cases (84 percent) ended with a restrictive outcome. (Restrictive outcomes include cases that reached an affirmative final determination or that were superseded by a restrictive agreement with the exporter.) But negotiated export restraints were more often used against developed countries—74 percent of the cases compared with 49 percent for developing countries. A country that possesses the countervailing power to retaliate is accorded the courtesy of a negotiated settlement. Others are restricted in the normal course of administrative procedures. Korea, in this regard, is treated as one of the powers—84 percent of restrictive outcomes against Korea were VERs.

- The U.S. government almost always finds that the foreign exporter is unfair or is benefiting from the unfair actions of its government. Only 11 percent of dumping and subsidy determinations resulted in negative decisions.[9]

- When no action is taken against the foreign exporter, more than six times out of seven it is because no competing U.S. producer has been hurt.

Taking into account both the sequencing of the dumping and injury tests and the patterns of outcomes of each in the 1980s, a typical one hundred antidumping or countervailing cases would end up with the following outcomes:

	Number
Negotiated export restraint	45
Antidumping or countervailing duty order	23
Case formally dismissed because of	
Negative injury determination	27
Negative dumping or susbsidy determination	5
TOTAL	100

Cases against Korea

From 1980 through 1988, the U.S. government processed twenty-two antidumping and fourteen countervailing duty cases against Korea. The largest part of these—twenty-two, in total—involved Korean exports of steel and steel products. These were part of an avalanche of cases the U.S. steel industry filed to force the U.S. government to negotiate quantitative limits on all imports into the United States. Consumer electronics, particularly color television sets, are another part of Korean exports that have come under antidumping attack.[10] Korea has not, however, negotiated a quantitative restraint on television sets: they remain under antidumping order. Comparing the way Korean producers have adjusted in the steel case, where quantitative limits have been put in place, with the way producers of television sets have adjusted, provides an important insight into contemporary trade policy. The two outcomes are compared below.

Quotas on steel. For thirty years after World War II, world consumption of steel grew by 5 to 6 percent a year. But the oil crisis of late 1974 and the following world recession brought dramatic challenges to the steel industry: consumption in 1975 was 10 percent less than in 1974, and growth of demand disappeared. It took ten years, until 1984, for world demand to make up the 10 percent drop recorded in 1975, and growth after that was much slower. Besides the change of demand and the resulting overcapacity of the world industry, significant changes in the competitive structure had also occurred. These changes allowed Japanese and eventually Korean producers of standardized products to enjoy a cost advantage over traditional producers in Europe and North America. In response to this challenge, both the United States and the European Community established comprehensive systems of quantitative restrictions on imports.

David Tarr has published an analysis of the effects of these U.S. and EC restrictions on exporting countries, particularly Korea. He found, first of all, that though the cutback of export sales caused the price of steel to fall in Korea, the comprehensive systems of controls in place in the United States and the EC actually allowed Korean export prices to rise. Korea's output of steel was reduced, and because Korea has comparative advantage in world trade in steel, there were efficiency losses to the world economy and specifically to Korea. But Tarr estimates that the rent Korean exporters collected by way of the higher-than-competitive prices in the U.S. and EC markets is several times larger than the efficiency losses, leaving the Korean economy more than $32 million a year better off than it would be if U.S. and EC steel imports were not controlled.

Antidumping orders against color television sets.[11] The Korean electronics industry achieved modernity in 1958 when it first produced radios on an assembly line. By 1988, total production was $24 billion. Of this output, $15 billion, almost two-thirds, was exported.

The Korean industry includes more than 150 small firms but is dominated by three large ones: Gold Star, Samsung, and Daewoo. Through the 1980s the big three accounted for virtually 100 percent of Korean production of all major consumer electronics products, including color television sets.

Although Korean production of color television sets is concentrated, the international market is very competitive. Yoon-Wook Jun (1988) lists twenty producers that sell color TVs in the U.S. market under the manufacturers' names. In addition, a number of major retailers such as Sears, K-Mart, and J.C. Penney sell color TVs under their own brand names. The intensity of competition is illustrated by changes in relative prices. Over the twenty years from 1967 to 1986, the U.S. consumer price index more than tripled. But prices of TVs and tape recorders actually fell, *in nominal terms*, while prices of radios and sound equipment went up by less than 10 percent.

The Korean government has supported development of the industry in several ways, including tax breaks and loans at below-market rates of interest. But the major form of government support of consumer electronics producers has been through import restrictions—during the formative years of the Korean companies, imports of competing products were banned—and the consequent opportunity to charge monopoly prices at home. In 1958, when other controls were still in effect, the tariff rate on consumer electronics was 40 percent. That import protection allowed Korean companies to collect a 40 percent premium on their domestic sales over the competitive price they had to charge in export markets where they had no monopoly power. That premium collected on the one-third of output sold domestically amounted to a 20 percent bonus on the two-thirds of production that was exported.[12]

During the 1980s, Korea supplied less than 2 percent of world exports but was the respondent in 6 percent of the world's antidumping cases. (These figures relate to antidumping cases in and exports to *all countries*. The ratios of exports to and antidumping plus countervailing duty cases *in the United States* were roughly proportional.) What is the rational response to antidumping actions by companies in the position of the Korean consumer electronics producers? They have considerable control over their prices in Korea and thus could make adjustments there. But in export markets they are entirely at the mercy of market forces. To raise export prices by the amount necessary to avoid antidumping duties would be to price themselves out of these markets. Thus reducing prices in Korea—which provides, after all, only one-third of their sales—would seem the better business alternative.

Political reactions in Korea also made the lowering of internal prices the better political option. The antidumping cases emphasized to Korean consumers and politicians that Koreans were being asked to pay considerably higher prices than foreigners for Korean products. This pricing soon became a hot political issue, leading eventually to congressional hearings at which industry officials were pressed to explain their high domestic prices.

The evidence supports the contention that the major adjustment Korean producers would make would be to the prices they charged in Korea. Take color TVs. Bark (1991) shows that before the U.S. antidumping cases, export prices (approximated by unit values) had been declining sharply, by 15 percent from 1980 to 1983. The antidumping order did not change this downward trend: export prices fell another 5 percent from 1983 to 1984 and 10 percent more by 1988. As for prices in Korea, before the U.S. antidumping case their trend was level—the same in 1983 as they had been in 1980. But when the Korean companies began to adjust to reduce the bite of the antidumping orders, Korean prices began to fall. By 1985 they were 20 percent below the 1983 level, and by 1988, 30 percent below.

Conclusions

David Tarr's study shows that restrictions on Korea's steel exports had a positive impact on Korean economic welfare. We have no similar calculation for the impact of antidumping actions against Korean exports of TVs, but Bark's evidence does show that Korean consumers benefited from considerably lower prices, while importing-country consumers seemed not to have been burdened by higher prices. The main effect, it seems, is that the antidumping orders provided a disincentive for Korean producers to exploit the monopoly power they hold over the Korean market.

Judged on a global basis, the effects of antidumping actions against Korean exports of color TVs seems to have been welfare enhancing.

Although the Korean economic interests were advanced by restrictions on Korea's and other countries' exports of steel to the United States and the EC, the outcome, judged on a global basis, was probably negative. Rent transfers to Korean and other exporters are, on a global basis, transfers from U.S. and EC users and hence net to zero. That leaves only the efficiency effects, which Tarr estimates the sum to be a global loss of about $36 million a year—based on prices and the size of the industry in 1984.

The major differences between the two cases are (1) the restrictions on steel imports were against all producers, not just Korea, and (2) TV-importing countries did not offer a price-supporting quantitative restraint as an alternative to their antidumping orders.

As to 301, I have focused on its *results* rather than on its *process*. Anyone may reject 301 as an unacceptable process—and I do not quarrel with the fact that it is gunboat diplomacy—but one should be aware of the results that would thus be given up. I have not argued the point here, but access to the U.S. market has been the one major avenue to development in the post–World War II era. Except for the matter of multilateral consent—and again I do not question that this matter is an important one—301 modulates access to the market in the way the World Bank and the International Monetary Fund modulates access to the capital these institutions can provide.

As to the changes in U.S. trade policy, my contention at the beginning of the essay was that it is now a particularized policy; the importance of trade remedies and 301 means that U.S. policy is no longer most favored nation, but tailored to the politics and the economics of each bilateral relationship. Indeed, it is possible to say that U.S. trade policy is domestic policy first and trade policy second. Its primary concern is to take care of the interests of individual domestic constituents; what happens to foreigners is, within the bounds of what determines what policy will be, hardly more than fallout.

Notes

1. This sequence and how the shift came about are explained at greater length in Finger and Dhar (1992).

2. It is difficult to develop a measure of total coverage (i.e., by all nontariff barriers) because it is difficult to determine, at the margin, whether certain regulations or licensing requirements have a trade-restricting effect. The categories in table 1 are roughly additive, but there are instances in which a product under voluntary export restraint is also the object of an antidumping or countervailing duty order.

3. The section has been modified and extended in the Trade Acts of 1979, 1984, and 1989. Until the 1989 amendments, 301 authority rested with the president.

4. Since 1988, retaliation may not have been on the case's subject product or services (e.g., if the subject practice affects U.S. exports of rice, retaliation cannot be a restriction on U.S. imports of rice).

5. The 1988 act introduced a provision to permit foreign governments to defend themselves against accusations of unreasonableness by pointing out that the United States does the same thing (Hudec 1990, 22).

6. The USTR (1991b) reports twenty-eight petitions that did not lead to investigations.

7. All six are on topics being negotiated at the Uruguay Round. Three concern disputes over European Community agricultural subsidies date back as 301 cases to 1981. A fourth, concerning Argentine marine insurance, began in 1979.

8. The United States is not alone in this. Many countries review their imports for instances of unfairness. Since 1980, the three other major users of GATT-based import screens, Australia, Canada, and the European Community, have processed more than a thousand antidumping and countervailing duty cases but only seventeen safeguard cases.

9. No country-by-country tally is available for this summary statement or for the following one.

10. Bark (1991) reports that color television sets and other Korean consumer electronics have also been hit by antidumping actions in Australia, Canada, and the European Community.

11. This subsection draws from Bark (1991).

12. There have been no countervailing duty cases against Korean consumer electronics, but evidence from countervailing duty cases against other Korean products that have benefited from programs similar to those available to consumer electronics producers indicates that the value of direct bonuses plus tax benefits and other programs that might be construed as subsidies ranged from 1 to 3 percent.

References

Ahearn, Raymond J.; Mendelowitz, Allan; and Alfred Reifman. 1991. "Congress and U.S. Trade Policy in the '90's." In Robert E. Baldwin and J. David Richardson, eds., *The Uruguay Round and Beyond: Problems and Prospects*. Cambridge, Mass.: National Bureau of Economic Research.

Bark, Taeho. 1991. "The Korean Consumer Electronics Industry: Reaction to Anti-dumping Actions." PRE Working Paper WPS 781. World Bank, October.

Finger, J. Michael, and Murray, Tracy. 1990. "Policing Unfair Imports: The United States Example." *Journal of World Trade* 24, no. 4 (August 1990): 39–53.

Finger, J. Michael, and Dhar, Sumana. 1992. "Do Rules Control Power? GATT Articles and Agreements in the Uruguay Round." In Robert M. Stern and Alan V. Deardorf, eds., *Problems in the International Trading System*. Ann Arbor: University of Michigan Press.

Hudec, Robert E. 1990a. "Mirror, Mirror on the Wall: The Concept of Fairness in

United States Trade Policy." Paper presented at the 1990 annual meeting of the Canadian Council of International Law, Ottawa, October 19.

———. 1990b. "Talking about the New Section 301, Beyond Good and Evil." Paper presented at a conference entitled Super 301 and the World Trading System, Columbia University, December 1–2.

Jun, Yong-Wook. 1988. *The Structural Analysis of the Global Consumer Electronics Industry and the Oligopolistic Behavior of Korean Firms in Their Internationalization.* KIET Occasional Paper no. 88–07. Seoul: Korea Institute of Economics and Technology.

Tarr, David G. 1987. "Effect of Restraining Steel Exports from the Republic of Korea and Other Countries to the United States and the European Economic Community." *World Bank Economic Review.* 1, no. 3 (May).

United States International Trade Commission. Annual. *Operation of the Trade Agreements Program,* Washington, D.C.

United States Trade Representative. 1991a. *Section 301 Table of Cases.* Washington, D.C.: USTR, August 15. Photocopy.

———. 1991b. *Section 301 Petitions—No Investigation Initiated.* Washington, D.C.: USTR, August 15. Photocopy.

———. 1991c. *1991 National Trade Estimate Report on Foreign Trade Barriers.* Washington, D.C.: U.S. Government Printing Office.

———. Semiannual. "Report to Congress on Section 301 Developments Required by Section 309(a)(3) of the Trade Act of 1974." Washington, D.C., beginning January–June 1975.

Appendix*

A List of United States 301 Cases against Korea (see appendix table 1)

(301-20)

Complaint.   The American Home Assurance Company on November 5, 1979, alleged that Korea was discriminating against the petitioner by failing to write insurance policies covering marine risks, not permitting the petitioner to participate in joint venture fire insurance, and failing to grant retrocession from the Korea Reinsurance Corp. to the petitioner on the same basis as Korean insurance firms.

Disposition.   USTR initiated an investigation on July 2, 1979, invited public comments on the petition and on proposals for retaliation. USTR held several rounds of consultations with the government of Korea, resulting in a

---

*SOURCES: U.S. International Trade Commission (annual), various issues. U.S. Trade Representative (1991a, 1991b, 1991c).

Appendix Table 1. United States 301 Cases, July 1975–July 1991, by Country and Outcome (number of cases)

Target country	Total	Negative	TARGET COUNTRY LIBERALIZED			U.S. retaliation	Other restrictive outcome	Pending
			Multilateral	Bilateral	Total			
Developed countries								
Austria	1	0	0	0	0	1	0	0
Canada	7	1	0	2	2	1	2	1
European Community	29	6	9	3	12	6	1	4
Japan	12	0	8	3	11	0	1	0
Norway	1	0	0	1	1	0	0	0
Sweden	1	0	0	0	0	0	1	0
Switzerland[a]	1	0	0	0	0	0	0	0
Developing countries								
Argentina	5	0	3	0	3	1	0	1
Brazil	5	1	4	0	4	0	0	0
China, Peoples Republic	2	0	1	0	1	0	0	1
Guatemala	1	0	0	1	1	0	0	0
India	4	0	1	0	1	0	0	3
Korea	8	0	5	2	7	1	0	0
Taiwan	5	2	3	0	3	0	0	0
Thailand	3	0	1	0	1	0	0	2

Eastern Europe								
USSR	1	1	0	0	0	0	0	0
All countries								
Number of cases	86	11	35	12	47	10	5	12
(% of total)	(100)	(13)	(41)	(14)	(55)	(12)	(6)	(14)
Developed countries[a]								
Number of cases	52	7	17	9	26	8	5	5
(% of total)	(100)	(13)	(33)	(17)	(50)	(15)	(10)	(10)
Developing countries								
Number of cases	33	3	18	3	21	2	0	7
(% of total)	(100)	(9)	(55)	(9)	(64)	(6)	(0)	(21)
Developing excl. Korea								
Number of cases	25	3	13	1	14	1	0	6
(% of cases)	(100)	(12)	(52)	(4)	(56)	(4)	(0)	(24)
Korea								
Number of cases	8	0	5	2	7	1	0	0
(% of total)	(100)	(0)	(63)	(25)	(88)	(13)	(0)	(0)

SOURCE: Tabulated from Office of the United States Trade Representative, "Section 301 Tables of Cases," Washington, D.C., USTR, August 15, 1991, photocopied.

[a] In 1979 a U.S. firm complained about the Swiss customs service's testing of the gold content of eyeglass frames. The USTR's investigation revealed that U.S. standards for testing and making gold content were different from those used by many other countries. The U.S. industry agreed to shift to the more common standards and markings, which the Swiss customs service would accept without further testing. This action is classified as "liberalization by the United States," and does not fit into any of the categories listed in this table.

commitment from the government of Korea to promote more open competition in the insurance market. Upon withdrawal of the petition, USTR terminated the investigation on December 29, 1980.

(301-51)
Complaint.   On September 16, 1985, at the president's direction, USTR initiated an investigation into Korean practices that restrict the ability of U.S. insurers to provide insurance services in the Korean market. This was one of the cases initiated by the president in response to pressure from Congress over the lack of success achieved in this matter and in other matters involving several countries.

Disposition.   There were intense consultations with Korea from November 1985 through July 1986. In July 1986 the United States and Korea announced an agreement whereby the government of Korea agreed to (1) license two U.S. firms to underwrite compulsory fire insurance, effective July 31, 1986; (2) admit two U.S. firms to the compulsory fire insurance pool effective the same date; license at least one U.S. firm to underwrite life insurance by the end of 1986; (3) license additional qualified U.S. firms to underwrite both life and nonlife insurance (no specified deadline); (5) reach specific understandings on certain technical and administrative matters including reinsurance by the end of 1986.

(301-37)
Complaint.   October 25, 1982, the Footwear Industries of America, Inc. et al. filed a petition alleging that import restrictions on nonrubber footwear by Korea, the EC, and seven other countries divert exports to the United States and deny U.S. access, are inconsistent with the GATT, are unreasonable and/or discriminatory and a burden on U.S. commerce.

Disposition.   On December 8, 1982, the USTR opened investigations of the alleged restrictive practices—other than allegations that GATT-bound tariffs are excessive and about trade diversion—made against Korea, Brazil, Japan, and Taiwan. The United States and Korea consulted in February and in August 1983. The USTR reported to the Senate on April 18, 1985, that Korea reduced tariffs on footwear items and removed all leather items from the import surveillance list.

(301-39)

Complaint. An association of U.S. wire rope and specialty cable manufacturers filed a petition on March 16, 1983, alleging that production of Korean steel wire rope is subsidized, that Korean limits on imports from Japan diverts Japanese exports to the United States, and that Korean producers infringe on U.S. trademarks.

Disposition. The USTR initiated an investigation on May 2, 1983, with respect to claims of production subsidies, held a domestic hearing, and requested consultations under the subsidies code. The petition was withdrawn in November 1983. In 1984 the U.S. government put in place a comprehensive system of (negotiated) quotas on steel imports.

(301-52)

Complaint. At the president's direction, on November 4, 1985, the USTR initiated an investigation of Korea's lack of protection of U.S. intellectual property rights.

Disposition. The United States consulted with Korea from November 1985 through July 1986. On July 21, 1986, the White House announced agreement with Korea.

On copyrights, the government of Korea agreed (1) to present to the National Assembly for enactment by mid-1987 comprehensive copyright bills including coverage of traditional literary works, sound recordings, and computer software (2) to accede during 1987 to the Universal Copyright Convention and the 1971 Geneva Phonograms Convention.

On patents, the government of Korea agreed (1) to submit for enactment by mid-1987 a comprehensive bill to amend Korean patent law to include patent protection for chemicals and pharmaceutical products and new uses thereof, provide patent protection for new micro-organisms (2) to accede to the Budapest treaty in 1987.

On trademarks, Korea eliminated (1) its requirement for technology inducement (trademarks already subject to technology inducement agreements will continue beyond the life of that agreement); (2) its requirement that trademarks be licensed only for joint ventures or if there were an accompanying materials supply agreement; (3) export requirements on goods covered by trademark licenses; (4) restrictions on royalty terms in licenses. Several other matters related to trademarks were also agreed.

The government of Korea also agreed to give high priority to enforcement and to enact effective penalties for intellectual property rights violations.

The agreement is being monitored on the U.S. side by an interagency task force.

(301-64)

Complaint.   On January 22, 1988, the U.S. Cigarette Export Association filed a petition complaining that the policies and practices of the Korean Government Monopoly Corporation unreasonably denied access to the Korean cigarette market.

Disposition.   After consultations, the government of Korea agreed to open the Korean market for cigarettes on July 1, 1988, in several ways, including the following: (1) the tax on imported cigarettes will be cut by two-thirds (from approximately $1.50 to approximately $0.50); (2) all foreign firms will be permitted to advertise in certain Korean magazines and to do specified types of sales promotion including the sponsoring of promotional events; (3) U.S. firms will be allowed to import cigarettes and to sell them independently of the Korean Monopoly Corporation; (4) U.S. cigarettes will be permitted to be sold in all retail outlets that carry Korean brands.

(301-65)

Complaint.   On February 16, 1988, the American Meat Institute filed a petition alleging that the government of Korea maintained a restrictive licensing system on imports of bovine meat, in violation of GATT Article 11. The petition alleged that since May 21, 1985, the approval of the government of Korea had been required for each shipment of beef imported and that all applications had been denied except for a single shipment of 49 tons imported for the annual meetings of the International Monetary Fund and the World Bank in Seoul.

Disposition.   The United States had already consulted with Korea under this matter under GATT dispute settlement procedures. On May, 4, 1988, The GATT Council established a panel on the matter, a parallel panel on a similar Korea-Australia dispute.

On May 27 the Korea-U.S. panel issued a report favorable to the United States, but Korea did not agree to council adoption of the report. The USTR, acting on authority given by 301, announced on September 28 that if there were no substantial movement toward a resolution by mid-November, a proposed retaliation list would be published.

On November 8, 1989, Korea allowed the GATT panel report to be adopted; consultations began to find an acceptable way to implement the panel's recommendations. In April 1990 letters were exchanged between the governments of Korea and the United States setting out an agreed mode of implementation of the GATT panel's recommendations. The USTR is monitoring Korea's implementation.

(301-67)

Complaint.   On April 27, 1988, the Wine Institute and the Association of American Vintners filed a petition complaining of policies and practices of the Korean government that unreasonably deny access to the Korean wine market.

Disposition.   After consultations, the government of Korea agreed, in January 1989, to provide foreign manufacturers of wine and wine products nondiscriminatory and equitable access to the Korean market.

4

Korean Import Barriers: Structure, Evolution, and Consequences for U.S.-Korea Trade

Byung-Il Choi

Introduction

Korea's trade policy accounts for much of its remarkable economic performance since the early 1970s. Like most industrializing countries, Korea initially tried to develop new industries by erecting high import barriers. Such a strategy cannot be maintained indefinitely because it ultimately angers trading partners and causes new, serious economic problems at home.

How have Korean import barriers since 1980 influenced Korea's economy and its trade relationships? I first describe the structure and evolution of Korean import barriers, the conventional import barriers such as import licensing and tariffs, new import controls that have emerged since the late 1980s, and sectoral import barriers. This account makes it possible to address these questions: how restrictive is the Korean import regime? Is the increase in Korean imports since the late 1980s related to the lowering of Korean import barriers? What effect has Korean trade liberalization throughout the 1980s had on Korea-U.S. trade?

The Structure and Evolution
of Import Barriers in Korea[1]

An Overview

Throughout the 1960s and 1970s, Korea relied greatly on import barriers like restrictive import licensing, high tariffs, and complex procedures to regulate all imports not directly related to export promotion. As the Republic of Korea's government-backed export drive achieved success, the government decided to restructure the nation's industrial base by promoting the heavy-industry and chemical sectors. This action brought about new government intervention in the economy, causing a dismal economic performance in the late 1970s.

This experience convinced the policymakers to favor the market mechanism, and as a result the Korean government shifted toward import liberalization in the early 1980s. Many import barriers erected and operated during the 1960s and 1970s were dismantled, and despite vehement debate on this program, the restructuring of import policy moved forward in the belief that it would enhance Korea's international competitiveness by reducing resource allocation distortion, diminishing rent-seeking activity, and encouraging research and development.

The scope of import liberalization was expanded as trade friction intensified with Korea's major trading partners, including the United States, in the latter half of the 1980s. Korea's trade surplus, which began in 1986, reached a high of $11.4 billion in 1989, thus attracting the attention of Korea's trading partners, who began to demand more access to the Korean market. Korea's heavy dependence on trade, particularly with the United States, forced it to accommodate these foreign demands.[2] In the 1980s the Korean government dramatically increased the number of products eligible for automatic import license approval, reduced tariffs, streamlined import procedures, and opened the services market to foreign participation.

Quantitative Import Restrictions

As Korea began to enjoy balance-of-payments (BOP) surpluses in the early 1980s, its protection policies were increasingly challenged by the GATT BOP Committee. At the committee meeting in October 1989, Korea agreed to phase out all remaining quantitative restrictions or to justify such restrictions under other GATT articles by July 1, 1997.

Quantitative import restrictions are implemented through the import-

Table 1.   Import Licensing Liberalization by Product (in percent)

	1981	1982	1983	1984	1985	1986	1987	1988	1989	1990
Primary product, food and beverages	68.5	70.6	73.2	75.8	78.2	79.7	79.9	75.3	76.1	79.9
Chemical products	93.4	94	94	95	95.6	97.7	99	100	100	100
Steel and metal products	88.9	89.7	90.9	92.8	95.6	98.6	99.5	100	100	100
General machinery	64.2	65.5	68.7	78	83	89.5	93.6	100	100	100
Electrical and electronic machinery	40.9	46.1	53.6	62.4	73.9	87	96.6	100	100	100
Textile products	65.4	68.4	80.4	90.3	93.1	96.1	97.7	98.8	99.5	99.5
Total liberalization ratio	71.2	76.6	80.4	84.8	87.7	91.5	93.6	94.8	95.5	96.4

SOURCE: Ministry of Trade and Industry

NOTE: Numbers show proportion of items subject to automatic import approval. Items are classified at the 8-digit level under CCCN before 1987, and at the 10-digit level under HS after 1988.

licensing system, which is designed to protect the weak base of many manufacturing sectors and increase the incomes of those completely dependent on agriculture, livestock, and fishing. Since 1967, when Korea signed the GATT, the list of items subject to prior license approval and review has been specified in the Export and Import Notice required by the Foreign Trade Act.

From the early 1980s on, however, Korea began import liberalization on the basis of a preannounced schedule with a view to providing a stable and predictable economic environment. This process has, however, proceeded in a gradual and uneven manner (see table 1). But as Korea's competitiveness in manufactured consumer goods grew and domestic demand for capital goods for export production increased, quantitative import restrictions on these goods had been almost completely lifted by 1988. By 1991, 97.2 percent of the items listed under the harmonized system (HS) of Korea tariff classification were eligible for automatic license approval: out of 10,274 items, only 283 items remained restricted, a great advance from the 70 percent in 1980.

Despite sweeping liberalization after 1980, import controls on some primary goods (agriculture, livestock, and fishery) continue. The government's liberalization plan for these products will increase automatic license approval to 85 percent of them in 1991 and 92 percent by 1994.

By removing many quantitative restrictions, Korea made a special effort to accelerate imports from the United States: in 1986, motor vehicles and ceramic products; in 1987, organic chemicals, computers, and electrical equipment; and in 1988, machinery and mechanical appliances. Before the May 1989 agreement with the United States, Korea announced plans to introduce automatic import license approval for 237 agricultural products between 1989 and 1991. Under that agreement, Korea agreed to automatically approve sixty-two products of particular concern to the United States, a development that dramatically increased U.S. imports.

Tariffs

In Korea's tariff structure, tariffs on agricultural products are much higher than those on manufactured products; tariffs on manufactured products vary according to fabrication intensity. This tariff structure reflects Korea's growth strategy of promoting the export of consumer goods locally fabricated from imported industrial supplies and capital goods. Yet this same tariff structure has promoted noncompetitiveness in Korea's agricultural sector.

The Korean government actively pursued tariff reduction as an instrument of import liberalization, launching two successive five-year tariff re-

Table 2.   Korea's Average Tariff Rate on Agricultural and
              Manufacturing Products (in percent)

	1983	1986	1987	1988	1989	1990	1993*
Agricultural products	31.4	27.1	26.4	25.2	20.6	19.9	16.6
Manufacturing products	22.6	18.7	18.2	16.2	11.2	9.7	6.2
Raw materials	11.9	10.0	9.8	9.8	3.9	3.9	2.8
Intermediate materials	21.5	18.1	17.8	17.1	11.7	10.7	7.0
Finished materials	26.4	21.8	21.1	19.1	13.3	11.2	7.1
Average	23.7	19.9	19.3	18.1	12.7	11.4	7.9

SOURCE: Ministry of Trade and Industry

duction plans, starting in 1984. As a result, Korea's average tariff rate on all
goods declined from 23.7 percent in 1984 to 11.4 percent in 1990. Progressive
reductions through 1994 will bring the average tariff rate down to 7.9
percent. Nevertheless, the tariff structure's underlying bias still is intact (see
table 2).

Korea's average tariff rate on manufactured goods fell from 22.6 percent
in 1983 to 9.7 percent in 1990 and will decline by 1994 to 6.2 percent, a
level comparable to that of OECD member countries.[3] During the same
period, the average tariff rate on agricultural goods was reduced from 31.4
percent to 19.9 percent and will decline to 16.6 percent in 1994. The 1989
tariff reduction lowered the modal tariff rate from 20 percent, when applied
to 72.1 percent of all imports, and to 15 percent, when applied to 64.2
percent of all imported items. The portion of items subject to a rate of 20
percent or less increased from 84.9 percent in 1988 to 94.8 percent in 1989.

The Korean tariff reduction policy certainly accommodated U.S. concerns. In 1987, the Korean government reduced tariff rates by 5 percent for
twenty-four items, including raisins, almonds, chocolate, photographic film,
and Oregon pine lumber; by 5–20 percent for eighty-three items, including
lemons, beer, wood products, paper products, telecommunication equipment,
and large passenger cars; and by 5–30 percent for fifty items, including
cosmetics, hand tools, machine tools, and furniture. In 1987 and 1988, the
Korean government reduced tariff rates for 1,877 items of concern to the
United States. In July 1989, Korea announced temporary tariff reductions of
between 5 and 15 percent on eighty-six items, including almonds, pistachios,
avocados, raisins, red and white wines, and certain seed grains of particular
interest to the United States.

Tariff Quotas

Since 1967, the Korean government has flexibly implemented tariff quotas under the Customs Act, setting them within 40 percent of a general rate. The Customs Act, revised in 1990, allows tariff quotas to facilitate import of specific items, to stabilize domestic prices of items using foreign inputs whose import prices sharply increase, and to rectify extreme imbalances in the tariff structure. In such cases, a low tariff quota is levied. A high tariff quota, in contrast, may be imposed on all items above their preset limits to restrict the importation of specific items. As of 1991, a tariff quota is applied to 329 items at the ten-digit level of the HS. Of these, only bananas and soybean oil are subject to a high tariff quota.

The Import Surveillance System

The import surveillance system adopted in 1979 mitigated the impact of market opening on domestic industries and helped maintain a healthy balance of payments. Most items subject to import surveillance were luxury consumer goods and agricultural goods.

The import surveillance system was constantly criticized as unfair and a "de facto import restriction" by Korea's major trading partners and international economic organizations. Korea's post-1986 trade surplus and foreign pressure compelled the government to abolish the system in late 1988.

Technical Barriers

The Republic of Korea has "individual laws" regulating the import of certain goods. Although Korea's restrictions generally comply with GATT rules, the government has worked to eliminate ambiguous and complicated procedures impeding market access. Since 1987, the Korean government has eliminated import restrictions on more than eight hundred items under twenty-five individual laws.[4] In September 1987, for example, Korea abolished import restrictions on 550 items under the Industrial Products Quality Control Act and the Pharmaceutical Act by limiting quality certification to the time of initial importation. In December 1987, the Ministry of Agriculture, Forestry, and Fisheries eliminated the Fertilizer Management Act's recommendation requirement for fertilizer imports. In April 1988, import restrictions on another fifty-four items under the Industrial Products Quality Control Act, the Pharmaceutical Act, and the Atomic Act were abolished. Korea also streamlined import procedures for medical equipment of particular interest to the United States.

In October 1988, Korea announced that it intended to reduce various import restrictions and simplify import procedures by reviewing potential technical barriers in thirty-nine special laws. Shortly afterward, a new task force of officials from several ministries eliminated or substantially relaxed barriers under thirty special laws covering approximately 1,500 items. For example, the number of imported agricultural chemicals will increase to 416 by 1993; a trade license for petroleum and its products is no longer required; documentation requirements for electrical products have been simplified, and the effective approval period has been extended from three to seven years; small shipments of food products may have Korean-language labels affixed after custom clearance, and labeling requirements have been streamlined for most foods except alcoholic beverages; films and videotapes are subject only to a single review by the Public Performance Ethics Committee; and a service charge on importation of medical equipment and radioisotopes has been eliminated.

In addition, changes in technical standards and regulations have eliminated a variety of restrictions on a large number of products. For instance, Korea revised testing and registration requirements for cosmetics to bring them into line with international standards and simplified preimport documentation requirements through such actions as eliminating the requirement for Korean-language documents on drugs and sanitary products. The preimport notification requirement was eliminated for 25 percent of the products to which it was applied and will be abolished on the remaining products by 1992.

Government Procurement

Government procurement often has been used to support domestic industry through discriminatory practices.[5] The calculus of cost and benefit from such a "buy national" policy varies by economic sector, but classic rent-seeking behavior has sometimes led to noncompetitive domestic industry and disservice to the procuring public sector and the general public. The Ministry of Trade and Industry no longer tries to determine whether its requirements can be met from local sources, and offsets are seldom required except for major military procurement.

Under U.S. pressure to open its government procurement market, Korea decided to seek accession to the GATT Government Procurement (GP) Code, and in June 1990 submitted its offer to the GATT. Korea's accession negotiations are taking place during the GP Code expansion negotiations, which cover the previously "excluded sectors" of telecommunications, transport, energy, and water.[6] Even if GP Code negotiations prove unsuccessful, Korea has agreed to open the telecommunications procurement contracts of its Office of Supply and Korea Telecom to the United States on a bilateral basis.

Import Source Diversification

The Ministry of Trade and Industry maintains a list of 258 items imported from Japan (at the ten-digit HS level) that require prior approval. That discrimination against Japanese imports is Korea's response to its huge, chronic trade deficit with Japan dating from the early years of industrialization; it increases U.S. exports to Korea by encouraging Korean companies to switch their sources of supply away from Japan to the United States.

Investment

Since 1984, when a negative list system was introduced into the foreign investment approval process, Korea has made progress in gradually opening its market to foreign investment. As of January 1991, 79 percent of all sectors in Korea's standard industrial classification system were open to foreign equity investment: some 98 percent of industrial areas and 61 percent of service areas are open to such investment. As of April 1991, foreign investment in Korea totaled $8.14 billion in 3,846 projects, with Japan the leading investment source (47.9 percent of total foreign investment), followed by the United States (28.5 percent).

The Emerging Import Control Structure in Korea

As the Republic of Korea's conventional import control system was dismantled throughout the 1980s, other import controls emerged in the form of safeguards and antidumping and countervailing duties, a regime more in line with the multilateral trade system.

Safeguards

Safeguards to neutralize imports' possibly inordinate impact on domestic industries were first established under the Foreign Trade Act of December 1986 and implemented by the creation of the Korea Trade Commission (KTC) in July 1987. In response to trading partners' constant attacks on that act for its alleged noncompliance with GATT Article 19, the Foreign Trade Act was revised to strengthen the KTC and improve its ability to investigate and determine injury. Under this system, if a domestic industry is deemed threatened or materially injured by imports of certain goods or trade and distribution services, concerned parties or the head of an administrative agency with jurisdiction over that industry may petition the KTC to investigate those imports' injurious effects on the domestic industry.[7]

Since the institution of safeguards in 1987, seventeen petitions have been filed for investigation. Four were withdrawn during investigation, twelve received affirmative rulings, and one case is still under investigation.[8]

Antidumping and Countervailing Duties

Korea became a signatory to the GATT Anti-Dumping Code in February 1986 and to the GATT Code on Subsidies and Countervailing Duties in June 1980. Domestic regulations on antidumping and countervailing duties enforced by the Customs Act are deemed consistent with GATT Article 6 and relevant multilateral trade negotiation (MTN) codes.

Under Article 10 of the Customs Act, either those who have been injured by dumping practices or appropriate ministers may ask the minister of finance to impose an antidumping or countervailing duty on the article concerned, after presenting sufficient proof of injury caused by dumping or subsidized importation. The minister of finance must decide within three months whether to investigate. Such investigations have two separate dimensions: (1) the Customs Administration's investigation of dumping or subsidization and (2) the KTC's inquiry to determine whether a dumped or subsidized import causes or threatens material injury to a domestic industry or materially retards the establishment of a domestic industry. The KTC's investigation must be completed within 180 days of the minister of finance's decision to investigate.[9]

If an exporter offers to revise his price or cease to export, and if the minister of finance accepts that undertaking, the investigation ends. If local industries are believed to have been injured by dumping or subsidization, and if it is deemed necessary to mitigate injury during the investigation period, the minister of finance may impose provisional antidumping or countervailing duties. If the Customs Administration finds dumping or subsidization and the KTC determines that it has caused material injury, the minister of finance finalizes his decision to impose dumping or countervailing duties after deliberation by the Customs and Tariff Deliberation Committee.[10] Unless another duration is specified, such duties remain in effect for three years.

Since the establishment of the antidumping system in 1986, eight requests for antidumping investigations have been lodged. The first antidumping ruling was made by the KTC in April 1991 on a polyacetal resin of DuPont, Hoechst Celanese, and Asahi Chemical. In July 1991, the minister of finance subsequently imposed 4 percent antidumping duties on polyacetal resin supplied by the three foreign companies.[11] No countervailing duty has been levied to date.

Rules of Origin

The import liberalization of the Korean market in the late 1980s gave more choices to consumers. This is a mixed blessing, as demonstrated by the confusing variety of low-quality, low-cost products like textiles and accessories arriving from South Asia without marks of origin, a condition allowing retailers to set prices for such goods to match those of domestic goods.

To promote fairness and protect consumers from inaccurate product information, the government introduced a mark of origin requirement in July 1991[12] that applies to 326 items at the four-digit level of HS (3,232 items at the ten-digit HS level), including food, consumer electronics, clothing, toys, and stationery.[13] The rules of origin outlined in the Kyoto convention (International Convention on the Simplification and Harmonization of Customs Procedures) form the basis of the Korean system.[14]

Dismantling Sectoral Barriers

Since 1986, Korea and the United States have entered into a series of agreements to increase access to Korean markets and to rectify their trade imbalance. The United States has requested increased market access to all sectors of the Korean economy in which its products and services are perceived to have the competitive edge; those requests have invariably been unilateral and accompanied by the threat of cross-sectoral retaliation against Korean products in the U.S. market. In many cases, the United States has specifically targeted Korea as a country whose policies and practices require correction to promote greater market opportunity for U.S. companies.

The most far-reaching of these agreements came in May 1989, when the Korean government agreed to enact substantial and domestically unpopular measures to facilitate foreign investment in Korea; to eliminate technical import restrictions; and to further open its market to agricultural imports. More examples are cited below.

Intellectual Property

Under the 1986 Intellectual Property Agreement with the United States, Korea expanded its copyright law to cover foreign works and adopted a new law to extend protection to computer software. It also enacted a patent law in July 1987 to cover chemicals, pharmaceuticals, and microorganisms, all areas of U.S. concern. To ensure adequate enforcement of intellectual property rights, Korea established an interagency Intellectual Property Task Force in

1988 and significantly increased penalties for copyright and trademark law violations.

In February 1991, a new law was passed to increase penalties for video piracy. Bills to protect trade secrets and semiconductor masks were submitted to the National Assembly in September 1991.

Banking Service

Since 1984, Korea has moved to extend national treatment to foreign banks by allowing their membership in the Korean Federation of Banks and the Korean clearinghouse association; broadening the definition of capital for foreign bank branches; approving the use of the Bank of Korea's rediscount facility for commercial paper; approving participation in the trust business; and approving the issuance of certificates of deposit and liberalizing interest rates on them.

Insurance

Korea entered into and honored three successive agreements on the establishment of U.S. branch offices and joint venture companies. Accordingly, Korea now considers all applications of U.S. insurance companies to underwrite insurance in Korea, and new guidelines became effective in January 1988 that permit U.S. insurance firms to form Korean joint ventures.

Motion Pictures

Korea streamlined the import and screening of foreign motion pictures by abolishing the Ministry of Culture's required preimport review program. Limits on the number of prints will be removed entirely in 1994.

Distribution System

Korea has undertaken a five-year, three-phase plan to liberalize its wholesale and retail distribution system. The first phase, implemented in 1989 and 1990, provides for foreign investment in wholesale distribution. In the second phase, begun in July 1991, the government will decrease the number of barriers to foreign investment in retail distribution. Finally, Korea will further liberalize foreign access to the retail market.

Wine

In 1990, Korea lowered the tariff on wine and wine products, abolished limits on the number of wine and wine product importers, and removed quantitative restrictions on imports of wine and wine products. Automatic import license approval for sparkling wines, brandy, and grain-based wine also became effective in January 1990. Finally, foreign alcoholic beverage manufacturers are now permitted to invest directly in the importation and distribution of all alcoholic beverages.

Beef

Korea adhered to the principles of its March 1990 agreement on beef, which provides for a gradual increase in base quota levels of beef imports over a three-year period. In addition, under the agreement between Korea's Livestock Product Marketing Organization and the livestock industry organizations of four beef-exporting countries (the United States, Canada, Australia, and New Zealand), Korea will implement a simultaneous buy/sell system in 1991 for 7 percent of the base quota level for imported beef.

Cigarettes

The May 1988 agreement to provide open and nondiscriminatory access for imported cigarettes has been implemented. In December 1988, Korea rescinded its Tobacco Monopoly Act and enacted the Tobacco Business Act, which permits foreign cigarette manufacturers to directly import and sell their products in Korea.

Telecommunications

After the United States designated Korea a priority foreign country for telecommunications trade negotiations in February 1989, the two countries engaged in three years of negotiations, ending in February 1992.[15] The agenda for those talks was complicated yet broad enough to cover the entire spectrum of telecommunications. As a result of the bilateral agreement, value-added services in Korea are being domestically and internationally liberalized, with foreign investment restrictions being relaxed by 1994. Transparency in standard setting and type approval has been institutionalized. Moreover, Korea has agreed to open its government procurement contracts in the telecommunications sector, and key tariffs have been cut by 40 percent.

Korean Import Barriers and U.S.-Korea Trade

Korean Import Barriers from a Comparative Perspective

Although Korea has maintained a system of *ex ante* import controls relying largely on quantitative restrictions, the United States also relies on import restrictions such as antidumping and countervailing duties, safeguards, and voluntary export restraints. The conventional perception of U.S. policymakers and businesspeople is that import barriers in Korea are so prohibitive that the United States is denied fair market access. To many Koreans, however, that assessment is unfair; in their eyes, the Korean market is open and fair to foreign imports.

No direct test is available to verify or disprove such assertions, so we resort to the indirect method (see Bergstern and Cline [1987] for a similar test on U.S.-Japan trade) to compare the relative efficacy of Korea's formal import barriers during the 1980s with those of other advanced economies. The test is whether larger economies have a lower ratio of imports to GNP than do smaller economies. If Korea's ratio of imports to GNP is relatively low, one might conclude that the Korean economy is more closed than other major economies.

See table 3 for the average ratio of imports of goods and services to gross national product (GNP) during 1982–1989 for Korea and other major economies.[16] The ratio tends to decline as GNP rises (see figure 1). The regression line drawn in figure 1 is

$$Z = 0.4598 - 0.1009 \log Y; R^2 = 0.712$$
$$ (9.58) (4.97)$$

where Z is the ratio of imports of goods and nonfactor services to GNP, Y is real GNP in billions of 1985 dollars, and t-ratios are in parentheses.

Korea lies far above the trend line (see figure 1), and in fact, its deviation from the trend line is the largest. The finding that Korea's imports were disproportionally large compared with its size does not necessarily imply that import barriers in Korea are trivial. Rather, it shows that Korean import barriers are not necessarily any more prohibitive than those of advanced economies, including the United States.[17] It would be fair to state that, considering its economic growth stage, the Korean market is fairly accessible to foreign products and relatively open vis-à-vis advanced economies.

Industrial supplies and capital goods represent almost 90 percent of total

Table 3.   A Comparison of Import-GNP Ratio to Size of
               National Economy (1982–1989)

	GNP (billion$)	Import/GNP (%)
United States	4,148.1	8.87
European Community	3,510.0	11.20
Japan	1,933.1	8.33
Canada	376.5	22.33
Australia	178.2	15.99
Switzerland	141.0	28.40
Sweden	127.6	27.66
Korea	115.3	33.38
Austria	111.3	27.99
Finland	68.3	24.66
Norway	66.8	27.88
New Zealand	27.6	24.92

SOURCE: IMF International Financial Statistics, various issues
NOTE: Average during 1982–1989, constant value, 1985

foreign exports to Korea, with capital goods' share increasing over time (see tables 4 and 5). Negligible as they may appear, manufactured consumer goods show an upward movement both in absolute sales and in share (see tables 4 and 5).

The Recent Upsurge in Korean Imports

After 1980 the Korean trade balance continuously improved until it peaked in 1988 at $8.9 billion. Since then, Korea's trade deficit has accumulated swiftly, reaching $9.7 billion in 1991. It took only four years for the Korean trade balance to change from the largest surplus to the largest deficit. A sudden surge in imports was the dominant factor in that process. Imports increased by $29.7 billion during 1988–1991. Exports grew by only $11.2 billion during the same period, indicating that Korean exports were losing competitiveness.

It is noteworthy that imports for domestic consumption rose by 86.8 percent, while imports of export-processing goods increased by only 15.4 percent during 1988–1991. Korean economic growth has been driven by the export of products fabricated locally from imported raw materials,

Figure 1. Relationship of Import-GNP Ratio to Size of Economy
(for period 1982–89)

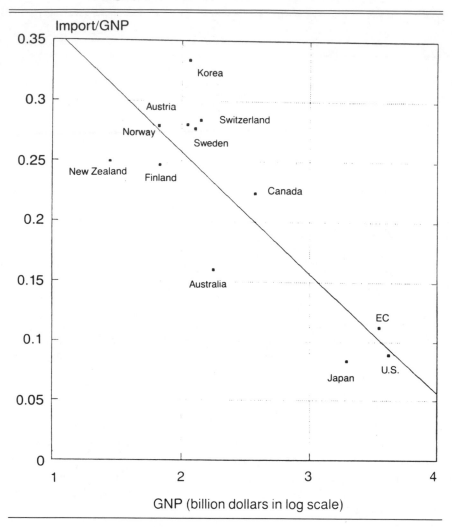

Table 4.   Foreign Exports to Korea (in billions of dollars)

	1980	1985	1988	1989	1990
Industrial supplies	14.48	17.41	27.72	32.77	37.43
Capital goods	5.12	11.1	19.04	22.4	25.46
Food and direct CG[a]	2.03	1.68	2.74	3.56	3.7
Nondurable CG[a]	0.08	0.12	0.39	0.59	0.9
Durable CG[a]	0.58	0.83	1.92	2.15	2.36
TOTAL	22.29	31.14	51.81	61.47	69.84

SOURCE: *The Statistics of Foreign Trade*, Korea Foreign Trade Association, 1989, 1990
[a] Consumer goods

Table 5.   Composition of Foreign Exports to Korea (in percent)

	1980	1985	1988	1989	1990
Industrial supplies	65	55.9	53.5	53.3	53.6
Capital goods	23	35.6	36.8	36.4	36.5
Food and direct CG[a]	9.1	5.4	5.3	5.8	5.3
Nondurable CG[a]	0.4	0.4	0.7	1.0	1.3
Durable CG[a]	2.6	2.7	3.7	3.5	3.4

SOURCE: *The Statistics of Foreign Trade*, Korea Foreign Trade Association, 1989, 1990
[a] Consumer goods

components, and machinery. The recent surge in imports for domestic consumption hints that the Korean economy has been undergoing a structural transformation since the late 1980s. The new import trend resulted from rapid, government-fueled expansion of the construction industry, business investment in production equipment (to cope with increasing labor costs), and expanding domestic demand.

A close look at the composition of Korea's imports in the manufacturing sector reveals that a dramatic turnaround in the heavy industrial sector is one of the main culprits in the recent surge in imports. Imports in heavy industry increased from $25.7 billion in 1988 to $33.6 billion in 1990, while exports rose slightly, from $30.9 billion in 1988 to $33.4 billion in 1990.

However, the overheated economy was not the only reason for the recent growth in imports. Baek (1991) shows that the lowering of Korean import barriers accounts for much of what cannot be explained in terms of exchange rate, the relative prices of imports and domestic goods, and domestic demand. According to Baek, tariff reduction accounts for 78 percent in 1989, 76 percent in 1990, and 64 percent in 1991 of residuals left unexplained by macroeconomic variables.

The impact of trade liberalization has been most drastic in agricultural products and manufactured consumer goods. Korea's trade deficit in agricultural and fishery products has steadily increased since the mid-1980s. Imports increased from $5.8 billion in 1990 to $9.8 billion in 1991, but exports grew only 5 percent, from $2.9 billion to $3.1 billion over the same period. The 1991 deficit of $6.7 billion in agricultural trade accounts for about 70 percent of the overall 1991 trade deficit. Imports of nondurable consumer goods went up 131 percent during 1988–1990, while overall imports increased 22.6 percent in the same period.

Import Liberalization and U.S.-Korea Trade

Probably the most remarkable result of Korean import liberalization has been the rapid decline in Korea's trade surplus with the United States, from the peak of $9.6 billion in 1987 to a $0.3 billion deficit in 1991.

Two factors were at work: a poor export performance in the United States market and an increased domestic demand for U.S. imports. Korean exports were losing their cost-competitiveness in the United States market, which was already in a prolonged recession. Overheated domestic demand for foreign capital goods and industrial supplies, coupled with increasing market access for U.S. products, was equally responsible. Translated into trade statistics, Korea's imports from the United States grew more than 114 percent from 1987 to 1991, but its exports to the United States increased only 3 percent in the same period. Korean exports to the United States actually declined after 1988.

It is not easy to determine how much of the recent rise in U.S. exports to Korea has resulted from the lowering of Korean import barriers, yet it would be useful to examine the causal relationship between import barriers and U.S. exports to Korea. For this purpose, we turn to U.S. export performance in previously protected sectors, particularly capital goods such as general machinery and electrical machinery, manufactured consumer goods, and agricultural products. By the late 1980s, import barriers to capital goods and manufactured consumer goods had been almost completely removed. There appears to be a strong positive correlation between the elimination of Korean restrictions on imported capital goods and the U.S. export performance. Between 1985 and 1990, U.S. exports increased 182 percent in capital goods, 933 percent in nondurable consumer goods, and 207 percent

Table 6.   U.S. Exports to Korea (in billions of dollars)

	1980	1985	1988	1989	1990
Industrial supplies	2.32	2.99	5.71	6.67	7.44
Capital goods	1.29	2.52	5.23	6.9	7.11
Food and direct CG[a]	1.19	0.81	1.37	1.68	1.66
Nondurable CG[a]	0.02	0.03	0.17	0.24	0.31
Durable CG[a]	0.07	0.14	0.28	0.43	0.43
TOTAL	4.89	6.49	12.76	15.91	16.94

SOURCE: *The Statistics of Foreign Trade*, Korea Foreign Trade Association, 1989, 1990
[a] Consumer goods

Table 7.   Composition of U.S. Exports to Korea (in percent)

	1980	1985	1988	1989	1990
Industrial supplies	47.4	46	44.8	41.9	43.9
Capital goods	26.3	38.9	41	43.3	42
Food and direct CG[a]	24.8	12.4	10.7	10.5	9.8
Nondurable CG[a]	0.4	0.4	1.3	1.5	1.8
Durable CG[a]	1.5	2.2	2.2	2.7	2.5

SOURCE: *The Statistics of Foreign Trade*, Korea Foreign Trade Association, 1989, 1990
[a] Consumer goods

in durable consumer goods, all exceeding the overall rate of increase in U.S. exports to Korea, which was 161 percent (see table 6). These products also took increasing shares of U.S. exports to Korea (see table 7). Furthermore, U.S. market shares in the Korean market increased in all these categories (see table 8), especially nondurable consumer goods and capital goods.

For an overview of the market performance of foreign products for which import licensing has been abolished, we examine the 972 items that received automatic licensing during 1986–1990 (see table 9). First, we find that the growth rate of U.S. imports in these liberalized items was larger than those of Japan and the EC. Second, the growth rate of U.S. imports constantly increased, while the opposite was true for Japan and the EC. As a result, U.S. products replaced their Japanese counterparts, thereby reducing the import share gap between those two countries in the Korean market. Of the 298

Table 8.   Share of U.S. Exports in the Korean Market (in percent)

	1980	1985	1988	1989	1990
Industrial supplies	16	17.1	20.6	20.4	19.9
Capital goods	25.1	22.7	27.5	30.8	27.9
Food and direct CG[a]	58.6	47.9	49.9	47.1	44.7
Nondurable CG[a]	25.3	21.8	42.8	40.4	34
Durable CG[a]	12.5	17.1	14.7	20.1	18.1
TOTAL SHARE	21.9	20.8	24.6	25.9	24.3

SOURCE: *The Statistics of Foreign Trade*, Korea Foreign Trade Association, 1989, 1990
[a] Consumer goods

items liberalized in 1986, the import share gap of 37.5 percent between the
United States and Japan narrowed considerably, down to 7.4 percent in 1990.
This pattern was replicated for items liberalized after 1986 as well.

One outcome of U.S.-Korean trade disputes was trade diversion from
Japan. Since the mid-1980s, the U.S. share of total Korean imports has
dramatically surged to nearly match the Japanese presence in Korea's market.
In 1986, 36 percent of Korea's imports were from Japan, and 21 percent
from the United States. By 1991, the gap had narrowed to 3 percent, with
Japan enjoying 26 percent and the United States 23 percent. Much of this
diversion resulted from the government's import source diversification program. The Korean government strongly recommended that OSROK and
many government-owned public corporations attach top priority to importing
U.S. products. The United States has been an immediate beneficiary of that
program (see table 10). Between 1982 and 1991, agricultural imports from
the United States increased from $1.3 billion to $3.2 billion, yet aggregate
U.S. agricultural exports stagnated during the same period.

Conclusion

As trade conflicts with its trading partners intensified and it
became clear that increased foreign competition was necessary to improve
Korea's economic competitiveness, in the 1980s Korea undertook a complete
overhaul of its import policy. As of 1994, most trade barriers have already
been eliminated or are scheduled to be phased out. For the barriers that
remain, the Korean government is trying to reduce their restrictiveness by

Table 9.   Share of Import-Liberalized Products by Country
            (in millions of dollars and percent)

	1986	1987	1988	1989	1990
Total imports	$2,787	$3,697	$4,536	$5,189	$2,813
Import share by country					
U.S.	17.6%	20.2%	23.4%	23.9%	26.3%
Japan	55.1	47.4	37.5	38.1	33.7
EC	12.6	13.9	14.9	15.2	17.5
Total imports		$3,528	$3,495	$3,868	$1,778
Import share by country					
U.S.		28.8%	33.6%	33.7%	33.8%
Japan		46.6	39.4	41.9	40.4
EC		8.4	12.6	10.7	11.8
Total imports			$2,927	$3,798	$2,129
Import share by country					
U.S.			23.5%	28.6%	28.6%
Japan			42.5	33.9	30.9
EC			10.4	10.8	12.6
Total imports				$33	$9
Import share by country					
U.S.				14.5%	45.5%
Japan				35.2	4.8
EC				6.6	18.4
Total imports					$287
Import share by country					
U.S.					66.9%
Japan					5.0
EC					8.4

SOURCE: Sang-ho Song, 1991. "Korea's Import Liberalization and Imports from the U.S.," KIET Occasional Paper, p. 13.

Table 10.   Source Diversification and Share by Country
             (in millions of dollars and percent)

	1986	1987	1988	1989	Annual avg. growth rate
Total imports	$1,248	$1,512	$2,142	$1,973	$16.5
Import share by country					
U.S.	19.4%	23.0%	29.6%	31.4%	36.9%
Japan	56.1	50.0	42.8	38.5	2.8
EC	15.0	16.7	19.1	20.4	29.3
Total imports		$462	$830	$868	$37.1
Import share by country					
U.S.		16.2%	17.2%	26.5%	76.3%
Japan		65.1	56.4	42.8	11.0
EC		14.4	19.1	17.9	53.2
Total imports			$1,076	$1,348	$25.3
Import share by country					
U.S.			12.7%	17.9%	77.1%
Japan			61.5	43.5	−14.1
EC			10.4	12.3	47.3

SOURCE: Sang-ho Song, 1991. "Korea's Import Liberalization and Imports from the U.S.," KIET Occasional Paper, p. 13.

making them more transparent and less arbitrary. Korea now relies less on traditional "*ex ante* trade barriers" such as quotas and import licensing than on "export regulations" such as safeguards and antidumping provisions.

Recent trade liberalization had the intended effects on foreign imports into Korea. Overall foreign imports rose dramatically. The rates of increase in imports have been particularly high in recently opened sectors.

Notes

1. The import barriers discussed in this chapter are mainly *formal import barriers*, which are defined as import-restrictive measures that are not informal. *Informal import barriers* include but are not limited to discretionary customs procedure, distribution system discrimination against foreign products, exclusionary business practices, pricing mechanisms to adjust price differentials between domestic and foreign markets, most of which are discussed in the Structural Impediments Initiatives between the United States and Japan. The list of import barriers is adopted from the GATT Trade Policy Review Mechanism. For more, refer to GATT (1990, 1991).

2. The Korean ratio of export to GNP is measured at 32.6 percent during the 1980s, with a high of 36.7 percent in 1987 and a low of 28.9 percent in 1980. Per capita ratio of export to GNP in 1989 is 29.7 percent, compared with 9.4 percent in the United States, 7.4 percent in Japan, 22 percent in West Germany, 22.8 percent in the United Kingdom, 18.8 percent in France, 23.8 percent in Canada, and 29.2 percent in Switzerland.

3. The average tariff rates for manufactured goods in 1988 are reported as 4.6 percent in Japan, 6.1 percent in the United States, 6.7 percent in the EC, and 7.3 percent in Canada. Korea's achievement of lowering tariffs by 67 percent in a span of a decade, if the current plan is implemented as scheduled, will be remarkable in light of the fact that it took from 1953 to 1984 for the United States to lower its average tariff rate from 12.8 percent to 4.2 percent.

4. The following discussion draws on Ministry of Trade and Industry (1989).

5. *Government procurement* in Korea is defined as the procurement by government agencies and corporations in which the government holds a majority of shares.

6. Korea's offer in June 1990 is its fourth bid to accede to the GP Code. This offer was revised in May 1992 to include more procuring entities and fewer exceptions.

7. Interested parties include industrial associations, individual firms, and labor unions.

8. Tariff increase was involved in several cases, including canned pork and wooden chopsticks.

9. In complex cases or at the reasonable request of the parties concerned, an extension may be granted.

10. The factors considered by the KTC for the determination of injury to a domestic industry are generally the same as in safeguards.

11. The estimated dumping margin ranged from 20.6 percent to 107.6 percent. However, this first antidumping duty in Korean history faced a hostile response from the United States and Japan. This case is now being bilaterally consulted in the context of the GATT Anti-Dumping Code.

12. Exports from Korea have been required to carry a mark of origin in accordance with the Foreign Trade Act since the 1960s.

13. Some "individual laws" prescribe the mark of origin. At the ten-digit level of

HS, this consists of 169 items by the Industrial Products Quality Control Act, 304 items by the Electrical Products Safety Control Act, 1,392 items by the Food Sanitation Act, and all imported items under the Fair Trade and Competition Law. This list and the list established in July 1991 largely overlap.

14. Forty-three of the items at the ten-digit HS fall under value-added or process criterion.

15. The U.S. designation of Korea as priority country was partially based on an increasing U.S. deficit in telecommunications equipment trade with Korea. The U.S. trade deficit with Korea in this sector reached above $100 million in 1985 and a record high of $443.7 million in 1987.

16. I treat the twelve countries of the EC as a single large group as in Bergstern and Cline (1987).

17. One needs to notice that my empirical exercise is done for the period 1982–1989 due to limitations on data. I conjecture that my finding will be robust, even if the time span extends to years after 1989, during which Korea underwent a dramatic upsurge in imports.

References

American Chamber of Commerce in Korea. 1990, 1991. *United States-Korean Trade Issues*. Seoul.

Baek, Ehung Gi. 1991. "Factors for the Recent Changes in Trade Volume." *Quarterly Economic Outlook*, KDI (in Korean).

Bergsten, C. Fred, and Cline, William R. 1987. *The United States-Japan Economic Problem*. Washington, D.C.: Institute for International Economics.

Chae, Wook. 1991. *Safeguards in Korea*, KIEP Policy Report no. 91–12 (in Korean).

Choi, Byung-Il. 1990. "Optimal Regulatory Response to Trade in Telecommunications Services." *Korean Journal of Information Society*, Fall.

GATT. 1990. *Trade Policy Review: Japan*. Geneva.

———. 1991. *Trade Policy Review: EC*. Geneva.

IMF. Annual. *International Financial Statistics Yearbook*. Washington, D.C.

———. Annual. *Direction of Trade Statistics Yearbook*. Washington, D.C.

Kim, Jung-Soo, et al. August 1989. *Korea, The Trading Partner*. Seoul: Korean Institute for Economics and Technology. KIET.

Korea Foreign Trade Association. Annual. *Statistics of Foreign Trade*. Seoul.

Ministry of Trade and Industry. March 1989. *Responsive and Responsible*. Kwachon, South Korea.

———. February 1990. *Partnership in Progress*. Seoul.

———. April 1991. *United States–Korea Trade Relationship: A Working Partnership*. Seoul.

Sohn, Sang-Ho. 1991. "Korea's Import Liberalization and Imports from the U.S.," KIET Occasional Paper.

United States Trade Representative. 1990, 1991, 1992. *National Trade Estimate Report on Foreign Trade Barriers.* Washington, D.C.

Young, Soogil. 1988. "Trade Policy Problems in the Republic of Korea and Their Implications for Korea-U.S. Cooperation," KDI Working Paper.

———. 1986. "Import Liberalization and Industrial Adjustment in Korea," KDI Working Paper.

PART THREE

FOREIGN-EXCHANGE-RATE REFORM

5

Liberalization of Korea's Foreign-Exchange Markets and the Role of Trade Relations with the United States

Jeffrey A. Frankel

In October 1988 the Department of the Treasury, in its "Report to the Congress on International Economic and Exchange Rate Policy" required by the Omnibus Trade and Competitiveness Act of 1988, concluded that Korea and Taiwan "manipulated" their exchange rates within the meaning of the legislation. In its October 1989 report, the Treasury announced that it would soon launch negotiations with Korea to induce that country to liberalize its financial markets, with improved treatment for U.S. financial institutions specified as one major goal and appreciation of the won presumed to be another. The Financial Policy Talks took place in two rounds, in February and November 1990.

It is unusual for one nation to include on its agenda for bilateral negotiations with another nation such matters as financial and exchange-rate policies alongside standard trade issues; financial and exchange-rate policies are normally thought to be purely a matter of sovereign choice. But Korea is not the only example. U.S. trade policy has recently included demands for structural reform in several Asian macroeconomies, in contrast to the usual focus on microeconomic trade issues concerning barriers to specific American exports. As nations go beyond arms-length merchandise trade and become more deeply entangled financially in one anothers' economies, and as world leaders fail to adapt adequately the multilateral trade negotiation framework to new issues such as services and investment, we may see more bilateral negotiations of the U.S-Korean type.

To understand the impetus behind recent financial and exchange liberalization in Korea, we must begin by briefly considering trade developments in the United States. We shall then review the two areas of negotiation between the Korea and the United States: exchange-rate issues and other issues of financial liberalization. We will conclude with some empirical tests of the removal of financial barriers in Korea, and among other East Asian countries, and of the strengthening of financial ties with financial centers in New York and Tokyo.

The U.S. Trade Deficit and Policy in the Reagan Years

Each of the years 1982 to 1987 set records for the U.S. trade deficit, particularly with respect to East Asian countries. Many in Congress and the private sector saw the deteriorating trade situation as requiring an immediate response. Proposed responses included efforts to try to reverse the 1981–1985 appreciation of the dollar, and even more often included "get-tough" trade policies.

Officials in the first Reagan administration, 1981–1984, often interpreted trade complaints as special-interest pleading. They pointed out three fallacies: the belief that all trade deficits are bad, the belief that foreign trade barriers could best be addressed by unilateral retaliation, and the belief that the U.S. trade deficit could be attributed to foreign trade barriers.

In these points, the officials of the first Reagan administration were on firm economic ground. Trade complaints *do* most often take the form of special-interest pleading. Trade deficits, in some circumstances, *can* be good. (For example, the large Korean deficits of the 1970s reflected borrowing from abroad to finance investment in plants and equipment, which left Korea in the 1980s with the capacity for output and foreign-exchange earnings needed to service the debt.) It *is* true that the United States unilaterally ruling that a foreign trading practice is unfair often does more to undermine the liberal world trading system than to promote it.

Finally, there *is* convincing evidence that the U.S. trade deficit of the 1980s cannot be attributed to foreign barriers. First, the U.S. current account deficit averaged zero in the 1970s. In the early 1980s, when the trade deterioration occurred, trading partners in East Asia and elsewhere were, if anything, somewhat *reducing* trade barriers against the United States. Second, the deterioration in the U.S. trade balance took place against almost all trading partners, which suggests that the cause lies not with specific foreign countries engaging in unfair trade practices but within the United States itself.

Other aspects of the early Reagan policy were on less firm ground. We will leave aside the point that free trade Reaganite rhetoric was belied by interventionist and protectionist trade actions (such as the negotiation of supposedly voluntary export restraints in autos and steel) that were more numerous and more serious than had been undertaken by previous administrations. Enthusiasm for an activist trade policy among Democrats and moderate Republicans was sufficiently great that one can only assume that others would have done a worse job than the Reaganites. The problem was failing to realize that the major source of the U.S. trade deficit was the switch in the monetary/fiscal mix that raised real interest rates sharply during 1981–1984, causing the dollar to appreciate and U.S. producers to lose competitiveness on world markets. The trade deficit and capital inflow financed not an increase in investment but a deterioration in the federal budget and in private saving rates. (The first Reagan administration pointed instead to a combination of other factors, which were admittedly somewhat relevant: more rapid growth in the United States than among trading partners, the loss in exports to heavily indebted countries when the international debt crisis hit, and stimulus to investment from changes in the tax code.)

In January 1985, with James Baker taking the helm at the Treasury Department, U.S. policy with respect to the trade deficit changed. Now it was agreed that the appreciated dollar was a major cause of the deficit and that both the exchange rate and the deficit were problems that needed to be addressed. The reversal was most complete with respect to intervention in the foreign-exchange market. Whereas the first Reagan administration, as personified in this area by Under Secretary of the Treasury Beryl Sprinkel,[1] abjured intervention almost completely, the second Reagan administration plunged into the foreign-exchange market with gusto. The selling of dollars, which was coordinated with other industrialized countries most visibly at the Plaza Hotel in September 1985, helped reverse almost the entire 1981–1984 appreciation over the subsequent two years.

By 1986, there was still no sign of the U.S. trade balance improvement that some economists promised would rapidly materialize. The search began for explanations as to why the trade deficit continued to worsen despite the substantial depreciation of the dollar since February 1985. One of the many reasons given was that, although the dollar had depreciated substantially against the yen, deutsche mark, and other currencies of the largest industrialized countries, it had not yet depreciated against the currencies of newly important exporters such as the East Asian NICs.[2]

Speaking in Seoul in July 1986, C. Fred Bergsten urged Korea to allow the won to appreciate. U.S. Treasury assistant secretary David Mulford soon picked up the idea and began to urge all four dragons to appreciate.[3] Because Hong Kong and (to a lesser extent) Singapore had open trade and financial markets, American attacks on the smaller two of the four rang hollow. But with a tradition of heavy intervention in all aspects of the economy, and rapidly growing trade surpluses, Taiwan and Korea were obvious targets. Taiwan was at first the more vulnerable politically in that it was rapidly amassing what was almost the largest stock of foreign-exchange reserves in the world (irrespective of GNP), while Korea could and did point to its large international debt (larger relative to GNP in 1982 than the most problematic Latin American debtors) and the need to service the debt with export earnings.

Taiwan began to let the new Taiwan dollar (which had ceased being pegged to the U.S. dollar in 1978) appreciate sharply in mid-1987, and the pressure switched to Korea. In 1987 the Korean current account surplus, which had first gone into surplus the previous year, doubled to $9.9 billion. The bilateral trade surplus with the United States reached a record $9.6 billion.[4] In a November 1987 speech in San Francisco, Mulford accused all four countries of artificially depressing the value of their currencies to run up huge trade surpluses with the United States but reserved the harshest criticism for Korea and Taiwan. The attack on Korea was seen as somewhat surprising in light of the special U.S. military relationship with Korea and the delicate political transformation under way there at the time.[5]

Meanwhile, congressional proposals for a more activist trade policy, which had been held in abeyance by Baker's Plaza initiative, resurfaced with as much force as ever. The final outcome was the Omnibus Trade Bill of 1988. The bill included super 301 provisions mandating that the administration identify "unfair traders" and negotiate elimination of the barriers in question, with automatic retaliation if progress were not satisfactory. There was a requirement (Section 3005) that the U.S. Treasury submit reports and updates to Congress twice a year on exchange-rate policy and other aspects of international economic policy. Although Japan was the single target that the Congress had most firmly in mind, the Treasury reports devoted many pages to the East Asian NICs.

Three threads in U.S. financial policy toward Korea came together in 1989. First, the dollar depreciation strategy of 1985–1986 had left a precedent for pressuring the East Asian NICs, particularly Korea, to appreciate their currencies against the dollar. Second, bilateral negotiations over Korean treatment of U.S. insurance companies had created a precedent, and the Primary Dealers Act of 1988 (the Schumer Amendment to the Omnibus Trade Bill, aimed mainly at Japan), required the government to push East Asian countries for better treatment of U.S. financial institutions through a new policy of "reciprocal national treatment." Third, negotiations with Japan beginning in the yen/dollar talks of 1983–1984 (and continuing through the

Structural Impediments Initiative of 1989–1990) constituted a precedent for the U.S. Treasury to pass judgment on the appropriateness of financial regulations in East Asian countries.

The Precedent of the Yen/Dollar Talks

The 1990 talks with Korea hark back to the campaign launched by the Treasury in October 1983 to induce Japan to liberalize its country's financial markets, where appreciation of the yen was the major goal, a campaign that reached fruition in the Yen/Dollar Agreement of May 1984 with the Japanese Ministry of Finance. Indeed, Treasury officials cite the earlier agreement with Japan as a precedent for the negotiations with Korea. The similarities and dissimilarities between the yen/dollar talks of 1983–1984 and the Korean financial policy talks of 1990 are discussed in Frankel (1989).

Changes in Korea's Exchange-Rate Policy

Korea maintained a fixed exchange rate against the dollar in the late 1970s. As the inflation rate was higher at home than abroad, the won became progressively more overvalued in real terms and exports suffered as a result. (The value of the won is graphed for the period 1970–1990 in figure 1, measured three ways, in terms of [1] the dollar, [2] a nominal trade-weighted average of foreign currencies, and [3] a real average of foreign currencies.) In 1979 the government enacted an important and needed program of macroeconomic stabilization and microeconomic reform. In January 1980 the won was devalued by 20 percent. This devaluation, and the contractionary macroeconomic measures taken the preceding year (though interrupted by social and political turmoil in the spring of 1980), succeeded in stimulating rapid export growth and reducing the current account deficit. This left Korea as one of the few major debtors that was well positioned when the 1982 international debt crisis hit.[6]

The official exchange-rate policy in 1980 became one of defining the won's value in terms of a basket of five foreign currencies, rather than just the dollar.[7] In principle, pegging to a basket leaves a small country less vulnerable to movements in exchange rates among major trading partners over which it has no control, particularly the yen/dollar rate in the Korean case, and is otherwise similar to pegging to a single currency. In practice, however, almost all countries that officially claim to be on a basket-peg regime do not publicly announce what the currency weights are and frequently

Figure 1.   Korean Exchange Rates

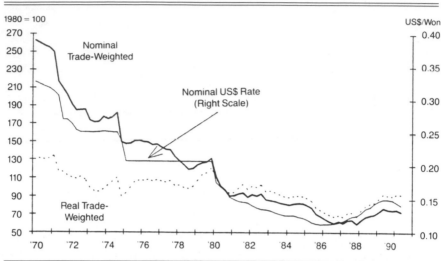

SOURCE: Pacific Basin Center for Monetary and Economic Studies, Federal Reserve Bank of San Francisco

NOTE: Trade-weighted indexes use 1980 bilateral trade weights with United States, Japan, and Germany

secretly change the weights or the level or both at which they peg to the basket, with the result that the exchange rate is as flexible as if the authorities made no commitment at all.[8] Korea in the 1980s was a clear example of basket-pegging in name only.[9] The equation that related the value of the won to the value of the dollar, yen, and other currencies included an additional "alpha" term that in practice could be varied at will. The IMF was perceptive enough to classify Korea as a "managed floater" rather than a "basket-pegger."

The phase of dollar depreciation that began in 1985, as represented by the Plaza Accord, was welcomed in Korea as one of "three blessings" in the world economic environment: low dollar, low interest rates, and low oil prices. For two years Korea kept the won close to the dollar, which meant a substantial depreciation against the yen and other currencies, and basked in the stimulus to its exports. But the country responded to U.S. pressure by appreciating the won against the dollar in 1987 and 1988.[10] The Korean government also claimed to have adopted current account convertibility: "By deregulating a substantial portion of external transactions in November 1988, Korea accepted the obligations of IMF's Article VIII."[11]

Despite the won appreciation, the U.S. Treasury, in its first three reports to Congress called for by the 1988 Trade Bill—October 1988, April 1989, and October 1989—pronounced Korea a country that manipulates its exchange rate. It sought further appreciation, citing as recently as the third report continued "indications of exchange rate 'manipulation' during the six months since the April report" (p. 26).[12]

The Treasury's October 1989 report included the following announcement: "Recently, the Treasury Department and the Korean Ministry of Finance have agreed to initiate talks on financial policies, including the exchange rate system and capital market issues. We hope to encourage a more market-oriented exchange rate system in Korea within the framework of these talks" (p.29). As noted, the financial policy talks took place in February and November of 1990. Evidently, the 1990 talks did not explicitly focus on the level of the won/dollar rate per se. Rather, the Treasury sought to "encourage the liberalization of Korea's exchange rate system and of the capital and interest rate controls that impede the full operation of market forces." A likely consequence of this liberalization of the system was, however, under the 1989 economic circumstances, to allow the won to appreciate further. The Treasury did say that, parallel with the talks on financial policy, would be negotiations "to press for exchange rate policy to support further external adjustment," that is, for more appreciation of the won to reduce the current account surplus.[13]

On March 2, 1990, the Korean authorities adopted a "market average rate" (MAR) system of setting the exchange rate each week (Hwang 1990, 15). This reform led the Treasury to drop charges of exchange-rate manipulation in its April 1990 report, whereas the earlier won appreciation was apparently not sufficient to convince it to do so.

The MAR system sets the won/dollar exchange rate at the beginning of each business day at the weighted average of transactions in the interbank market on the preceding business day. Interbank and customer rates are allowed to float freely within specified margins.[14] Presumably the width of the margins puts an upper limit on the amount by which the central rate can be adjusted each day (somewhat like so-called circuit breakers imposed on some countries' stock markets). This leaves out the most important questions: Will the authorities systematically intervene and if so how? Will they exercise influence over the banks? Also, the question that is of secondary importance except to the United States, how fully will foreign banks be allowed to participate in the developing foreign-exchange market?

A year later, the U.S. Treasury report (p.15) found that "during the first thirteen months of the MAR system (through April 12, 1991), the won depreciated 4.4 in nominal terms against the dollar. . . . Foreign banks accounted for a large share of transactions in the inter-bank market, generally 40–60 percent of the total. The Bank of Korea (BOK) was not a direct participant in the market, and other government-owned banks accounted for only a small share of inter-bank activity." This would seem to suggest a genuinely market-oriented system.

We are also told, however, that "the Korean authorities maintain a comprehensive array of controls on foreign exchange and capital flows. These controls prevent market forces of supply and demand from playing a fully effective role in exchange rate determination, distort trade and investment flows, and provide the Korean authorities with tools for indirectly manipulating the exchange rate." In other words, Korea has moved to a floating exchange rate before removing capital controls or progressing with other aspects of financial liberalization. This unusual response to a campaign for free markets is discussed in the next section.

On the surface, it appears from the report that the Treasury cares primarily about the Korean foreign-exchange *system*—that it be fair, or free, or market-oriented—rather than about the level of the exchange rate per se. This appears to follow from the fact that the Treasury continued to accuse Korea of manipulating the exchange rate after the won had appreciated substantially and terminated the accusation during a period when its value fell but was set by the MAR system. If U.S. motives are interpreted more pragmatically, however, the key change between 1988 and 1991 was the disappearance of the Korean current account surplus in 1989. (The two most important reasons for the deterioration in the trade balance were probably the large effective appreciation of the won in 1988–1989 and rising labor activism.) Indeed the report concludes that "with a return to external surpluses likely in 1992, we would expect to see a renewed trend toward appreciation of the won" (p.18).

The view from Korea is that the trade deficit is likely to remain in deficit in 1992 and 1993. Nevertheless, capital inflow may create a potential surplus in the *overall* balance of payments and thereby put upward pressure on the won. In current circumstances, allowing the won to appreciate very much would probably be unwise from the Korean viewpoint. It seems likely that the government would react by resuming sales of won to dampen such an appreciation, abandoning the floating-rate system.

Do Free Markets Imply
Freely Floating Exchange Rates?

In one respect, the case for appreciation of the won was less confused than the 1984 argument for appreciation of the yen: the Korean central bank had indeed been buying dollars and selling won in foreign-exchange intervention in 1987 and 1988, which is not what the Japanese were doing in the early 1980s. Thus a move to a freely floating exchange rate system would have entailed a stronger appreciation of the won in the late 1980s. Also there are some respectable economic arguments for letting the won appreciate, beyond the goal of helping to reduce the U.S. trade deficit. When a country such as Taiwan or Korea attempts to keep the currency from appreciating, it may experience an inflow of reserves too large to sterilize, resulting in undesired monetary expansion and inflation.

In general, my advice to a less developed country experiencing unwanted reserve inflows and fearing real appreciation of its currency is as follows: (1) liberalize with respect to capital outflows, thus reducing the magnitude of the net inflows and (2) liberalize with respect to domestic bond markets, thus allowing scope for central bank operations to sterilize reserve inflows. In 1986–1989 Korea did the right things: paying off external debt and sterilizing reserve inflows by selling monetary stabilization bonds and raising reserve requirements.[15] But the actions were not strong enough to prevent inflationary growth in the money supply. The absence of active domestic bond markets in which the Bank of Korea might have been able more fully to sterilize its purchases of dollars in exchange for won (by selling domestic bonds in exchange for won and thereby preventing the supply of won in the hands of the public from expanding) has been attributed to the cessation of financial liberalization in the period 1984–1987.[16] Further financial liberalization is indeed a good idea for Korea; facilitating sterilization operations in the future is one of the reasons.

In any event, the case against Korea, and the other Asian NICs dampening appreciation of their currencies against the dollar, has none of the legal or principled basis that is imputed to it by the Omnibus Trade Act of 1988. Small countries should be perfectly free to seek to maintain fixed exchange rates. There is nothing in the Articles of Agreement of the GATT or IMF, nor is there anything in idealized free market principles, that discourages the attempt to maintain a fixed exchange rate. Indeed, the original goal of the IMF was to promote stable exchange rates even for large countries.[17] Such fathers of supply-side economics as Robert Mundell and Jack Kemp consider a return to exchange-rate stability essential to their creed. (They actually consider proposals to solve world trade imbalances by depreciating the dollar against Asian currencies to be similar to protectionism!)

Even those who are more enamored of floating exchange rates for major currencies like the dollar and yen recognize that there is little point in a sufficiently small country—whether less developed, newly industrializing, or fully industrialized—having a floating exchange rate. The optimum currency area argument of undergraduate textbooks in international economics reminds us that for a small open economy like Hong Kong—or the San

Francisco Bay Area—the advantages of a floating exchange rate (monetary independence and automatic adjustment of the balance of payments) are probably outweighed by the advantages of a fixed exchange rate (no exchange-rate uncertainty and a credible commitment to low money growth and inflation). It would not be unreasonable for a country the size of Korea to opt for a fixed exchange rate. The countries of Europe claim to be in the process of doing so. (For Korea, if it chose to go this route, I would recommend a true basket peg, with the weights publicly announced to enhance credibility.)

This is not to say that there might not be some valid economic reasons for Korean appreciation. The point is rather that Americans are mistaken to accuse small Asian economies of violating any rules of free market economics or international commitments when they intervene in the foreign-exchange market. The case for negotiating reductions in barriers to international trade has strong justification in the principles of economic theory and of international commitments like the GATT. The case for reducing barriers to international capital flows is also respectable, though its justification in principle is somewhat weaker, both in theory and under international commitments. The case for abstaining from intervention in the foreign-exchange market has no such basis in principle. When Americans apply terms like *unfair* or *manipulate* indiscriminately, they undermine the rules and principles that are truly important.

A presidential commission on economic restructuring, established in April 1988, submitted a report to President Roh in October 1988 that called for internationalization of the Korean economy, including reduction of the country's then-surplus on the current account by means of liberalization of import restrictions *rather than by rapid appreciation of the currency.*[18] As Korean minister of finance Il SaKong (1989, 15) has pointed out, pressuring Korea into further appreciation of the won could undermine import liberalization there by adding to domestic opposition:

> Korea's first order of business at this point must be to eliminate existing market-distorting elements. In this regard, Korea has been doing its utmost to get rid of nontariff barriers still remaining in the economy and to reduce the average tariff. By so doing, Korea will be able to import more from the United States, provided that US firms take full advantage of these measures. This, more than anything else, will help to restore a favorable bilateral trade balance. Accelerating the appreciation of the Korean won would act to preserve, and perhaps heighten, distortions in the economy, with negative ramifications for both Korea and the United States.

Americans would be as well advised as Koreans to keep clear the distinction between policies that are based in principle and those that are based in expediency.

Korean Financial Liberalization in the 1980s

Issues of financial liberalization fall into three areas: domestic liberalization, removal of international capital controls, and treatment of foreign providers of financial services.

In the 1970s, Korea met the description of a financially repressed economy. The banking system was kept underdeveloped (although an informal "curb market" became very large), securities markets were largely nonexistent, and interest rates were kept negative in real terms to stimulate investment in favored sectors (especially heavy industry).[19]

By end of the 1970s, the government recognized that financial repression was an obstacle to further growth. An early aspect of a financial liberalization program was the establishment of two open-end trust funds.[20] The road to banking deregulation started in 1982 with the privatization of five national commercial banks.[21] Restrictions on bank management were reduced. The requirement that loans be made at preferential rates for policy purposes became less common in 1982. Further steps toward liberalization of interest rates were taken in early 1984. But the most effective agents of liberalization were the rapidly growing nonbank financial intermediaries. There seems to be general agreement that the pace of liberalization has been slow since 1984. "During [the 1984–1987] period no important steps were taken to further liberalize the financial sector."[22]

In December 1988 more-serious interest-rate decontrol was undertaken by the outgoing finance minister, Il Sakong.[23] (This process was soon slowed, however, when interest rates—rather predictably—started to rise.) At the same time, "citing unexpected economic changes, the Korean Government revised its original 1981 schedule to liberalize the securities industry."[24] A new timetable was announced for the removal of controls on capital inflow and outflow. The measures announced in December 1988 included a schedule under which substantial liberalization was to take place in 1992.

Many Korean officials believe that further domestic liberalization "could further raise the market interest rates, pushing up the firms' financing costs."[25] One would think that *international* liberalization is the answer, allowing the firms to borrow much more cheaply abroad. But apparently the government position is the reverse: "It is recognized that in order to minimize the negative effects on the economy as a whole, the deregulation of interest rates and domestic financial markets need[s] to precede the liberalization of foreign exchange and capital transactions." It is not clear what these negative effects are. Perhaps the authorities wish to avoid overborrowing like Chile did in its 1970s liberalization, which caused writers on the Optimal Order of Liberalization to warn against beginning with the removal of capital controls. According to Nam (1989, 157), "The fear of massive capital inflows attracted by relatively high domestic real interest rates and anticipated foreign exchange appreciation has prompted controls on capital inflows."

One possibility is that the authorities are worried that a large capital inflow would bring about a real appreciation of the won; if the authorities intervened to resist the pressure toward nominal appreciation (which would itself require abandoning the free float spirit of the MAR), then the inflow of reserves would be inflationary. Korean exporters would lose competitiveness. The solution, as I noted above, is to resist the nominal appreciation but to sterilize the increase in reserves so as to prevent inflationary growth in the money supply.

Another possibility is that the authorities are worried that Korean "domestic financial institutions, especially banks, are not efficient and competitive enough compared to their foreign counterparts."[26] One could argue that there are three natural stages of development in a country's financial system. In stage 1, business investment is financed out of family savings or—in a country where the government plays a more *dirigiste* role—by official loans. This is the stage where Korea has been until now. One should hesitate before condemning Korean "financial repression," given how successful the development process has been over the last thirty years.[27] Nevertheless, it may be time to move on to a new stage.

In stage 2, financial intermediation by investment banks allows a more effective channeling of funds from savers to business. The Japanese postwar main bank system illustrates this system at its best, with the banks efficiently monitoring the activities of the firm managers to make sure they are not diverting the funds from productive investment projects toward their own purposes.[28] DeLong (1991) has argued that in the nineteenth century investment banks served this role in the United States as well.

In stage 3, well-established corporations find that it is more efficient still to disintermediate. They switch from reliance on bank loans to issuing securities directly in developed financial markets, where a corporation with a good reputation and credit rating can obtain capital cheaply. The United States and the United Kingdom have been at stage 3 for some time, and Japan is apparently beginning to move there (though it is unclear whether this will constitute an improvement). The question is whether it is premature for Korea to jump to stage 3 without first having passed through stage 2.

Recent U.S.-Korean Negotiations over Financial Issues

The U.S. Treasury evaluation of progress in the 1990 Financial Policy Talks regarding financial services was negative. With respect to treatment of foreign banks, even though Korea had in 1984 declared national treatment for foreign-owned banks as part of a three-year deregulation plan,[29] the report found that "progress in resolving problems has been very slow and no timetable for dealing with them has been produced."[30] With regard to the treatment of foreign securities firms, even though Korea had in 1988 declared that twenty-four foreign firms would be allowed to establish branches,[31] the report found (p.11) that "U.S. financial firms do not receive national treatment in Korean securities markets."[32] With regard to overall financial liberalization, the report found that "until the Korean Government allows domestic banks to compete in a market environment, fully liberalizes interest rates, and eliminates credit allocation and exchange controls, there is little likelihood of major advances in equality of competitive opportunity for foreign financial service providers in the Korean market."[33]

In 1991, foreign securities companies were for the first time allowed directly into the country, as had been promised in the negotiations with the United States. The Ministry of Finance in March approved four out of nine applications for branch office securities licenses,[34] two of them American,[35] turning down all four Japanese securities companies (and a French-owned one) that had applied. The reason given was reciprocity: Korean firms would be more able to enter American and British markets than would Japanese and French firms. But in the interpretation of *The Economist*, "Few people doubt that dislike and fear of Japan had more to do with it." Such developments are of interest because there is the potential that as U.S. political pressure forces Korean financial markets open, the capital and financial firms that come in will be Japanese rather than American. On economic grounds, the flow of money from Japan to Korea is natural. On political grounds it is more difficult.

In June 1991 restrictions were lifted on the establishment of multiple branches of foreign banks. It was also announced that application of national treatment for banks will be "stepped up" (Oum 1991, 8) and that the government of Korea was preparing a "master plan" to liberalize interest rates and to "rectify distortions in its term structure."[36]

At the beginning of 1992, foreign investors are to be free to invest in individual Korean stocks on the stock market.[37] Other reforms are planned as well. On December 17, 1991, the National Assembly approved revisions in a number of laws, including a revision to permit banks to engage in all foreign-exchange business that is not specifically prohibited.[38]

Tests of Financial and Monetary Links to the United States and Japan

A useful way of empirically measuring the magnitude of barriers separating a country's financial markets from the outside world is to look at differentials between onshore and offshore interest rates, usually with adjustments of some kind to make them more comparable. The idea is that if barriers are low, then arbitrage should equate onshore and offshore rates of return. We will review some empirical evidence on three questions:

1. How open are financial markets in Korea compared, for example, with other Asian countries?
2. Are financial links tighter with New York or Tokyo?
3. Of the barriers that remain, which are more important: currency factors or country factors?

Are Korean Financial Markets Becoming More Open?

A recent study by Reisen and Yeches (1991), through a time-varying coefficients model, estimates the degree of Korean links with foreign interest rates. The study finds an increase in financial openness in the first half of the 1980s, following the financial deregulation package that was part of an overall liberalization of the economy in 1981. But the degree of openness declined during 1985–1987 (and remained below its 1985 peak as recently as 1990). This is the period when the won appreciated against the dollar as the result of dollar depreciation against major currencies followed by U.S. pressure on Korea not to keep its currency tied to the dollar. Reisen and Yeches point out that despite the switch from a depreciation trend to an appreciation trend, which one would expect in a fully liberalized system to eliminate the premium demanded by investors to hold Korean assets, Korean interest rates remained far higher (16 to 20 percent) than U.S. interest rates. These are curb-market rates;[39] their still-high level represents some unknown combination of controls on capital inflow and the higher credit risk of curb-market obligations. But the fact that low-risk, market-determined interest rates are still not available is even more direct evidence that the market is not liberalized.

The Korean consumer price index (CPI) inflation rate averaged 4 percent during the period 1982–1989, almost exactly as low as the U.S. CPI inflation rate. This suggests a differential in real interest rates between Korea and the United States in excess of 16 percent. For purposes of comparison, the real interest differentials in other Asian Pacific countries averaged as follows: Japan − 0.6 percent, Hong Kong − 2.9 percent, Singapore + 0.1 percent, Malaysia + 0.8 percent, Australia + 1.2 percent, and New Zealand + 1.0 percent.[40] This list of six countries is unrepresentative of Asia and the Pacific in that their financial markets are the most developed and open; the list was chosen because these countries are the only ones for whom data from the London forward-exchange market are available.[41] But the contrast between Korea and these six makes clear how far the former is from having open and fully developed financial markets.

Are Financial Links Tighter with New York or Tokyo?

To tell whether a small country is more tightly linked to one major world financial center or another, one can run a regression of its interest rate against interest rates in the foreign countries. A regression of monthly Korean interest rates (three-month interbank rate) against major foreign interest rates over the period December 1977 to March 1989 suggests that U.S. interest rates have the most influence, with Japan close behind.[42] These effects appear to be highly significant statistically.[43] One would expect that this relationship would have changed over time, particularly since Korea did not even begin to deregulate its interest rates until 1982. One way to address this issue is to allow for simple time trends in the coefficients. (These results are reported in table 3 of Frankel, 1992b.) The influence of Japanese interest rates, though high, appears to be decreasing over time. The same is true of German interest rates. The British interest rate is gaining influence over time; the United States shows no significant trend. When one takes first differences,[44] the significance of the results regarding the role of Japanese interest rates remains.

During most of this period, Korean interest rates were still tightly regulated. U.S. pressure to liberalize in that direction dates from 1988. I tried the interest-rate regression, against U.S. and Japanese interest rates, during the more recent time period, 1988–1991. New York and Tokyo appear to have equal effects on the Korean interest rate.[45] For purposes of comparison, the influence of Japanese interest rates in Taiwan and Singapore now appears to be greater than the influence of U.S. interest rates, while in Hong Kong (which is pegged to the dollar) it is the U.S. influence that is larger. (It is not a coincidence that Hong Kong is the one country of the four that is currently pegged to the U.S. dollar.)

Which Sort of Barrier Is More Important: Currency Factors or Country Factors?

There are many factors or barriers that can separate a country's interest rates from world interest rates. The barriers can be sorted into two categories: those that pertain to the political jurisdiction in which an asset is issued (capital controls, tax differences, default risk, risk of *future* capital controls, and information costs) and those that pertain to the currency in which it is denominated (expected currency depreciation and the exchange risk premium). To separate the two factors, one needs some way of adjusting for the prospect of exchange-rate changes, such as forward-rate data. Out of the twenty-five countries for which forward-rate data are available, all but a few (none of them in the Pacific) show currency premiums that are larger than country premiums. For some, covered interest parity holds almost precisely, showing evidence of no country barriers at all. But these twenty-five are typically countries with relatively liberalized financial markets.[46]

Without forward-rate data, which do not exist for Korea, it is difficult to decompose definitively the interest differential into a currency component and a country component. Survey data can be used in place of forward-rate data to correct for expectations of exchange-rate changes.[47] The hypothesis of a unit coefficient in the interest-rate regression then becomes the condition of uncovered interest parity, rather than covered interest parity.

I tried the Korean interest-rate regression with foreign interest rates adjusted for expected depreciation using the survey data.[48] The apparent significance of the Japanese effect in Korea now disappears (as it does in Singapore and Taiwan). This finding suggests that the link between Korean and Japanese interest rates during the recent period may be due in part to currency factors: the won is less closely tied to the dollar than it used to be, partly as the result of U.S. pressure, and perhaps more closely to the yen. We now turn to a test of this question.

The hypothesis that the implicit weights assigned to major foreign currencies by the won changed during the course of the 1980s can be tested by regressing changes in the value of the won against changes in the value of other major currencies. There is a methodological question of what numeraire should be used to measure the value of the currencies. A simple solution is to use the special drawing right (SDR) as numeraire. This approach suffers a bit because the SDR is itself a basket of five major currencies including the dollar and yen. An alternative approach is to use purchasing power over Korean goods (the inverse of the Korean price level) as the numeraire.

Regressions of the change in the real value of the won reported here in table 1 show a statistically significant weight on the value of the dollar throughout the period April 1980 to March 1986, with an estimated coefficient of .4 to .7. There is also a significant constant term (the alpha) during this period: the value of the won declined during the early 1980s, whether measured by inflation or depreciation, relative to foreign currencies. The dollar, like the other major currencies, is insignificant during the period April 1985 to March 1987. Its influence reemerges from April 1986 to March 1988. But during the final two-year subperiod, April 1988 to March 1990, the yen (with a significant coefficient estimated at .09) suddenly eclipses the dollar (with an insignificant coefficient).[49] This evidence appears to confirm that Korea has loosened the link between the won and the U.S. dollar, as the United States urged, and has developed a link with the yen.

Another sign of the increased influence of the yen in Korea is the yen share of external debt, which increased from 16.6 percent in 1980 to 29.5 percent in 1988. For an average of five major debtors in the region (Korea, Indonesia, Malaysia, Philippines, and Thailand), the yen share increased from 19.5 percent to 37.9 percent over this period. In the Asian region, the share of the yen in official reserve holdings rose from 13.9 percent in 1980 to 26.7 percent in 1988 (and then declined back to 17.5 percent in 1989).[50] To the extent that the emergence of a "yen bloc" in East Asia would not be welcomed by the United States, it is ironic that internationalization of the yen was originally a goal of U.S. policy.

Conclusion

Financial liberalization is a good thing for Korea, so long as proper SEC-type regulation is maintained. Allowing in providers of financial services, like allowing in foreign agricultural products, is consistent with comparative advantage and would benefit both countries.

The beneficial implications for U.S. "competitiveness" through Asian liberalization in the area of exchange-rate policy are less clear than one would infer from observing the amount of U.S. pressure applied. It is misguided for Americans to appeal to free market principles to justify pressure on Asian countries to allow their currencies to appreciate against the dollar. It is perfectly appropriate for a small country to seek exchange-rate stability if it so desires. American negotiators would perhaps be better advised to concentrate on negotiating the liberalization of trade in goods and services, where the appeal to principle is on secure ground.

Table 1. Weights Assigned to Yen and Dollar in
Determining Changes in Value of Korean Won
(ordinary least squares regression estimates)

| Period | VALUE DEFINED IN PURCHASING POWER | | | | |
	Constant	Yen	Dollar	R^2	D.W.
80.4–91.9	−.0040	.02	.42	.33	.69
	−7.22***	1.21	7.80***		
80.4–82.3	−.0098	−.01	.72	.58	1.00
	−5.95***	−0.22	5.36***		
81.4–83.3	−.0051	.05	.72	.76	1.26
	−6.13***	1.78	7.67***		
82.4–84.3	−.0036	.02	.47	.54	1.28
	−5.54***	0.67	4.84***		
83.4–85.3	−.0030	.09	.47	.71	−1.20
	−5.63***	2.97***	6.61***		
84.4–85.3	−.0034	.04	.38	.37	1.28
	−4.16***	1.89*	3.31***		
85.4–85.3	−.0017	.00	.11	.05	1.78
	−2.37**	0.05	0.98		
86.4–88.3	.0012	−.03	.48	.71	2.21
	1.14	−1.51	7.12***		
87.4–89.3	.0012	.01	.42	.55	1.90
	0.76	0.25	4.97***		
88.4–90.3	−.0026	.09	.09	.29	1.51
	−2.19**	2.75***	0.94		

NOTES: t-statistics reported below coefficients.
  * Statistically significant at 90% level.
 ** Statistically significant at 95% level.
*** Statistically significant at 99% level.

Notes

1. The starting team at the Treasury included, in addition to monetarists like Sprinkel who viewed free market philosophy as requiring freely floating exchange rates, supply-siders who viewed free market philosophy as requiring fixed exchange rates (in order that the money constitute a stable store of value). In the first administration the issue was decided firmly on the side of the free-floaters by Secretary Don

Table 1.   (*continued*)

| Period | VALUE DEFINED IN TERMS OF SDR | | | | |
	Constant	Yen	Dollar	R^2	D.W.
80.4–91.9	−.0017	−.02	+.83	.71	.41
	−2.25**	−0.41	+14.72***		
80.4–82.3	−.0069	−.08	+.79	.74	1.26
	−3.67***	−1.02	+6.28***		
81.4–83.3	−.0042	−.01	+.84	.89	1.09
	−4.32***	−0.16	+9.91		
82.4–84.3	−.0034	−.04	+.69	.86	1.07
	−3.68***	−0.75	+6.80***		
83.4–85.3	−.0033	+.04	+.71	.78	.89
	−3.60***	+0.52	+7.26***		
84.4–85.3	−.0055	+.12	+.96	.90	1.08
	−5.40***	+1.66*	+10.60		
85.4–85.3	−.0005	−.01	+.96	.82	.34
	−0.32	−0.67	+7.09		
86.4–88.3	+.0072	−.04	+1.04	.84	.53
	+4.42***	−0.34	+7.81		
87.4–89.3	+.0098	−.02	+.90	.85	.80
	+6.34***	−0.11	+7.77***		
88.4–90.3	+.0060	+.55	+1.11	.91	1.44
	+4.96***	+5.87	+14.98***		

NOTES: t-statistics reported below coefficients.
  * Statistically significant at 90% level.
  ** Statistically significant at 95% level.
  *** Statistically significant at 99% level.

Regan, who came to view negative statements about the strength of the dollar as equivalent to negative statements about the president's economic policies.

2. In retrospect, the trade balance responded to the dollar depreciation with close to the standard two-year lag that economists had always specified. Many observers think that there was a bit of an unusual delay because the pass-through of the exchange-rate change into dollar import prices was slower than in the past, though even this bit of revisionism has more recently been attributed to a problem with the proper measurement of computer prices (Krugman, 1991). The role of the NIC

currencies was in any case only a relatively minor element of the overall U.S. trade situation.

3. The first discussions with the Korean government took place in September 1986. (Wang 1991, 14—15, details the chronology of U.S. demands in this area.)

4. Ohm (1991, 9). (The bilateral surplus was to decline to $2.4 billion in 1990 on Korean reckoning, $4.1 billion on U.S. reckoning [U.S. Treasury, 1991, 30].)

5. Preparations for elections were under way in Korea (Kim 1990, 17).

6. Balassa and Williamson (1990), Collins and Park (1989), and K. Kim (1990).

7. Including the U.S. dollar, yen, mark, pound, and Canadian dollar (Wang 1991, 3).

8. One can ascertain whether a country that is officially pegging to a basket is in fact doing so by regressing the value of its currency against the value of major trading partner currencies, allowing for occasional changes in weights and in level. A true basket-pegger will show up with an R-squared close to one. Such tests are reported in the last part of this paper.

9. Balassa and Williamson (1990, 48).

10. Bergsten (1989), Layman (1988, 374), Noland (1990, 49–50), Oum (1989), Williamson (1989), Kwack and Kim (1990), Park and Park (1990), and Wang (1991).

11. Oum (pp. 4–5). (See also Wang [1991, 19].) But the government still requires documentation in support of foreign currency transactions. According to 1989 Federal Reserve records, "Korean export proceeds must be deposited in foreign-exchange accounts in domestic banks (if not surrendered to the government), payments for imports of services are restricted, foreign borrowing by financial in situations is subject to ceilings, and all outward-bound capital requires approval."

12. See also Balassa and Williamson (1990, 58).

13. Fall 1990 footnote.

14. (U.S. Treasury Report May 1991.) The margins were widened to 0.8 percent in July 1992 (from 0.6 percent, to which the range was widened in September 1991 [Lindner 1991a, 8]).

15. Lindner (1991) and Kwack (1993).

16. Kim 1990, 17, and Kwack 1993, 3, 26–27.

17. Noland (1991, 176) notes that the IMF did not agree with the Treasury position that Korea should appreciate its currency after 1985.

18. In-June Kim (1991, 55–56).

19. See, for example, Kihwan Kim (1990, 3–6), who argues that the resistance to currency depreciation in the late 1970s was in part due to the desire to keep interest rates low.

20. Kim (1991, 22).

21. Oum (1991) and K. Kim (1990, 11).

22. Kihwan Kim (1991). Others who note the slow pace of Korean financial liberalization include Fry (1990, 42–44) and Park.

23. For example, Kihwan Kim (1991, 21).

24. U.S. Treasury (1990b) National Treatment Study, p.261.

25. Oum (1991, 7).

26. Ibid.

Figure 2.   Korean Interest Rates

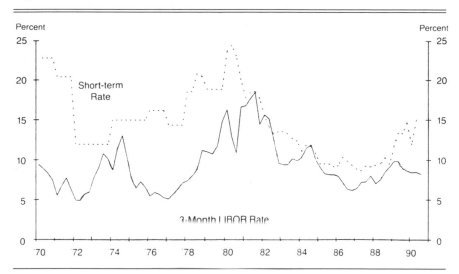

SOURCE: Pacific Basin Center for Monetary and Economic Studies, Federal Reserve Bank of San Francisco
NOTE: Short term = Korea Call Money Rate

27. See Yung Chul Park (1991) on this point.

28. For a survey of this and other aspects of corporate finance in Japan, see Frankel (1991b).

29. Ohm (1991, 7).

30. U.S. Treasury 1990, 243.

31. Eight of them American (Ohm 1991, 7).

32. U.S. Treasury 1990, 261.

33. U.S. Treasury 1990, 258.

34. "The Korea That Can Say No," *The Economist*, March 23, 1991.

35. Oum 1991, 10.

36. Oum 1991, 10–11. Evidently there is a need to encourage more saving in longer-term securities, as opposed to short-term securities (Fry 1990).

37. Kihwan Kim (1991, p.22) and Oum (1991, p.9). But apparently there will be a 10 percent limit on foreign ownership (*Economist*, March 23, 1991).

38. *Korea Times*, December 19, 1991.

39. The Korean call money rate is lower, occasionally as low as offshore dollar interest rates (as shown in figure 2).

40. Over the period September 1982 to January 1988. Further statistics and data details are given in Frankel (1991a). For more tests of real interest parity in the region, see Glick (1987) and Glick and Hutchison (1990).

41. These data allow tests of covered-interest parity, which show that capital controls and similar barriers to the movement of capital across national boundaries are as low in Japan, Hong Kong, and Singapore as in any European country.

42. These results, which use monthly observations of the Korean call money rate, are reported in table 1 of Frankel (1992b). The foreign interest rates are three-month interest rates. Regressions using a Korean three-month financial bill rate from *World Financial Markets* show a greater role for U.K. interest rates during this sample period but are otherwise similar.

43. This significance disappears, however, when one tries the regression on first differences in response to the evidently high level of serial correlation, as reported in table 2, ibid.

44. In table 4, ibid.

45. Frankel (1992a), table 4, or (1992b) table 5.

46. Frankel (1991a, 247–49).

47. There are a number of surveys of forecasts of participants in the foreign-exchange market, but most deal only with the major five or so currencies. One, however, covers more currencies, including a number of Asian ones: *Currency Forecasters' Digest* of White Plains, New York. This is the source for our survey data, obtained by subscription of the Institute for International Economics where the author is a visiting fellow.

48. Frankel (1992a), table 4.

49. When values are measured in terms of the SDR, the dollar appears to maintain its significance much more strongly, but the finding of a highly significant yen in the last two years remains, as the table shows. The corresponding table in Frankel (1992b) reports tests that include the Canadian dollar and other major currencies, in addition to the yen and dollar. It shows better fit and lower serial correlation (as measured by R^2 and Durbin-Watson statistic). The qualitative conclusions are similar.

50. Tavlas and Ozeki 1991.

References

Balassa, Bela, and Williamson, John. 1990. *Adjusting to Success: Balance of Payments Policy in the East Asian NICs*, Policy Analyses in International Economics no. 17. Washington, D.C.: Institute for International Economics.

Bergsten, C. Fred. 1989. "Currency Manipulation? The Case of Korea." Statement before the Senate Committee on Finance, Subcommittee on International Trade, May 12.

Collins, Susan, and Park, Won-Am. 1989. "External Debt and Macroeconomic Performance, in South Korea." In Jeffrey Sachs, ed., *Developing Country Debt and Macroeconomic Performance*. Chicago: University of Chicago Press.

DeLong, J. Bradford. 1991. "The Great American Universal Banking Experiment." In Peter Temin, *Inside the Business Enterprise*, Chicago: University of Chicago Press.

Frankel, Jeffrey. 1984. *The Yen/Dollar Agreement: Liberalizing Japanese Financial Markets*, Policy Analyses in International Economics no. 9. Washington, D.C.: Institute for International Economics.

————. 1989. "And Now Won/Dollar Negotiations? Lessons from the Yen/Dollar Agreement of 1984." In *Korea's Macroeconomic and Financial Policies*. Seoul: Korean Development Institute.

————. 1991a. "Quantifying International Capital Mobility in the1980's." In D. Bernheim and J. Shoven, eds., *National Saving and Economic Performance*. Chicago: University of Chicago Press, pp. 227–60.

————. 1991b. "The Japanese Financial System and Cost of Capital: A Survey." In Shinji Takagi, ed., *Handbook of Japanese Capital Markets*. Cambridge, Mass.: Basil Blackwell, forthcoming.

————. 1992a. "Is Japan Forming a Yen Bloc in Pacific Asia?" J. Frankel and M. Kahler, eds., *Regionalism and Rivalry: Japan and the U.S. in Pacific Asia*. Chicago: University of Chicago Press, forthcoming.

————. 1992b. "The Recent Liberalization of Korea's Foreign Exchange Markets, and Tests of U.S. Versus Japanese Influence." *Seoul Journal of Economics* 5, no. 1 (March 13).

Fry, Maxwell. 1990. "Nine Financial Sector Issues in Eleven Asian Developing Countries." International Finance Group Working Papers, United Kingdom: University of Birmingham, October.

Glick, Reuven. 1987. "Interest Rate Linkages in the Pacific Basin." *Federal Reserve Bank of San Francisco Economic Review*, no. 3: 31–42.

————, and Hutchison, Michael. 1990. "Financial Liberalization in the Pacific Basin: Implications for Real Interest Rate Linkages." *Journal of the Japanese and International Economies* 4: 36–48.

Hwang, Eui-Gak. 1990. "Trade Policy Issues between South Korea and the United States, With Some Emphasis on Korea's Position." Academic Symposium on the Impact of Recent Economic Developments on US/Korean Relations and the Pacific Basin," University of California at San Diego, November 9–10.

Kim. In-June, 1991. "Republic of Korea." In Sylvia Ostry, ed., *Authority and Academic Scribblers: The Role of Research in East Asian Policy Reform*. San Francisco: ICS Press.

Kim, Kihwan. 1990. "Deregulating the Domestic Economy: Korea's Experience in the 1980s." Paper presented at Senior Policy Seminar, Caracas, Venezuela, revised December.

————. 1991. "The Political Economy of U.S.-Korea Trade Friction in the 1980s: A Korean Perspective." Chapter 2 in this volume.

Krugman, Paul. 1991. "Has the Adjustment Process Worked?" Policy Analyses in International Economics no. 34. Washington, D.C.: Institute for International Economics, October.

Kwack, Sung. 1993. "Sterilization of the Monetary Effects of Current Account Surpluses and Consequences: Korea, 1986–1990." In *Foreign Exchange Rate Policy in Pacific Basin Countries*, organized by R. Glick, Federal Reserve Bank of San Francisco, revised February.

Kwack, Sung, and Jin Kim, Seung. 1990. "Managed Adjustment in the Korean Won-Dollar Exchange Rate: Hypotheses and Empirical Evidence." Unpublished paper. Washington, D.C.: Howard University.

Layman, Thomas. 1988. "Monetary Policy and Financial Reform in Korea." In Hang-

Sheng Cheng, ed., *Monetary Policy in Pacific Basin Developing Countries*. Boston: Kluwer Academic Publishers, pp. 353–79.

Lindner, Deborah. 1991. "Foreign Exchange Policy, Monetary Policy, and Capital Market Liberalization in Korea." Washington, D.C.: Federal Reserve Board. Presented at Allied Social Sciences Association meetings, New Orleans, January 1992.

Nam, Sang-Woo. 1989. "Liberalization of the Korean Financial and Capital Markets." In *Korea's Macroeconomic and Financial Policies*. Seoul: Korea Development Institute, December.

Noland, Marcus. 1990. *Pacific Basin Developing Countries: Prospects for the Future*. Washington, D.C.: Institute for International Economics.

Ohm, Young-Suk. 1991. "U.S.-Korea Trade Relations." National Institute for Economic System and Information. Presented at A New Economic Order: A U.S.-Korea Forum, Woodrow Wilson Center for Scholars, Washington, D.C., June.

Oum, Bongsung. 1989. "Korea's Exchange Rate Policy in the 1980s: Evaluation and Prospects." In *Korea's Macroeconomic and Financial Policies*. Seoul: Korea Development Institute, December.

———. 1991. "Liberalization of Korea's Financial and Capital Markets." Paper presented at New Economic Order: A U.S.-Korea Forum, Washington, D.C., June 25.

Park, Yung Chul. 1993. "The Role of Finance in Economic Development in South Korea and Taiwan." In *Finance and Development: Issues and Experience*, ed. Alberto Giovannini. Cambridge, Eng.: Cambridge University Press for the Centre for Economic Policy Research.

———, and Park, Won-Am. 1990. "Exchange Rate Policy for the East Asian NICs." Korean Development Institute Working Paper no. 9010, May.

Reisen, Helmut, and Yeches, Helen. 1991. "Time-Varying Estimates on the Openness of the Capital Account in Korea and Taiwan." OECD Development Centre Technical Papers no. 42, August. *Journal of Development Economics*, forthcoming.

SaKong, Il. 1989. "The International Economic Position of Korea." In Thomas Bayard and Soo-Gil Young, eds., *Economic Relations between the United States and Korea: Conflict or Cooperation?* Washington, D.C.: Institute for International Economics, Special Report 8, January.

Tavlas, George, and Ozeki, Yuzuru. 1991. "The Japanese Yen as an International Currency." IMF Working Paper WP/91/2. International Monetary Fund, January.

U.S. Department of the Treasury. 1989. "Report to the Congress on International Economic and Exchange Rate Policy." October.

———. 1990a. *National Treatment Study: Report to Congress on Foreign Treatment of U.S. Financial Institutions*. November, pp. 242–71.

———. 1990b. "Report to the Congress on International Economic and Exchange Rate Policy." December.

———. 1991. "Report to the Congress on International Economic and Exchange Rate Policy." May.

Wang, Yen Kyun. 1991. "Exchange Rate and Current Account Balance of Korea and U.S.-Korea Negotiations on Exchange-Rate Policy." Chapter 7 in this volume.

6

Fluctuating Foreign-Exchange Rates and Price Competitiveness

In-June Kim

Introduction

This chapter analyzes the deviation of exchange rates from the long-term equilibrium exchange rate and its impact on the Korean economy. A simple model estimates long-term equilibrium exchange rates, which are defined as exchange rates that maintain the price competitiveness of Korean goods in the world market. That model is then used to compare actual foreign exchange-rates over the past fifteen years with long-term equilibrium exchange rates in order to assess the impact of their deviations from equilibrium exchange rates on the balance of payments.

The Model

The model tries to estimate the long-term equilibrium exchange rates to maintain price competitiveness for Korean goods in the world market. Price competitiveness is achieved with a trading partner when the real exchange rate is held constant. Even if the Korean-U.S. exchange rate is fixed, however, the price competitiveness of Korean goods in the world market will vary with the fluctuation of Korea's exchange rates with its major trading partners because of the magnitude of capital flows. To maintain price competitiveness, the real effective exchange rate should remain constant, but this is not sufficient to maintain price competitiveness. For both traded and nontraded goods, price competitiveness is only guaranteed when the real, effective exchange rates of traded goods are held constant.

The following method estimates the change in the won-dollar exchange rate required to hold the real effective exchange rates of traded goods constant.

In equation (1), the nominal effective exchange rate is defined as the geometric mean of Korea's exchange rates with its trading partners:

$$I = \prod_{i=1}^{n} (E_i)^{w_i}. \tag{1}$$

In the following equations, the subscript i indicates country i. Here, I, E_i, and w_i represent, respectively, nominal effective exchange rate, exchange rate vis-à-vis country i, and weight of country i, which is determined as a share of the trade volume of country i to total trade volume. For convenience, let us assume that $\dot{E}_1$ is the won-dollar exchange rate. After taking the log and differentiating with respect to time, we can derive the rate of change in the foreign-exchange rate with the U.S. dollar that makes the nominal effective exchange rate constant:[1]

$$\dot{E}_1 = \sum_{i=2}^{n} w_i \dot{E}_{i1}, \tag{2}$$

where $\dot{E}_1$ and $\dot{E}_{i1}$ represent the rate of change in the foreign-exchange rate with the U.S. dollar and the rate of change in the exchange rate between the United States and country i, another of Korea's trading partners. As $\dot{E}_{i1}$ increases, the currency of country i depreciates against the U.S. dollar.

The real effective exchange rate is defined as follows:

$$J = \prod_{i=1}^{n} \left(\frac{E_i P_i}{P_0} \right)^{w_i}, \tag{3}$$

where J, P_i, and P_0 are, respectively, the real effective exchange rate, the price level of country i, and Korea's price level. The rate of change in the exchange rate with the U.S. dollar that maintains a constant real effective exchange rate is

$$\dot{E}_1 = (\pi_0 - \pi_1) + \sum_{i=2}^{n} w_i (\pi_1 - \pi_i) + \sum_{i=2}^{n} w_i \dot{E}_{i1}, \tag{4}$$

where π_0, π_1, and π_i represent the inflation rates of Korea, the United States, and country i, respectively. Finally, let us derive the change in foreign exchange rates that makes the real effective exchange rates of traded goods constant. In equation (5), J^T (the superscript T indicates traded goods) represents the real effective exchange rate of traded goods:

$$J^T = \prod_{i=2}^{n} \left(\frac{E_i P_i^T}{P_0^T} \right)^{w_i}. \tag{5}$$

Thus, the rate of change in the exchange rate against a U.S. dollar that makes the real effective exchange rate of traded goods constant is

$$\dot{E}_1 = (\pi_0^T - \pi_1^T) + \sum_{i=2}^{n} w_i (\pi_1^T - \pi_i^T) + \sum_{i=2}^{n} w_i \dot{E}_{i1}, \tag{6}$$

where π_0^T, π_1^T, and π_i^T represent the inflation rates of the traded goods of Korea, the United States, and country i, respectively.

Because there are no data on the inflation rates of both traded and nontraded goods, we relate them to the growth rates of wages and productivity in both sectors. In the event that there should be no significant difference in the growth rate of wages between the two sectors, the inflation rate is linked to the inflation rate of traded goods as follows[2]:

$$\pi = \pi^T + \left(\frac{\theta^N}{\theta} \right) (I^T - I^N), \tag{7}$$

where θ^N, θ, I^T, and I^N indicate the total product of nontraded goods, the total product of both traded and nontraded goods, the growth rate of productivity in the traded sector, and the growth rate of productivity in the nontraded sector, respectively. In equation (7), superscript N indicates nontraded goods.

Substituting (7) into (6), we derive the rate of change in the exchange rate with the U.S. dollar that makes the real effective exchange rates of traded goods constant:

$$\dot{E}_1 = \left[\pi_0 - w_1\pi_1 + w_1 \left(\frac{\theta_1^N}{\theta_1} \right) (l_1^T - l_1^N) - \left(\frac{\theta_0^N}{\theta_0} \right) (l_0^T - l_0^N) \right]$$
$$+ \sum_{i=2}^{n} w_i \left[\left(\frac{\theta_i^N}{\theta_i} \right) (l_i^T - l_i^N) - \pi_i \right] + \sum_{i=2}^{n} w_i \dot{E}_{i1}. \quad (8)$$

From equation (8), we can easily conclude that the rates of change in the exchange rates that maintain price competitiveness depend on the differences in inflation rates between Korea and its trading partners, the gaps in growth rates of productivity between the traded and nontraded sectors, and the rates of changes in exchange rates among trading partners.

Empirical Analysis

Using equation (8), we estimate the long-term equilibrium exchange rate that maintains the real effective exchange rate of traded goods constant. First, we limit our trading partners to the United States, Japan, and Germany. These countries were Korea's major trading partners, and their exchange rates greatly fluctuated during the 1980s. After the cold war, their share of world trade still was very great. The Republic of China on Taiwan was later added to Korea's trading partners.

As for country weights, we calculate the average share of its trade volume in total trade during 1987–1990 and readjust to make the sum of the weights equal to one.

It is difficult to find operational counterparts to the traded and nontraded aggregates in equation (8). Manufacturing, mining, electricity, gas, and water supply were allotted to the traded sector. Wholesale and retail trade; restaurants and hotels; transport, storage, and communication; finance, insurance, real estate and business services; community, social, and personal services were classified into the nontraded sector. Although the agricultural and fishery sectors are heavily protected, about 52 percent of the total supply of agricultural and fishery products is imported from abroad. Therefore, classifying the agricultural and fishery sector poses some difficulty. In the third column of table 1, agricultural and fishery products are classified as traded goods, while in the fourth column, half of agricultural and fishery products were arbitrarily assigned to the trade sector and the other half to the nontraded sector.

To measure the deviation of exchange rates from the long-term equilibrium exchange rate, we must set a base year for the estimation of long-term equilibrium exchange rates. Because Korea was in balance-of-payments equilibrium in 1977 and 1985, those two years seem natural candidates for

Table 1.   Comparison of the Actual Exchange Rate with the Long-Term Equilibrium Exchange Rate

Year	ER	A	A'	B	B'	CA	GR
1977	484	484	484	484	484	12	9.8
1978	484	499	493	500	494	−1085	9.8
1979	484	562	564	563	564	−4151	7.2
1980	607	674	665	673	664	−5321	−3.7
1981	681	709	695	707	692	−4646	5.9
1982	731	769	767	767	765	−2650	7.2
1983	776	761	776	761	774	−1606	12.6
1984	806	762	774	760	772	−1373	9.3
1985	870	773	795	772	792	−887	7.0
1986	881	649	667	650	668	4617	12.9
1987	823	639	656	638	654	9854	13.0
1988	731	653	676	651	672	14161	12.4
1989	671	711	725	694	718	5055	6.8
1990	708	735	759	729	752	−2179	9.0

NOTES:
1. Weights for A and A': United States (0.5060), Japan (0.4221), Germany (0.0719).
2. Weights for B and B': United States (0.4904), Japan (0.4091), Germany (0.0697), Taiwan (0.0309).
3. A and B: Long-term equilibrium exchange rate with agricultural and fishery products classified as traded goods.
4. A' and B': Long-term equilibrium exchange rate with half of agricultural products assigned to trade sector.
5. ER: Actual exchange rate.
6. CA: Current accounts (in million dollars).
7. GR: Growth rate of gross national product (%).

a base year in which price competitiveness was maintained. If we take 1985, we know that in 1988 the Korean won was already overvalued even though the balance-of-payments surplus had peaked. Therefore, we select 1977 as the base year and consider the exchange rate of 1977 to be the long-term equilibrium exchange rate.

Measuring productivity in the traded and nontraded sectors was obtained by dividing output, at constant prices, by the number of people employed in each sector.

We observe that columns 2 and 3 in table 1 show long-term equilibrium exchange rates if the trading partners are the United States, Japan, and Germany. According to column 2, the Korean won was overvalued during 1978–1982, even though the degree of overvaluation was reduced by the exchange rate being devalued in 1980 and 1981. In 1983 no significant gap between the actual exchange rate and the long-term equilibrium exchange rate occurred, and the real effective exchange rate of traded goods of 1983 equaled that of 1977. The actual exchange rate almost converged with the long-term equilibrium exchange rate. Because of time lag and the remaining effects of the 1980 oil shock, the balance of payments was still in the red by a significant amount in 1983. The trend reversed in 1984, and the won became substantially undervalued until 1988, mainly due to the rapid appreciation of the Japanese yen and the deutsche mark. Despite that appreciation, Korea's actual exchange rate moved in the opposite direction, depreciating further against the U.S. dollar. The won's undervaluation became a major factor in explaining Korea's balance-of-payments surplus. The current account was in the red until 1985 but achieved a surplus in 1986, reaching a peak of US$14 billion in 1988.

Because Korea never experienced a current account surplus, the government failed to cope adequately with the new economic situation. The rapid growth of the domestic money supply caused by the sudden influx of foreign currency not only overheated the Korean economy but also led to speculation in real estate that dramatically increased real estate prices. On the positive side, high economic growth also provided room to accommodate labor's wage demands.

As hot money poured in and policies for the gradual liberalization of the exchange rate took hold, the trend reversed: by 1989 the won again became overvalued. That overvaluation was more evident in 1990, as table 1 reveals, and Korea again experienced a current account deficit. The same trend is also demonstrated in column 3 of table 1 when half the agriculture and fishery sector is classified as a traded sector. The size of overvaluation of the Korean won in 1990 was more evident here than when the agricultural and fishery sector is classified as fully traded.

Figures 1 and 2 show that deviations of actual exchange rates from the long-term equilibrium exchange rates significantly influenced Korea's trade balance. In the early 1980s, when the won was overvalued, Korea suffered from a balance-of-payments deficit. The undervaluation of exchange rates contributed materially to a balance-of-payments surplus, but when the exchange rate began to appreciate in 1990, the balance of payments again deteriorated.

Columns 4 and 5 in table 1 show the long-term equilibrium exchange rates when Taiwan is included as a trading partner. That addition makes no significant difference in long-term equilibrium exchange rates.

Figure 1.   Comparison of the Actual Exchange Rate with the
              Long-Term Equilibrium Exchange Rate

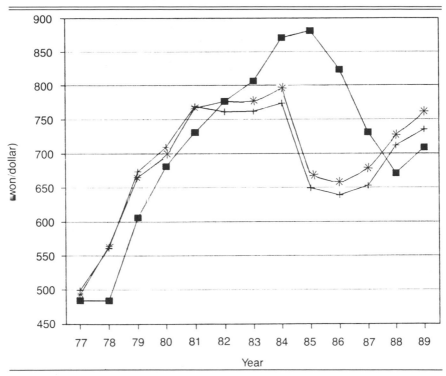

NOTES:
1. ■ : ER drawn from column 1 in table 1.
2. + : A drawn from column 2 in table 1.
3. ✳ : A' drawn from column 3 in table 1.

Conclusion

The model shows that the won's undervaluation in the mid-1980s contributed substantially to the growth of Korea's balance-of-payments surplus. As the foreign-exchange system was liberalized, however, exchange rates converged with the long-term equilibrium exchange rate and then became overvalued.

At the same time, institutional reforms of the foreign-exchange rate system were also undertaken, such as introducing the market-average ex-

Figure 2.   Trend of Current Account

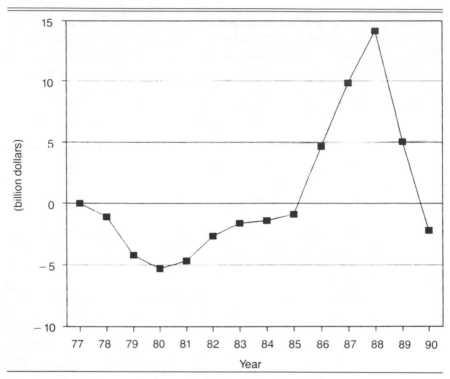

NOTE: 1. ■ : Current account drawn from column 6 in table 1.

change-rate system, relaxing regulations on foreign-exchange concentration, and revising the Foreign Exchange Control Act.

When capital movements were strictly controlled, capital transactions did not significantly affect the exchange rates. With the opening of the stock market to foreign investors in 1992, however, we expect a large inflow of capital into Korea. That inflow will undoubtedly serve to appreciate the won. As the Korean won is already overvalued, that appreciation will further increase the current account deficit (which for 1991 alone is expected to reach US$8 billion).

If the liberalizing of capital movements had been pursued in the late 1980s, when the won was undervalued, Korea would not have been concerned about the won's appreciation and the balance-of-payments problems.

Notes

1. $\log I = \log E_1 + w_2 \log(E_2/E_1) + \cdots + w_n \log(E_n/E_1)$. If we derive $\dot{E}_1$, which makes $\dfrac{d(\log I)}{dt} = 0$, then $\dot{E}_1 = w_2 \dot{E}_{21} + w_3 \dot{E}_{31} + \cdots + w_n \dot{E}_{n1}$.

2. If the growth rate of wage, w, is the same between two sectors, then (i) $\pi^T = w - l^T$, (ii) $\pi^N = w - l^N$. Because the inflation rate is a weighted average of the inflation rates of the traded and nontraded sector, (iii) $\pi = \pi^T + \dfrac{\theta^N}{\theta}(\pi^N - \pi^T)$.

Substituting (i) and (ii) into (iii), we will have $\pi = \pi^T + \dfrac{\theta^N}{\theta}(l^T - l^N)$.

References

Ballassa, B. 1974. "The Purchasing Power Parity Doctrine: A Reappraisal." *Journal of Political Economy* 72: 584–96.

Dornbusch, R. 1987. "Exchange Rate Policy for NICs." KIET Working Paper, March.

———, and Park, Y. C. 1986. "The External Balance of Korea." KDI Working Paper, December.

Feldman, R. A. 1986. *Japanese Financial Markets: Deficits, Dilemmas and Deregulation*. Cambridge, Mass.: MIT Press, pp. 37–78.

Funabashi, Yoichi. 1988. *Managing the Dollar: From the Plaza to the Louvre*. Washington, D.C.: Institute for International Economics.

Hsieh, D. A. 1982. "The Determination of the Real Exchange Rate: The Productivity Approach." *Journal of International Economics* 12: 355–62.

Jwa, Sung-hee. 1987. "Korea's Exchange Rate Policy: System, Effect and Issues." KDI Working Paper, October.

Kwack, S. Y. 1988. "Korea's Exchange Rate Policy in a Changing Economic Environment." *World Development* 1: 169–83.

———. 1987. "Exchange Rate Management of Korea." Korea Development Institute, unpublished manuscript, August.

Loopesko, B., and Johnson, R.A. 1988. "Realignment of the Yen-Dollar Exchange Rates: Aspects of the Adjustment Process in Japan." In R.C. Marston, ed., *Misalignment of Exchange Rates: Effects on Trade and Industry*. Chicago: University of Chicago Press.

Marston, R. C. 1986. "Real Exchange Rate and Productivity Growth in the United States and Japan." NBER Working Paper no. 1922. Cambridge, Mass.: National Bureau of Economic Research.

Officer, L. 1976. *Productivity Bias and Purchasing Power Parity: An Econometric Investigation*. IMF Staff Papers no. 23, pp. 545–79.

Yoshio Suzuki. 1986. *Money, Finance, and Macroeconomic Performance in Japan*. New Haven, Conn.: Yale University Press.

———. 1987. *The Japanese Financial System*. Oxford, Eng.: Clarendon Press.

7

Exchange Rates, Current Account Balance of Korea, and U.S.-Korea Negotiations on Exchange-Rate Policy

Yen-Kyun Wang

Introduction

A rapid increase in exports and investments enabled the Korean economy to maintain high economic growth rates in the 1960s and 1970s but did not avoid double-digit inflation and large, chronic current account deficits.

The government tightly controlled the financial, foreign exchange, and capital markets and rationed loans at regulated interest rates, mainly to government-designated industries. During most of the 1970s, real interest rates were negative. The manufacturing sector and export-related activities also benefited from substantial interest subsidies. These features of the real and financial sectors of the Korean economy yielded considerable inefficiencies and caused structural imbalances in the economy.

Between 1972 and 1981, the Korean economy suffered two major oil price shocks, which also contributed to very high rates of inflation. The average annual growth rate of the wholesale price indexes was 20 percent, and that of consumer price indexes was 17.3 percent. In contrast, the annual average growth rate of gross national product (GNP) during this period was 7.8 percent. After 1981, the rate of annual price increases declined to less than 10 percent owing to favorable external circumstances, strong demand management, and tight income policies.

During the first half of the 1980s, the government's primary economic concern was to reduce the country's large current account deficit and its growing foreign debt (the debt-service ratio exceeded 20 percent). From 1981 to 1986, a policy of depreciating the won was part of a large program to reduce the chronic current account deficit in the face of high domestic inflation.

During the second half of the 1980s, however, Korea was blessed with three new developments: low oil prices, low international interest rates, and the low exchange rate of the won (three lows). From 1986 to 1989, Korea enjoyed substantial current account surpluses, especially with the United States.

In the mid-1980s the United States initiated bilateral negotiations on Korea's financial, foreign exchange, and capital markets. These negotiations led to continued U.S. pressure to expedite a substantial appreciation of the won, which helped bring about a new exchange-rate system, the "market-average-rate" system, which proved more responsive to market forces. More policy changes encouraged the liberalization of the foreign-exchange, financial, and capital markets.

What was the relationship between Korea's new exchange-rate policy and the country's current account balances? How did U.S.-Korean negotiations on Korea's exchange-rate policy influence Korea's exchange rate and its financial and capital markets?

Exchange-Rate Policy and the Current Account Balance in Korea

In January 1980, Korea adopted a currency basket system to replace its dollar-gliding peg system, in which the won's exchange rate was linked to the U.S. dollar and adjusted from time to time to account for inflation-rate differences between Korea and the United States. The major reason for this change was to stabilize the exchange rate of the won vis-à-vis Korea's major trade partner countries. The formula for the currency basket system is as follows:

$$R = \beta \text{ (SDR basket)} + (1-\beta) \text{ (Korea's own basket)} + \alpha,$$

where R is the won/dollar rate and α is a policy variable to account for the relative inflation differential between Korea and abroad, exports and balance-of-payments prospects, and so forth.

The government does not inform the public about either the size of β or

Table 1.   Ratio of α to the Actual Exchange Rate, 1980–88
            (in percent)

1980	1981	1982	1983	1984	1985	1986	1987	1988
−0.2	13.6	24.7	29.1	33.0	38.5	27.5	14.6	−2.4

SOURCE: Based on Tae Woon Kwack, *Choice of the Exchange Rate System in Korea*, Seoul: Korea Economic Research Institute, Federation of Korean Industries, 1990, p. 90.

Korea's own basket and currency weights, but the basket is presumed to include five major currencies: those of the United States, Japan, Germany, the United Kingdom, and Canada. Currency weights are supposed to be based on trade amounts, but the weight attached to the U.S. dollar should be greater than the trade volume between the United States and Korea would imply because the dollar has served as the payment currency for more than 90 percent of external transactions in Korea. More specifically, the won/U.S. dollar exchange rate is determined mainly by two factors: the weighted average change in major trading partners' exchange rates vis-à-vis the U.S. dollar and an adjustment factor based on policy considerations.[1]

Kwack (1990) estimated α (the policy variable) using the 1975–1979 trade weights of the five major trading nations and assuming β = 0.4. The sign of α was computed as

$$\text{actual} \frac{\text{won}}{\$ \text{ exchange rate}} - \beta \text{ (SDR basket)}$$

$$- (1 - \beta) \text{ (Korea's own basket)}.$$

The ratio of α to the actual exchange rate (AER) is seen in table 1. The policy variable increased gradually, reaching 38.4 percent of the exchange rate in 1985, and declined to −2.4 percent in 1988. This evidence shows that policy considerations played a major role in determining exchange rates in Korea during the 1980s (see figure 1).

During the first half of the 1980s, the government's primary economic goal was to curtail the expanding current account deficit and foreign debt (see table 2). In that period, Korea became the fourth-largest debtor among developing countries, and in 1985 the gross foreign debt of $46.7 billion reached 55 percent of Korean GNP.

The government's second major objective was to lower the inflation rate. Both objectives were eventually achieved in 1985 by strong government control over market demand, income distribution, and the declining price of

Figure 1.   Nominal Effective Exchange Rate
             (won/currency basket) (1985 III to 1986 II = 100)

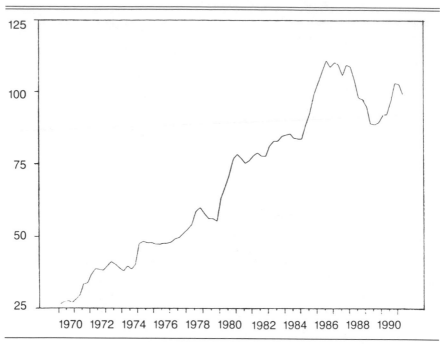

SOURCE: Bank of Korea, *Economic Statistics Yearbook*, various issues.

imports. Korea also continued import liberalization efforts to improve economic efficiency and price stabilization and abolished interest-rate subsidization for export-related industries in 1982.

In 1985, the already mentioned three lows began to have favorable effects
on the Korean economy. Low international interest rates reduced the interest
burden of businesses. The U.S. dollar's depreciation pulled down the value of
the Korean won and appreciated the Japanese yen. The won's nominal
effective exchange rate (NEER) and real effective exchange rate (REER)
dramatically depreciated in 1985 and 1986 (see table 3 and figure 2), making
Korean exports very competitive and creating large current account surpluses
from 1986 to 1989. Gross foreign debt declined from $46.7 billion at the
end of 1985 to $32.8 billion by the end of 1989 (table 2).

The pattern of change in REERs is similar to the pattern of change in
the ratio of trade balance to GNP (figure 3), but the won's NEER and REER

Table 2.   Balance of Payments and Foreign Debt in Korea
(in billions of dollars)

	Current A/C	Trade A/Cª	Gross foreign debt	Net foreign debt	DSRᵇ
1980	− 5.69	− 4.76	29.5	19.5	18.5
1981	− 4.65	− 3.63	33.0	24.2	20.1
1982	− 2.65	− 2.59	37.3	28.2	20.6
1983	− 1.61	− 1.76	40.4	30.8	18.8
1984	− 1.37	− 1.04	42.1	32.9	20.1
1985	− 0.89	− 0.02	47.1	35.5	22.1
1986	4.62	4.21	46.7	32.5	24.0
1987	9.85	7.66	39.8	22.4	27.5
1988	14.16	11.45	35.7	7.3	14.6
1989	5.06	4.60	32.8	3.0	11.4
1990	− 2.17	− 2.00	35.0	4.9	9.4
1991	− 8.73	− 6.98	40.5	13.5	NA

SOURCES: (1) Asian Development Bank, *Key Indicators of Developing Asian and Pacific Countries* 22 (July 1991): 191–93, various issues, Philippines. (2) DSR (1980–85) from Foreign Debt White Paper, Economic Planning Bureau, 1985, Korea, p. 25; DSR (1986–90) from *Asian Development Outlook*, 1989, various issues, Asian Development Bank, Philippines.

ª Free on board basis.

ᵇ Debt Service Ratio (DSR): (principal repayments + interest on long-term short-term payment) ÷ exports of goods and services.

appreciated sharply in 1988 and 1989 (table 3) for the following reasons. First, the U.S. increased pressure on Korea to significantly appreciate the won. Second, the current account surplus increased liquidity, and the rising value of the won attracted large capital inflows that caused rapid inflation in stocks and real estate.

As the result of an overheated economy, growth rates for 1986–1988 were 12.9 percent, 13.0 percent, and 12.4 percent, respectively. Wages increased at an annual rate of about 20 percent during 1988–1990, and labor-management relations were seriously strained by severe conflicts from 1987 to 1990 that lowered both labor productivity and the quality of outputs. The unit labor cost in terms of U.S. dollars increased by 16.2 percent, 25.5 percent, and 36.1 percent in 1987–1989, rates much higher than those in Taiwan and Japan during the same period (table 4). Furthermore, labor shortages in the manufacturing sector became very serious owing to fast growth in other sectors and the construction boom.

Table 3.   Rate of Depreciation of the Won[a] (in percent)

	1985	1986	1987	1988	1989	1990	1991
W/$[b]	7.6	−3.2	−8.0	−13.7	−0.7	5.4	6.2
W/¥[b]	34.2	21.3	19.3	−14.7	−13.8	12.8	14.0
NEER[c]	7.5	18.0	1.2	−6.1	−11.4	6.4	6.4
REER[d]	6.3	14.4	0.4	−7.0	−9.3	4.7	1.5

SOURCES: Korea Development Institute, *KDI Quarterly Economic Outlook* 10, no. 3 (1991): 15; Bank of Korea, *Economic Statistics Yearbook*, various issues.

[a] Minus ( ) means appreciation. A comparison is made based on the annual or quarterly average percentage change over the same period of the previous year.

[b] On an end-of-year basis.

[c] Nominal Effective Exchange Rate: geometric weighted average of the exchange rate of the won to a basket of currencies including the United States, Germany, Japan, France, the United Kingdom, the Netherlands, and Canada.

[d] Real Effective Exchange Rate: NEER ÷ (P_d/P_f) where P_d is the domestic wholesale price index and P_f is the geometric weighted average of the wholesale price indexes of the basket currency countries.

Labor costs in Korea's manufacturing sector became the highest among the four Asian NIEs (Taiwan, Hong Kong, Singapore, and Korea), although per capita income in Korea was approximately half that of Singapore. The current account surplus turned into deficits of $2.17 billion in 1990 and $8.73 billion in 1991, and considerable deficits are expected over the next few years unless the won depreciates significantly.

In the second quarter of 1991, the real effective exchange rate was overvalued by approximately 7 percent using the third quarter of 1985 to the second quarter of 1986, when the current account was in equilibrium, as the base year (figure 2).

As for the international competitiveness of Korean goods, it is much more appropriate to use labor cost indexes rather than wholesale price indexes (WPIs) because when labor costs and production costs increase, imports will increase, and the increase in production costs will not be fully reflected on price increases by international arbitrage.

Certain REERs emerge when the unit labor cost indexes are used in calculating relative prices between Korea and its trade partners (see table 5 and figure 4). The REER of the won turns out to be 30.7 percent overvalued relative to the basket currencies in 1990 (taking 1985 as the base year with an equilibrium exchange rate). This new situation requires that the won be depreciated against the major currencies, wage rates stabilized, and low-cost

Figure 2. Real Effective Exchange Rate
(won/currency basket) (1985 III to 1986 II = 100)

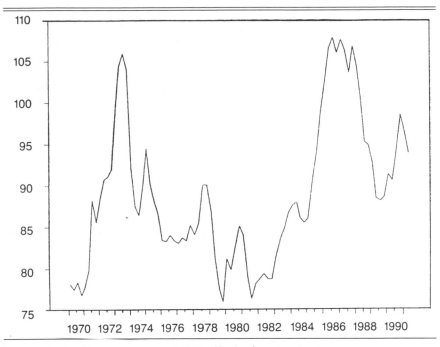

financing extended to trade and export-oriented industries. From these developments it seems that U.S. pressure forced the value of the won to rise too high.

Negotiations and the Deregulation of Exchange Rates

In 1986, Korea's large trade surplus with the United States prompted the American government to ask Korea to negotiate on foreign-exchange rates. The two countries held meetings on this issue in September 1986. In 1987, both the American automobile makers and the National Association of Manufacturers (NAM) asked the Treasury Department to insist that Korea adjust its foreign-exchange rate. The NAM specifically requested that the won be appreciated 15 to 25 percent in 1987.

Figure 3.   REER of the Won and Korea's Trade Balance[a] (1988 = 100)

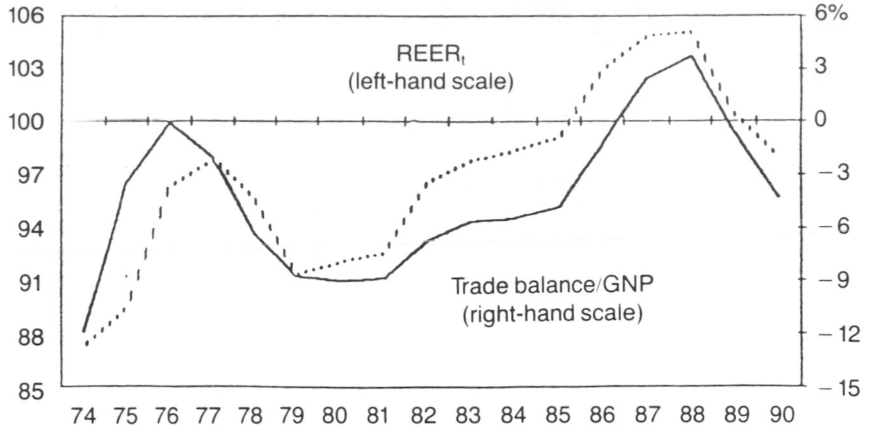

SOURCE: Se Hyung Choi, *A Study on the Exchange Rate Management in the Internationalization Process of the Korean Economy*, Korea Foreign Trade Association, August 1991, p. 75.
[a] $REER_t$ is a three-year moving average = 1/3 ($reer_t$ + $reer_{t-1}$ + $reer_{t-2}$).

In January 1987, Senators Baucus, Moynihan, and Sanford submitted the Fair Currency Exchange Rate and Trade Act of 1987 to Congress. The act requires the secretary of the Treasury to identify exchange-rate-manipulating countries and negotiate with them. If those negotiations did not produce fair exchange rates within six months, the U.S. trade representative would negotiate for trade concessions. If this did not work, the failed negotiations would be reported to Congress so that appropriate retaliatory measures would target Korea (or Taiwan). The Exchange Rate Adjustment Act, introduced by Senator Moynihan, and the Trade Package Act, introduced by Senator Bentsen, also provided for negotiating exchange-rate adjustments.

Lane Kirkland, president of the AFL-CIO, testified before the Senate Finance Committee in January 1987 that the Korean won depreciated by 45 percent between July 1980 and October 1986. At a symposium held by the Institute for International Economics in March 1987, Bela Balassa and John Williamson argued that Korea needed to appreciate its currency by 10 to 15 percent. A 10 percent appreciation of the won would lower exports by $3.5 billion and raise imports by $1.5 billion. In the same month, House Ways and Means chairman Daniel Rostenkowski and Trade Subcommittee chair-

Table 4.   Changes in Unit Labor Costs in the Manufacturing Sector and Exchange Rate (in percent)

	1986	1987	1988	1989	1990	Average 1986–90
Korea						
Wage	9.2	11.6	19.6	25.0	20.2	17.1
Productivity	8.3	2.9	7.5	0.0	8.3	5.4
ULC($)[a]	−0.1	16.2	25.5	36.1	5.3	16.6
W/$[b]	1.3	−6.7	−11.1	−8.1	5.4	−3.8
Taiwan						
Wage	10.1	9.9	10.9	14.6	13.5	11.8
Productivity	11.0	10.5	5.3	9.1	8.4	8.9
ULC($)[a]	4.5	18.2	17.3	13.7	2.8	11.3
NT/$[b]	−5.0	−15.8	−10.2	−7.7	−1.3	−7.5
Japan						
Wage	1.9	2.6	1.8	5.6	4.6	3.3
Productivity	−2.1	8.8	7.0	4.3	3.2	4.2
ULC($)[a]	47.5	9.9	7.3	−5.9	−3.4	11.1
¥/$[b]	−29.3	−14.2	−11.4	7.8	4.9	−8.4

SOURCE: Based on Korea Development Institute, *KDI Quarterly Economic Outlook* 10, no. 3 (1991): 20.
[a] Percentage change in the unit labor cost in terms of the U.S. dollar.
[b] On the basis of the average during the period. Minus (−) means appreciation.

man Sam Gibbons agreed that it might be a good idea to put an "exchange rate equalization tariff" on countries like Korea and Taiwan that pegged their currencies to the dollar. The won appreciation targets requested by the U.S. Treasury Department during 1987–1989 and the actual won appreciation are listed in tables 6 and 7.

Inside U.S. Trade (March 13, 1987) said:

> It's likely that a final Senate trade bill will contain language on exchange rates that would require trade concessions from countries such as Korea and Taiwan if they continue to manipulate their exchange rates after negotiations.

The Korean currency issue is a high priority for the United States, but its actions are somewhat constrained because Korea needs to export in order to pay off its $45 billion foreign debt.[2]

Table 5.   Real and Nominal Effective Exchange Rates
               Using the Unit Labor Cost Indexes (1985 = 100)

	REER	NEER	PPI[a]
1980	84.6	77.7	91.9
1981	93.2	85.3	91.5
1982	87.4	86.4	98.8
1983	89.4	91.6	102.5
1984	97.8	93.4	95.5
1985	100.0	100.0	100.0
1986	123.4	118.8	96.3
1987	115.8	120.7	104.2
1988	97.3	113.1	116.3
1989	73.9	100.3	135.8
1990	69.3	106.9	154.2

SOURCE: Bank of Korea, *Monthly Bulletin*, various issues; IMF, *International Financial Statistics*, various issues; Department of Labor, Bureau of Labor Statistics, various issues; *Monthly Labor Review*, December 1981.

[a] Unit labor cost indexes of Korea ÷ geometric average of unit labor cost indexes of seven trade partner countries.

At the ministerial meetings held in Washington, D.C., in September 1987, Treasury secretary Baker pointed out that between January and September, Taiwan's exchange rate had appreciated by 15.3 percent, Japan's by 10.3 percent, but Korea's by only 6.45 percent. Baker went on to say that the Korean won should be further appreciated.

Korean negotiators responded by asserting that Taiwan has no foreign debt and enjoyed continuous current account surpluses throughout the 1980s but that Korea experienced its first current account surplus in 1986, carried a huge foreign debt, and faced rapid wage and price increases.

Korea held presidential elections in December 1987 and National Assembly elections in April 1988 while preparing for the 1988 Summer Olympics. The government feared that these events would be costly and therefore tried to promote exports and a large reduction of foreign debt. Connected to these policies, the government decided to gradually appreciate the won and win popular compliance. But high domestic interest rates and the expectation of continuous won appreciation caused a large inflow of foreign capital, a jump in the money supply (especially for deposits in nonbank financial institutions), and a steep rise in the prices of stocks and real estate.

These arguments failed to convince the American side, which continued

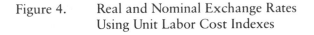

Figure 4.   Real and Nominal Exchange Rates
             Using Unit Labor Cost Indexes

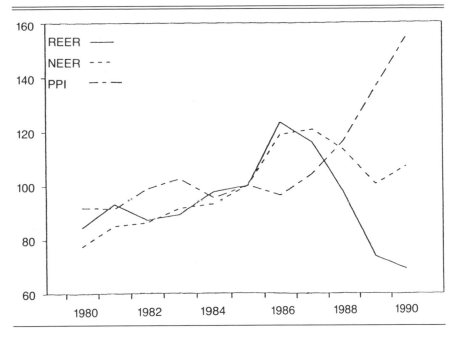

to exert pressure to appreciate the won and reduce the current account surplus with the United States. The Korean government capitulated and relaxed foreign-exchange controls as well as substantially appreciating the won. After the two elections, the won appreciated even more.

Under Section 3004 of the Omnibus Trade and Competitiveness Act of 1988, the U.S. secretary of the Treasury is required to "consider whether countries manipulate the rate of exchange between their currency and the U.S. dollar for purposes of preventing effective balance of payments adjustments or gaining unfair competitive advantage in international trade." The secretary is also required to submit a biannual report to Congress on "International Economies and Exchange Rate Policy."

The October 1988 report judged Korea and Taiwan to have engaged in exchange-rate manipulation as defined by Section 3004, a finding that required the Treasury to negotiate with Korea and Taiwan on a regular basis to adjust their exchange rates. The October report stated:

Table 6.   U.S. Requests for Appreciation of the Won

Negotiation date	Requested rate (end of month, won/dollar, percent)	Realized rate[a] (won/dollar, percent)
April 1987 ADB Meeting	*March–June* 846.9 → 780 (7.9%)	*June* 808.9 (4.5%)
April 1988 Baker and Dallara in Seoul	*March–June* 746.2 → 700 (6.2%)	*June* 728.3 (2.4%)
Dec. 1988 Assistant Treasury Secretary Meetings	Continuous appreciation	
Feb. 1989 Secretary and Minister of Finance Meetings	Appreciation of the won to the appropriate level	
March 1989 Assistant Secretary Meetings	*March–May* 671.9 → 650 (3.3%)	666.7 (0.8%)
April 1989 Assistant Secretary	*March–June* 671.9 → 657 (2.2%)	667.2 (0.7%)
Aug. 1989 Secretary Brady's letter	(1) Continuous appreciation (2) Propose regular meetings on financial and capital markets and exchange rates	

[a] end of each month

The value of the Korean won is established administratively by the Korean authorities based on an undisclosed basket of currencies of Korea's trading partners and on "policy variables," chiefly the balance of payments target. Tight restrictions on capital inflows coupled with severe monetary restraint and close control of the Korean financial sector enhance the authorities' ability to control the exchange rate and limit exchange rate appreciation. Given Korea's strong underlying economic fundamentals, further exchange rate appreciation within a framework of liberalized trade, exchange, and capital controls is clearly required.

The April 1989 report further described subsequent exchange-rate developments and negotiations as follows:

The October 1988 report to Congress and the subsequent initiation of exchange rate negotiations with the Korean authorities stimulated a period

Table 7.   Comparative Appreciation of Major Currencies
            since Plaza Accord
            (September 22, 1985, to end of second quarter, 1989)

	Korea	*Japan*	*Taiwan*
Nominal	32.4%	72.8%	53.3%
Real	18.6%	21.2%	18.4%

SOURCE: Korea Foreign Trade Association, *Korea's Exchange Rate Policy*, September 1989, p. 47.

of more intense apreciation of the won in late 1988. The won appreciated 11.1 percent in 1988 compared with 6.7 percent in 1987

Given the strengthening of the U.S. dollar against the other major currencies in 1988, the won's own appreciation vis-à-vis the U.S. dollar resulted in even greater appreciation against other major currencies. Thus, in 1988, the Korean won began to lose some of the advantage it had gained earlier in the decade. The won's appreciation against most major currencies continued in 1989, particularly with regard to the yen. The cumulative won appreciation still lagged behind that of the yen and the New Taiwan (NT) dollar in key periods. For example, in the interval from the Plaza Agreement in September 1985 to the end of 1988, the won appreciated 34 percent against the U.S. dollar, compared with 49 percent for the NT dollar and 83 percent for the yen. Thus, the won maintained an important, albeit diminished competitive edge.

The U.S. bilateral trade deficit with Korea increased just 1 percent in 1988 to $9.0 billion. This increase was significantly slower than in 1987 when the U.S. bilateral trade deficit with Korea increased 39 percent, from $6.4 billion to $8.9 billion. Korea's 1988 global trade surplus increased 51 percent to $11.6 billion on a balance of payments basis, and the current account surplus increased 44 percent to $14.3 billion.

The cumulative exchange rate appreciation, however, remains insufficient and there are no assurances that the won will appreciate further. In addition, Korea has not indicated that it intends to move to a market-based system of exchange rate administration over the medium term. Nor is Korea willing to engage in broader discussions on financial market liberalization. Therefore, our judgment is that, within the meaning of Section 3004 of the Omnibus Trade and Competitiveness Act, Korea continues to "manipulate" its currency.[3]

In late 1988, the Korean government decided to join the IMF Clause VIII countries, which were expected to liberalize receipts and payments originating from current account transactions, and to loosen some foreign-exchange controls. The Korean government also announced a program to liberalize some interest rates on bank deposits. That liberalization, however, did not start until November 1991.

The won appreciated by 8.1 percent, but a year-end comparison showed that it appreciated 0.66 percent in 1989. As a consequence, Korea's current account surplus dropped 64 percent, to $5.1 billion (2.5 percent of GNP) in 1989, compared with $14.2 billion (8.4 percent of GNP) in 1988. Its trade surplus also fell 61 percent, to $4.5 billion, compared with $11.4 billion in 1988, and the U.S. trade deficit with Korea fell 30 percent, to $6.3 billion.

In September 1989, the Korean Foreign Trade Association (KFTA) distributed a report entitled "Korea's Exchange Rate Policy" to the U.S. government, Congress, mass media, research institutes, various political groups in the United States, and many Korean organizations. One month before the October report to Congress was released, the KFTA report stated that the Treasury's designation of Korea as a "currency manipulator" was unjustified and could damage trade relations.

The report argued the following. First, Korea did not manipulate its currency any more than other countries. Its trading system alone could not be used as evidence of intent to gain unfair trade advantage. Second, Korea has not had "significant" or "sustained" surpluses. Its surpluses of 1986–1988 were the first after almost four decades of chronic, massive trade deficits. Finally, Korea's surpluses lasted only for a short period and were necessary to correct the huge imbalances created by years of massive trade deficits. Even these short-term surpluses rapidly disappeared.

The KFTA report also pointed out that since the Plaza Accord (September 22, 1985), the won had appreciated in real terms as much as the new Taiwanese dollar and only slightly less than the Japanese yen (table 7). The October 1989 Treasury report, however, designated only Korea for the third time as an exchange-rate-manipulating country, citing evidence of the won's insufficient appreciation, weak market forces in Korea, and widespread capital and interest rate controls that helped the government "manipulate" the exchange rate. The Korean government now worried that the U.S. trade representative might interpret Korea's exchange-rate operation as an export subsidy and retaliate.

On March 2, 1990, Korea introduced the "market-average exchange rate" system, in which the won/dollar exchange rate at the beginning of each business day was set at the weighted average of the transaction rate in the interbank market on the preceding business day. Exchange rates between the won and third currencies were set in accordance with dollar rates in international currency markets. During each business day the won/dollar interbank rate was permitted to fluctuate ±0.4 percent. Foreign-exchange banks were free to set customer rates within a range of ±0.4 percent for won/dollar telegraphic transactions and of ±0.8 percent for won/third-currency telegraphic transactions. The range for interbank and customer rates was widened to ±0.6 percent in September 1991. The U.S. Treasury Department responded by saying that more liberalization was necessary to give greater scope to market forces.

In February 1990 the Ministry of Finance and the Treasury Department began financial policy talks to help U.S. banks and securities firms gain access to the Korean financial services market. These talks encouraged further liberalization of Korea's financial, foreign-exchange, and capital markets. The April 1990 Treasury Department report to Congress finally concluded that Korea was no longer directly "manipulating" the won, giving these reasons. First, Korea had introduced a "market-average exchange rate" system. Second, the Korean government did not conduct transactions in the interbank market to influence the exchange rate directly. Third, Korean wage rates had rapidly increased, and the current account surplus had become a deficit during the first quarter of 1990. The cumulative current account deficit amounted to $2.2 billion in 1990. The U.S. bilateral trade deficit with Korea in 1990 fell to $4.1 billion, down 38 percent from 1989. The won depreciated 5.4 percent in 1990.

The Korean government eased certain foreign-exchange and capital controls in March 1990. The Treasury's October 1990 report, however, pointed out the following:

> The various controls and restrictions on foreign exchange and capital flows prevent market forces of supply and demand from playing a fully effective role in exchange rate determination and provide the Korean authorities with tools for indirectly "manipulating" the exchange rate. One of the most onerous controls is the requirement that foreign exchange banks obtain and review, prior to entering into most foreign exchange transactions, original documentation of an underlying commercial transaction. This "real demand" rule seriously hampers the development of Korea's foreign exchange market.[4]

In October 1991 the Korean government announced a plan to reform the strict 1961 foreign-exchange management law from the current prescriptive system to a proscriptive one that would regulate foreign-exchange transactions only in exceptional cases; however, foreign-exchange transactions related to capital movements in general would still be regulated. The Korean capital market was to be opened to a limited extent to foreigners from January 1992 onward.

Treasury secretary Nicholas F. Brady proposed regular discussions about Korea's financial markets, capital markets, and exchange-rate policy. Following three such financial policy talks between the United States and Korea,[5] the Korean government enacted measures to further liberalize the financial and foreign exchange markets by (1) expanding the ceiling on foreign-exchange holdings by foreign-exchange banks (September 1989); (2) establishing a dollar call market (December 1989); (3) introducing the market-average exchange-rate system (March 1990); (4) establishing a yen call market (March 1991) and liberalizing the foreign-exchange concentration system in such particulars as deposits of foreign exchange (May 1991); (5) relaxing overbought and oversold positions on foreign exchange and deregulating spot and forward foreign-exchange transactions (July 1991); and (6) liberalizing interest rates on some deposits and loans (November 1991). Immediately after deregulation, interest rates on liberalized loans increased about 2 percent and interest rates on liberalized deposits jumped about 1 percent. This first significant stage of interest-rate liberalization is scheduled to be completed around 1997.

Moreover, the Ministry of Finance took concrete measures in 1990 to improve the treatment of foreign financial institutions in Korea. These steps included raising the ceiling on the issuance of certificates of deposit by foreign banks, eliminating the ceiling on foreign banks' paid-in capital in Korea, and extending the operating hours of cash dispenser machines. However, foreign financial institutions are not yet treated on an equal footing with Korean firms.[6]

The November 1991 Treasury report to Congress emphasized the need for faster financial liberalization:

> Most troubling at this stage is that the Korean government appears to lack a "vision" and well-defined strategy for broader liberalization of its tightly controlled financial markets. Recently announced plans for the deregulation of interest rates, liberalization of foreign exchange controls, and the opening of Korea's capital markets are steps in the right direction, but do not appear to go fast enough or to be part of a coordinated strategy. The Treasury Department has called on the Korean government to develop and publish a comprehensive blueprint with clear timetables for the full liberalization of its financial sector.

There are limits to the speed with which the Korean government can liberalize financial markets. First, the government wants high rates of economic growth, higher than 7 percent a year, but liberalization of the financial markets and higher interest rates will ruin many marginal businesses and reduce investment. The business cycle has constantly pressured the government to maintain interest rates lower than the liberalized rates. Second, Korean banks carry a large portion of bad debts in their portfolios and are thus reluctant to see rapid liberalization of the financial market and face keen domestic and international competition.

Conclusion

Korea's efforts to reduce its chronic current account deficits and its large foreign debt during the 1980s conflicted with U.S. interests during the second half of the 1980s. The movement of exchange rates, especially the won's real effective exchange rates, significantly affected Korea's current account balances.

U.S.-Korea negotiations on exchange rates and financial, foreign-exchange, and capital markets have expedited deregulation in those markets. The won's exchange rate and real effective exchange rate were substantially overvalued by the end of 1991, spawning substantial current account deficits. Intense U.S. pressure was a major factor in the rapid appreciation of the won in 1988 and 1989.

Currently, Korea's exchange rate is closely linked to the short-term funds market. Because interest rates are controlled and the short-term funds market is limited, when the funds market becomes tight, banks sell foreign currencies, driving up the won exchange rate. In such cases, government intervention is needed to stabilize the REER. Furthermore, liberalizing the foreign-exchange market and modulating exchange rates should be implemented as the financial market is deregulated. Therefore, financial policy talks between the United States and Korea, along with the Uruguay Round of GATT talks, are very helpful in developing Korea's financial markets.

Notes

1. Once the won/U.S. dollar rate is determined, the exchange rates of the won vis-à-vis other currencies are determined by cross rates.

2. *Inside U.S. Trade*, March 13, 1987.

3. Department of the Treasury, *Report to the Congress on the International Economics and Exchange Rate Policy*, April 1989.

4. Department of the Treasury, *International Economic and Exchange Rate Policy*, November 1991.

5. These talks were held on February 26, 1990, October 31, 1990, and May 22, 1991.

6. Department of the Treasury, *International Economic and Exchange Rate Policy*, May 1991.

References

Asian Development Bank. 1988. *Key Indicators of Developing Member Countries of ABD* 19 (July).

Bank of Korea. 1991. *Monthly Bulletin*, October.

————. 1991. *Foreign Exchange System in Korea*, March.

Choi, Se Hyung. 1991. *A Study on the Foreign Exchange Rate Management in the Internationalization Process of the Korea Economy*. Seoul: Korea Foreign Trade Association, August.

Hong, Kap Soo. 1990. "An Analysis of the Correction between the Exchange Rate and Call Market Interest Rates under the Market Average Exchange Rate System." *Financial Economy Review*, no. 15 (August), Bank of Korea.

Korea Development Institute. 1991. *KDI Quarterly Economic Outlook* 10, nos. 1, 3/4.

Kwack, Tae Woon. 1990. *A Proposal for Choice of Foreign Exchange Rate System*. Seoul: Korea Economic Research Institute.

Oum, Bong Sung. 1991. "Korea's Exchange Rate Policy in the 1980s: Evaluation and Prospects." *Korea's Macroeconomic and Financial Policies*. Korea Development Institute, December.

Park, Won Am. 1989. "An Empirical Analysis of the Current Account Surplus of Korea." *Korea Development Review* 11, no. 2 (Summer), Korea Development Institute.

U.S. Dept. of the Treasury. Semiannual. *International Economic and Exchange Rate Policy*, various issues, 1988–1991. April 1989, October 1989, April 1990, October 1990, May 1991, November 1991.

Wang, Yen Kyun. 1990. *Foreign Exchange Liberalization and Development Policy of the Forward Foreign Exchange in Korea*. Seoul: Korea Chamber of Commerce and Industry, June.

————, and Kim, Wan-Soon. 1990. "A Reform of the Foreign Exchange Market and Foreign Exchange Rate Determination Policy in Korea with Foreign Exchange Policy Experiences of Taiwan." *Asian Economic Journal* 1, no. 1 (March), Osaka International University.

Williamson, John, and Balassa, Bela. 1990. *Adjusting Success: Balance of Payments Policy in the East Asian NIEs*. Washington, D.C.: Institute of International Economics, May.

PART FOUR

OTHER PERSPECTIVES

8

Politicizing Trade Issues and U.S. Business in Korea

Hi-Taek Shin

Lately, the trade relationship between the Republic of Korea and the United States has been politicized by acrimonious disputes, with the U.S. side taking the offensive posture. How have American businesses and their political activities, individually and collectively through organizations such as the American Chamber of Commerce, influenced bilateral trade relations over the last decade? What have been the factors underlying these disputes, and which measures have been utilized by the U.S. side to resolve bilateral trade disputes?[1]

Underlying Factors of the Disputes

Formal Barriers

U.S. businesspeople who want to do business in Korea perceive certain barriers that interfere with their operations.

Korean regulations. One of their strongest complaints is that Korean regulations, whether or not by design, discriminate against foreign business. They point out that numerous Korean regulations are relatively unsophisticated and vague, giving strong discretionary powers to those enforcing them.

Such action has a chilling effect on businesspeople who are uncertain how the regulations are to be interpreted and how the regulators use their discretionary powers. Another problem is the wide discrepancy between the written regulations and their enforcement. There may be several reasons for this.

First, sanctions for violating the regulations are often less severe in Korea than in the United States. Therefore, some Korean companies are more willing to risk getting caught. Second, Korean regulatory agencies do not have sufficient personnel to monitor the business community and take punitive action. Third, Korean authorities may be willing to overlook violations because they believe the regulations are sometimes unfair or unnecessarily burdensome. However, foreign businesspeople who are required to comply with the laws in their home countries, often under threat of severe sanctions for violations, are inclined to follow the letter of the law and heed the unenforced regulations. Such behavior increases their costs of doing business.

Some U.S. businesses also have complained that Korean regulators have a hidden agenda and discriminate against them when applying their regulatory powers. Common complaints are that regulators reject or unduly delay applications for permits or licenses filed by U.S. businesses that would have been readily acceptable if filed by Korean companies or that regulators selectively enforce certain laws against foreign businesses. Of course, there are no data to confirm these charges, but the foreign business community strongly believes that to be the case.

Foreign businesses in Korea also complain that, even when regulations are clear, the regulatory authority is unknown. When a foreign business has a problem that needs to be addressed by a Korean regulatory agency, Korean regulators often respond by saying that, although they recognize a problem exists, they lack the authority to do anything. In other cases, more than one regulatory agency may claim authority to intervene.

Such perceptions may be valid for some Korean regulations and bureaucrats. But neither Korean regulations nor Korean bureaucrats are designed to discriminate against foreign businesses. Korea has not had sufficient time to develop and refine its regulations or to build rational administrative rulings or to hold enough court cases to interpret the regulations. In addition, modern Korea, which has a long tradition of strong Confucian bureaucracy, has been dominated by a "bureaucratic elitism" in which well-educated, intelligent government officials determine, both formally and informally, the operation of the private economy. Korean businesses willingly accepted their paternalistic regulations.

American companies, unfamiliar with such regulations, are skeptical of Korean bureaucrats. Actions perfectly understandable to Koreans may seem unfair or discriminatory to American businesspeople's standards. Although the ministries and agencies regulating foreign businesses understand the need to reform Korean regulations, such changes will come slowly.

Informal Barriers

Sometimes informal barriers to trade make the formal barriers worse.

Communication difficulties. One of the most significant impediments for U.S. businesses is dialogue with Korean regulators. English is taught in Korean schools as a major foreign language, but in general Korean regulators have little or no command of English. Most U.S. business executives do not speak Korean. Official translations of Korean laws and regulations are often not readily available, and U.S. businesspeople must hire translators. Moreover, incorrect translations often cause considerable misunderstanding.

Another complicating factor is the cultural differences between Koreans and Americans. Most American businesspeople are unfamiliar with Korean customs and social conventions. Well-intended acts by Americans may be interpreted by Koreans as rude or arrogant, which can discourage Korean officials' help. Similarly, Koreans may not effectively communicate with U.S. businesspeople because they misunderstand American behavior.

Some problems are self-inflicted by American businesses. Koreans feel that many U.S. businesspeople are arrogant and act as if they are above the Korean law. A good example is the recent exit ban imposed on foreigners against whom criminal charges have been filed and against whom criminal investigations are pending. Many of these criminal charges arise from business dealings between foreign businesspeople and their Korean counterparts or employees. Some Americans who have not been allowed to leave Korea have complained to the U.S. government.

The exit ban has its legal basis in the Entry and Exit Control Law and applies to both foreigners and Koreans likely to flee criminal prosecutions. Although it may be true that certain criminal complaints have been filed in order to harass foreign businesspeople and that the authorities may not have exercised proper discretion in some cases,[2] shifting the issue to the diplomatic level is seen by many Koreans as foreigners' lack of respect for Korean laws.

Admittedly, U.S. businesses have made substantial efforts to address language and cultural problems. They have hired many Koreans, some educated in America, and taken the advice of Korean counsel. However, the fundamental problem still exists: those with the ultimate power to decide, with few exceptions, neither speak Korean nor understand Korea's culture. This situation indicates a certain insensitivity by U.S. businesses. It is hard to imagine Korean companies sending executives to their American branches or subsidiaries who are unfamiliar with English or American culture.

Of course, this comparison is not necessarily fair because of the disparity between Korean and English as a means for business communications and the relative economic, cultural, and political power of Korea and the United States. It is more difficult for U.S. companies to find American managers who speak fluent Korean and understand Korea than it is for Korean companies to find Korean managers who speak fluent English and understand America. Yet U.S. businesses should give their executives in Korea extensive education and training in that country's language and culture.

Another factor contributing to politicizing business issues in Korea is that some U.S. businesspeople sent to Korea are simply not up to the task of conducting business there. Many problems and perceived barriers encountered by American businesses can be satisfactorily solved through local channels without violating legal or ethical standards. Instead of relying on local remedies, which require persistence and resourcefulness, some American businesspeople eagerly rely on diplomatic means to resolve their problems.

Another sensitive issue is the alleged corruption of Korean administrative officials. It is difficult to estimate how widespread corruption is in Korea or what happens to a company unwilling to "play the game." But many Americans feel that the Foreign Corrupt Practices Act penalizes American companies and businesspersons who have bribed foreign officials and that, because of their ethical standards, American companies are at a disadvantage vis-à-vis their counterparts when they compete for licenses or permits, seek exemption from restrictions, or negotiate with the Korean government. Because successful cases of bribery are rarely discovered, it is impossible to determine the accuracy of these concerns.

American Businesses Respond

When American businesspeople encounter unfair regulatory authorities who deny them licenses or permits or impose additional costs, they can appeal to officials, seek court action, or ask for political assistance. Some U.S. companies have been very successful in such efforts.[3]

Political Remedies through U.S. Government Channels

Despite the availability of domestic remedies and their successful use by some American companies, by and large domestic remedies are considered ineffectual. Thus most U.S. companies prefer using U.S. government channels to solve their problems.

American companies often ask the U.S. embassy in Korea to pressure the Korean government either to open Korean markets or to solve their difficulties. Or these same companies will use political channels in the United States to pressure the Korean government.

The American Chamber of Commerce (AmCham) in Korea has extensive political and diplomatic connections. Organized as a business and cultural information source for American businesspeople in Korea, one of its most important functions is to link American businesses in Korea to the U.S. government. The officers meet every month with the U.S. ambassador to Korea. AmCham members also send "door-knock teams" to the United States to visit American senators and representatives as well as executive officials. At those meetings AmCham asks the U.S. government to take action to remove hidden trade barriers. Many Koreans have responded by accusing AmCham of being a spy organization and engaging in inappropriate political activities.

In addition, AmCham publishes booklets highly critical, sometimes even mocking, of Korean laws, regulations, and regulatory agencies.[4] Many Koreans perceive that AmCham improperly acts as a political pressure group. Moreover, its controversial publications have made it a favorite target of the Korean press and public.

Yet many Koreans also admit the constructive, positive functions of AmCham, seeing AmCham as a means of resolving trade problems at the domestic level. The Korean government also receives early warnings of the important issues to be discussed in Korea-U.S. trade talks. Because AmCham is familiar with Korea's economic and social situation, it can influence U.S. trade policy-making toward Korea that is inappropriate or misinformed.

Some Consequences

Shifting certain business issues to the diplomatic level sometimes produces solutions. Some good examples include the market opening for beef, wine, tobacco, life insurance, and travel agents as well as improved business conditions for American bank branches in Korea. The Korean government also has used these publicized cases to rationalize Korean regulations, streamline its bureaucracy, and eliminate agencies having vested interests in the regulatory system.

Although the political resolution of trade disputes has solved some specific issues, the ultimate benefits for American companies can be small or slow in coming owing to the potential institutional resentment of the particular Korean government agencies. A good example is the Korean insurance market. In 1986, Korea agreed to open its insurance market to American life insurance companies after extreme political pressure from the U.S. side using Article 301 of the 1974 Trade Act. By late 1986, however, Korea had only licensed the LINA Corporation to conduct life insurance business in

Korea. American insurance companies believed that the Korean government had intentionally excluded AIG companies because of American strong-arm tactics.[5] The Korean government finally granted a license to the AIG companies in June 1987.

It is impossible to confirm whether licensing was delayed for the reasons the AIG companies suspected, yet as the once-powerful president's office in Korea relinquishes its power, individual regulatory agencies are able to retaliate against American companies. Those implementing agencies, often more nationalistic than the Korean trade negotiators, have a different view of the benefits of market liberalization. Therefore, top-level agreements between the U.S. and Korean governments do not guarantee that all regulatory agencies will treat American businesses fairly.

Another serious problem for U.S. businesses is the "free ride" effect. After the U.S. government has opened Korean markets through bilateral negotiations at some political costs, American businesses often find that they are less competitive than other foreign firms because of the most-favored-nation provisions of the General Agreement on Tariffs and Trade (GATT). After Korea opened most of its markets to manufactured goods, the real beneficiary of market opening, some Korean officials believe, was Japan. Similar effects have been observed in the beef market. After the U.S. government forced Korea to open its beef market by threatening to use Article 301, Australia and New Zealand quickly dominated the Korean beef market. Most Korean regulators believe that the free ride problem will apply to the financial and agricultural sectors.

Conclusion

Although the Korean language, culture, and unfair regulations have hindered American business activities, there is more the Korean government can do. Its officials can rationalize regulations and control their regulators. They can coordinate administrative agencies to guarantee that agreements with the United States are fully implemented and agencies cannot undermine those agreements by subterfuge. Such actions can help restore the credibility of Korean officials in American eyes.

U.S. businesses, however, can help increase understanding on Korea's side through the press and other channels, including AmCham, by arguing the merits of free trade. In addition, U.S. businesses and AmCham must tone down their accusatory rhetoric in press releases and information booklets. U.S. businesses also should recognize that Korean trade officials, especially in top levels of government, usually act in good faith, and they should be sensitive to the difficulties these negotiators face when accommodating both foreign pressure to open Korean markets and domestic pressure to restrict imports.

U.S. businesses also might resolve some of their problems by using local remedies before relying on diplomatic channels or other pressure tactics. U.S. companies ought to be certain their cases are not frivolous and have not originated from mere misunderstanding. The U.S. side could choose its market-opening targets more carefully. Market-opening disputes involve high political cost. U.S. businesses that pressure their government should first be sure their products are competitive with Korean products as well as other foreign products. It does not make sense for the U.S. to spend its political capital if others gain the market before their business firms can do so.

Finally, the U.S. side could demonstrate more sensitivity about the political situation in Korea. For example, the ten million people who still live on agriculture in Korea feel strongly about Korea feeding itself.[7] Continued attempts by the United States to open up the rice market will be met by violent opposition in Korea. The cultural significance of rice for Koreans will hinder negotiations between the two sides.

Notes

1. Although the writer has been personally involved in some of the cases discussed in this paper, specific details of the cases herein consist only of information that is publicly available.

2. For example, with respect to the foreign businesspeople named in criminal complaints, Korean authorities might have released them after obtaining a bond from them or their companies.

3. Most notably in the intellectual property protection area, several U.S. companies were successful in having the infringers of their intellectual property rights, including copyrights, criminally sanctioned by the Korean courts. These companies include Prentice-Hall and Appleton & Lange.

4. Some titles of the booklets are *Pillars of Protectionism in Korea* and *Fair Shake for American Finished Products for the 1990s: Tariff, Non-Tariff, and Structural Barriers in the Korean Market.*

5. U.S. Park, *Tongsang Machal ui Hyunjang* (Scenes of Trade Conflicts), p. 346. Seoul: Maeil/Economic Daily, 1988.

7. Most Koreans, who have long experienced the pains and the embarrassment of their nation not having the agricultural capacity to feed itself, consider this a national security issue.

9

The Perspective of U.S. Businesses in Korea

Marion Spina

The first American businessman to enter Korea after diplomatic relations were established in 1882 died within several days of his arrival, and his shipment of cargo disappeared. The Japanese consul identified the second American businessman as a "beggar-like fellow" who barely survived by peddling canned beans out of a hovel in which he died alone and ignored. The third American businessman, Walter Davis Townsend, spent several years in Japan before coming to Korea. In Korea, he learned how to contact the U.S. government representative for political assistance whenever his business ventures seemed threatened by official inaction and corruption. Walter Davis Townsend remained in Korea for thirty years and successfully managed businesses that have long since disappeared. His activities included gold mining, weapons sales, oil distribution, banking, insurance, real estate speculation, and selling medicine.[1]

One episode in Townsend's career is relevant for Americans conducting business in today's Korea. Townsend had purchased a house in Inchon, which Korean officials used as a telegraph station. When Townsend arrived in Inchon, he demanded that the officials vacate the house. They refused. The officials insisted that they needed the dwelling to perform their duties and that, because Townsend had another house in the city, he could live there. Although the legal owner of the house, Townsend could not occupy it. After exhausting all efforts to remove the officials, Townsend asked the U.S. consul for help. The U.S. consul wrote letters to the local officials and then to their superiors but never received any reply. Finally, he wrote to the commodore of a U.S. naval vessel stationed in Japan, requesting his assistance to force the Korean government to respond. A letter from a Korean official quickly followed, explaining that, it being midwinter, the officials could not leave Townsend's house because of the cold weather. In the spring, however, the officials evacuated the house without any explanation. Townsend's later requests for payment of rent were never answered.

This example set a pattern familiar to American businesspeople: they ask the U.S. government's help to negotiate with the Korean government, and the Korean government remains unresponsive until threatened with dire consequences. Even now, the typical American businessperson will state without equivocation that "the Koreans" (lumping businesspeople with government players) will not move until "hit on the head with a two-by-four."

Meanwhile, the Koreans wonder why a country as large and rich as the United States would bother to request anything from a small and insignificant country like Korea. How could anything in the Hermit Kingdom be of significance to such a distant, giant country? Intransigent nonresponses (such as "we can't do that because this is Korea") suggest the Koreans do not take the U.S. government demands seriously because those demands are so numerous and typically so petty.

Many examples in the last ten years reflect the Townsend pattern and suggest that each side judges the other as evil. Consider these examples. The recent foreign-exchange valuation dispute caused much ill will on both sides. To the Koreans it seemed yet another example of American bullying, while to the Americans it seemed insincere procrastination by the Koreans. The disputes originating from U.S. pressures to open the Korean markets for beef, motion pictures, cigarettes, alcohol, and (of course) life insurance (necessary before consuming the foregoing wholesome imported items) were ultimately resolved but only after much recrimination on both sides. Whatever goodwill the Koreans gained after meeting U.S. demands, the American side still believed the Koreans had not complied in good faith. Even after U.S. companies benefited from a more open Korean market, Korean public anger nullified some of those gains.

Ironically, when Korean officials met with American Chamber of Commerce representatives in 1988, the highest-ranking Korean official listened to the complaints and then said his government could act if the American side would supply detailed information on a specific-case basis. (In fairness to the Korean official, he did not ask the American Chamber of Commerce to distribute its detailed complaints to every member of the U.S. Congress and government.)

U.S.-Korean trade indeed did become politicized in the 1980s. Everyone agrees that the Koreans perceived the United States as bullies and that the

United States perceived the Koreans as insincere. U.S. officials view themselves as fair and cannot accept the bully label, insisting that America only wants fair access to Korean market, as Koreans have free access to American markets. Korean officials consider themselves as sincere and insist that they are making their best efforts to cope with difficult problems that require time to resolve. Both sides wish that trade issues could be separated from political process.

On the one hand, as many essays in this volume show, the United States did bully Korea. The United States adopted antidumping actions without fearing retaliation and worrying about due process. The United States applied Section 301 to Korea to open specific markets because it had the power to do so. The partial opening of Korea's land transport market in 1991, after years of demands by the United States, came because of the severe sanctions taken in the United States to harm Korean shipping companies.[6]

On the other hand, Korea has been insincere. The Koreans negotiate as a means to delay until the other side either gives up or threatens to act. This method of negotiation, well known to Korean entrepreneurs, has cultural underpinnings. Korean officials' claims of liberalizing financial markets but delaying because they must make difficult political adjustments are unbelievable when the government then raises taxes on real estate holdings that foreigners own. The Korean government often releases information on trade disputes to the local press to cover up the government's failure to take timely measures to comply with international obligations. This tactic misleads the Korean public, which then believes that the United States is unfairly pushing Korea to comply with its demands.

Korean officials sometimes raise the infant industry argument but ignore mentioning that Korea lacks the institutional infrastructure to accommodate foreign participation in specific sectors (e.g., financial services, telecommunications services, distribution businesses). Perhaps Korea does not wish to make the infrastructure issue the center of discussion because it fears the public will ask why its government has not reduced tax evasion or corruption.

For both sides, politicizing trade issues has become a convenient way to build up inexpensive domestic political capital. On the U.S. side, bullying Korea allows the U.S. government to show the American public that it is doing something meaningful to correct unfair trade behavior by foreign countries. The U.S. government can do that because it is afraid to bully Japan. The Koreans understand this very well. The Korean side announces difficulties in complying with U.S. pressure to open various markets to divert attention away from its failed economic policies and the corruption at every level of government as well as the wide disparity of income distribution.

Thus, both governments politicize trade issues. Most Americans believe that the Koreans are unreliable and unfair trading partners; most Koreans believe that the Americans are rapacious colonists intent on squeezing Korea's national wealth by exploiting its markets at the point of a gun.

To avoid the politicization of trade, I suggest the following:

1. U.S. officials should refrain from bullying, and Korean officials should desist from insincerity. The United States might refrain from making demands on Korea for market opening and cease applying antidumping duties. Korea could stop being insincere by declaring its honest position on specific bilateral issues and by faithfully implementing its obligations to liberalize markets. Each side should address its domestic economic and political problems without reference to the foreign scapegoat. Unfortunately, both sides stand to gain if they can win more domestic approval. For that reason, neither side will solve the problem by abandoning its current negotiation style.

2. The United States can try to persuade the Korean people it is not bullying, and Korea can try to persuade the American people it is not insincere. This approach is also beyond the capacity of the two governments because they would be trying to persuade the people to believe something that is not true.

3. The two governments could be more selective about the disputed issues. For example, the United States could decide not to promote market liberalization for products such as cigarettes and alcohol, which harm people. Such a decision would be altruistic and noble. The United States could also refrain from demanding a currency revaluation, which, even in the best case, would not likely substantially benefit the U.S. economy. Korea, meanwhile, could faithfully implement the agreements concluded.

4. The two countries could intensify their efforts at resolving specific disputes at the company or industry level. Korea might try to accommodate foreigners who are at a disadvantage in a nonlitigious society with a small court system. The United States might try to ensure that Korean companies are duly protected against or compensated for frivolous or excessively long-term antidumping procedures.

5. The two countries might establish methods of ensuring more balanced reporting about disputes. The Koreans' complaints about AmCham publications on trade issues are similar to the Americans' complaints about inaccurate reporting in the Korean press. AmCham exists to promote bilateral trade. It could receive Korean businesspeople's complaints about U.S. restrictions on Korean exports to the United States and articulate complaints, along with complaints about Korean gov-

ernment restrictions on U.S. business in Korea. The United States also might find better means to discuss trade issues in the Korean media.

6. Finally, other channels of communication between the U.S. and Korean governments, involving private organizations and individuals, might promote better understanding and defuse unnecessary controversy.

One writer[7] suggested that implementing a free trade agreement between Korea and the United States might reduce trade friction. At this time, a free trade agreement between the United States and Korea is probably inappropriate to reduce politicization of bilateral trade disputes. Korea has already lifted many formal restrictions on imports and allowed foreign businesses to expand in Korea; the remaining obstacles impeding U.S. penetration of the Korean market are associated with the weak institutional infrastructure of Korea. For example, even if a market is officially liberalized, Korea's primitive financial system operates only to restrict businesses, particularly foreign businesses. If both countries agree to free trade agreements and U.S. businesses have difficulty in entering or operating in the Korean market, trade issues could become more politicized.

Notes

1. See generally Harold F. Cook, *Pioneer American Businessman: The Life and Times of Walter Davis Townsend*, 1981. Seoul: Seoul Computer Press for the Royal Asiatic Society, Korea Branch.

2. Marcus Noland, chapter 1, this volume.

3. Kihwan Kim, chapter 2, this volume, and Noland, chapter 1, this volume.

4. Hi-Taek Shin, chapter 8, this volume.

5. Deuk-Hwan Yu, "The Influence of Noneconomic Factors on U.S.-Korean Trade Relations" (Paper delivered U.S.-Korea Economic Relations Conference, Hoover Institution, Stanford, California, December 5–7, 1991), p. 7.

6. The Federal Maritime Commission proposed a rule by which Korean flag carriers would face a $100,000 per voyage fee when they call on U.S. ports as a countervailing measure against unfavorable Korean laws that restrict U.S. companies who wished to engage in the transportation business. The proposed rulemaking proceeding was suspended, not terminated, upon agreement by the Korean government to open specific portions of the land transportation market to U.S. carriers.

7. Kihwan Kim, chapter 2, this volume.

10

A New Approach to Korea-U.S. Economic Relations

Okyu Kwon

The preceding chapters have reviewed the politicization of Korea-U.S. trade and the efforts to resolve the ensuing difficulties. As Korea-U.S. relations have a long history, reducing trade and financial frictions between the two countries is paramount for this partnership to improve. How might that be done?

Reexamining Korea-U.S. Economic Relations

Economic relations between Korea and the United States have expanded in both quantity and quality. The rapid increase in bilateral trade volume to $36.3 billion in 1990 from a mere $150 million in 1960 shows the strong interdependence between the two economies. That bilateral economic relationship has also included investment, technology transfer, and capital transactions.[1] Various types of frictions are bound to arise when bilateral economic relations expand so rapidly, and that was especially true in the 1980s. But in the 1990s tensions have been relatively low. This improved situation can be partly attributed to the resolutions of major bilateral trade issues by reliance on Section 301 or super 301 consultations since the mid-1980s.[2] Another factor was the substantial reduction of Korea's trade surplus with the United States, shifting from $9.6 billion in 1987, then to a trade balance, and finally into a deficit in 1991.

From the U.S. perspective, Korea's trade deficit cannot justify a rollback of market-opening policy. The U.S. government argues that there must be new institutions, customs, and legal systems commensurate with Korea's position in the international economic arena and that Korea's trade deficit owes much to greater imports of investment goods, which will eventually contribute to Korea's future growth.

U.S. domestic politics have also forced the U.S. administration to strengthen its pressures on the Asian export-oriented economies. This trend accelerated as American negotiations with Japan turned out to be unsatisfactory for the U.S. side.

There is a widespread perception in the U.S. Congress, the administration, and even the press that Korea and Japan have the same development strategy and trade policies. Many even believe that Korea is a second Japan. Such a shared perception might be why U.S. pressure seems to have been more assertive on Korea than other Asian countries.

From the Korean perspective, however, Korea's shift to a trade deficit is more a structural problem. I offer these two reasons. First, Korea's sluggish export to the United States is expected to continue, having recorded negative growth rates for the past three years. This slide in Korea's export is apparent in almost all its major export items to the United States such as textiles, shoes, electric and electronic equipment, and automobiles. The slowdown is partly due to the U.S. recession but, more fundamentally, to the loss of competitiveness of Korean products in the U.S. market.

Second, Korea's import from the United States will continue to grow in the future. In particular, the import of machinery and electric and electronics equipment is rapidly increasing; these items are necessary for Korea's economic structural adjustments.

But Korea's situation differs widely from that of Japan and Taiwan, which have maintained and even increased their trade surpluses with the United States. Korea also differs from China and those ASEAN nations whose trade surpluses with the United States have dramatically increased in recent years. Considering that Korea's bilateral trade deficit with the United States will persist for some period, Korea can legitimately argue that the United States should consider Korea's recent performance in its policy.

If the United States continues to pressure the Korean government without considering these broadly changing trade relations, substantial resistance from the Korean side will arise and advocates of liberalization within the Korean government will face greater difficulties to push market-opening policies.

Is Korea a second Japan? The Korean side maintains that the two countries are significantly different in many ways: their levels of income and pattern of development; their development strategy; their general attitudes toward market opening. Korea's GNP is only one-fifth that of Japan. Although both countries are heavily dependent on trade, Korea does not accumulate foreign exchange. In addition, Korean firms are suffering from the more competitive Japanese firms just as many U.S. companies are.

Resolving Korea-U.S. Economic Frictions

Considering the high volume and great diversity of Korea-U.S. trade, several prescriptions can be offered to resolve these frictions:

1. Multilateral negotiations: the Uruguay Round and three-way negotiations including Japan

2. A systematic approach: a SII (Strategic Impediment Initiative), a free trade agreement, or common report making

3. Firm-based microapproach: pursuit of local remedies

4. Greater efforts for mutual understanding: cultural and social exchanges

5. Enhancing the role of government officials

Let us consider these separately.

Multilateral Negotiations

Because the bilateral relationship with the United States is inherently unilateral and Korea does not have any meaningful leverage against the United States, the idea of multilateral negotiation is attractive for Korea. If many smaller countries cooperate in multilateral negotiations, bilateral pressure from more powerful countries can be diffused. This advantage of the multilateral approach does not seem to apply to Korea and the United States because the United States has brought many multilateral issues to the bilateral negotiation table. It is Korea's perception that the United States uses the Korean card in negotiations with other powerful counterparts such as Japan or the EC by first obtaining Korea's cooperation.

The U.S. government urges Korea to cooperate in many key areas such as the agricultural sector, service sector, trade-related intellectual properties, and so forth. The Korean government already has initiated a painstaking campaign to convince its people that the successful conclusion of the Uruguay Round is in Korea's best interest and has for the most part prevailed in obtaining general consensus. Pressure from the United States is constraining the Korean government's ability to persuade its people to accept the outcomes of the multilateral negotiations. For example, the United States insists on opening Korea's rice market so as to isolate the EC in agricultural negotiations. However, this politically sensitive and serious issue is very difficult for the Korean people to accept.[3]

The Korean government understands the U.S. position in the Uruguay Round and its concerns for successfully completing the round by pressuring participating countries, including Korea. Korea is just as eager to successfully conclude the round, if not more so. The United States need not excessively pressure countries such as Korea, which seeks a resolution but has little bargaining power. In agricultural negotiations, Korea should make every effort to make structural adjustments, regardless of U.S. pressure. In this sense, the United States does not need to pressure Korea on agricultural issues. If, on the contrary, the United States continues to push Korea, the United States will be censured by the Korean people.

It may be useful to consider Korea's suggestion that, if the Uruguay Round proves to facilitate free trade rather than reflecting the interests of advanced countries, the political compromise and mutual exception of one or two politically sensitive items of each country should be accepted. These compromises would not undermine the basic goal of the Uruguay Round or international free trade but, rather, might hasten the round to achieve a swift, successful conclusion.

As for three-way talks including Japan, the United States and Korea would agree on many points. However, Japan might be reluctant to join such negotiations if the two other countries appear to agree on means to rectify their trade imbalances with Japan rather than achieve three-way cooperation between the countries. For Korea, this approach might require a complete review of the Korean trade system in a three-way perspective. For example, the import diversification system of Korea, which is favorable to the United States, might be changed or lifted, which is by no means advantageous to the United States. Nevertheless, in terms of exchange-rate policy, the three countries have much to discuss.

A Systematic Approach

SII talks may be justifiable between the United States and Japan, but no serious structural imbalance exists between Korea and the United States as between Japan and the United States. The U.S. government is unhappy with the outcome of the SII talks with Japan. Therefore, this approach does not seem to be desirable from Korea's standpoint.[4]

As for a free trade agreement (FTA), further discussions are necessary. In the Uruguay Round, the United States suggested the zero-for-zero tariff rate approach in limited areas such as steel, fishery, furniture, electronics, paper, and construction equipment. The Korean government announced that it would join the steel area in full scale and for construction equipment on a partial scale. For the other industries, the Korean government cannot make any definite decisions until further studies have been made concerning objections from domestic industries. On the matter of zero-for-zero tariff setting, any FTA will require tremendous study and efforts on both sides, as in the case of the North American FTA. Therefore, the FTA is a policy option requiring enormous time and study. Despite its distinct merits, FTA discussions are still restricted to academic circles. Both countries will require a substantial period of time to review the consequences of agreeing to an FTA.

The third method, common report making, was originally raised by the United States. It can be regarded as a small-scale SII-type discussion related to a specific sector. During President Bush's visit to Korea in January 1992, the United States suggested this approach: to study and recommend ways to solve problems by forming joint working groups and making joint recommendations. Some suggested areas include customs and import clearance, standards and rule making, and investment. This approach may help expedite Korea's internationalization, especially in the day-to-day handling of working-level government officials.

The Korean government is expected to agree to this approach even if the United States had not suggested it. The Korean government would still undertake structural reforms to internationalize its economic system, including its institutions, laws, and customs. In other words, whenever minor problems occur in the daily routine of business, the Korean government will investigate their underlying causes and resolve them according to international standards. By doing so, similar problems may not occur again in the future. In any case, this approach could preempt the escalation of trade tensions at an early stage.

Firm-based Microapproach

Many U.S. firms in Korea, when facing difficulties in doing business, do not resolve these issues by their own initiative. Instead, they resort to diplomatic channels. Much of the agenda in the Trade Action Group (TAG) meeting[5] concerns the daily operation of doing business.

To solve such problems, the firm-based approach may be appropriate. Japanese firms, for instance, never raise the issues that U.S. firms do because Japanese firms usually seek local remedies and resolve problems at the working level, thereby avoiding the use of political means at the diplomatic level.

Seeking local remedies to solve trade issues is important from a firm's viewpoint; in fact, many firms admit that they may have "won the battle but lost the war" after a tedious and time-consuming negotiation process. Instead of resorting to diplomatic channels between the two governments, which politicizes trade issues, this approach is more promising. Both countries then avoid political tensions and minimize unexpected harmful effects on business-people.

Greater Efforts for Mutual Understanding

The importance of social and cultural factors in trade negotiations cannot be denied. Many trade frictions between two countries become unnecessarily serious because of the ignorance of each side's social behavior and cultural values. Expanding channels for communication and exchange of ideas can help to resolve bilateral trade frictions in their early stage, but this approach takes time. Official channels between the two governments can be improved to include new links between legislators, businesspeople, scholars, and interest groups.

Enhancing the Role of Government Officials

In many ways, U.S. trade policy can be seen as responding to constituents' pressure.[6] The U.S. Congress tends to respond most sensitively to the interests of constituents, because members of Congress face reelection every two years. Moreover, politicians strongly advance their initiatives because they believe such action will enable them to be reelected. The U.S. administration, not to mention Congress, operates with a short time frame because it worries about its political constituencies. As a result, the U.S. administration tends to pursue a short-sighted trade policy that may not promote the long-term interests of national welfare. A Korean proverb is applicable here: One who sees a tree in detail may not be able to see the forest. Therefore, government officials in each country should look at the substance of the issues and consider the overall national welfare on a long-term basis.

The Korean government abides by a basic policy line of internationalization. Regardless of the changing external environment, Korea will pursue liberalization for its own sake. Currently, Korea's comparative advantage is shifting toward technologically advanced industries. This structural adjustment process cannot continue because of domestic forces only; it requires foreign competition.

For example, economic power concentration, labor disputes, and equitable income distribution have become public disputes because both the elite and the public believe that the rich earn their wealth through illegitimate means. By encouraging more foreign competition and undertaking reform, such suspicions might disappear. Therefore, structural adjustment must be accompanied by domestic policy reform along with internationalization, just as in the USSR *perestroika* could not proceed without *glasnost'*.

It might be in the best interest of the United States for its administration officials who handle international negotiations to consider the long-term perspective of U.S. national welfare. For example, the United States has repeatedly expressed frustration about disputes involving customs clearance standards. The Korean side regards these as minor issues that will be resolved as soon as the Korean government allocates greater resources to those areas. U.S. pressure and effort might expedite this change, but more time will be required to change Korea's legal system, customs, and attitudes. The time frame I consider reasonable is not large, only a year or two. Therefore, these issues need not be a major area of focus in Korea-U.S. economic cooperation. Rather, the main area of cooperation should be in areas constructive and beneficial to both sides, such as technological cooperation. As business firms in both countries are suffering from weak competitiveness, exploring greater opportunities for technological cooperation and joint ventures can be beneficial. But this creative action cannot be taken up by the U.S. administration if it always responds to the political constituencies. There is a great opportunity for officials of both countries to work together and achieve fruitful results.

Notes

1. As of December 1991, the United States remains the largest capital-exporting country to Korea, comprising 21 percent of Korea's total capital inflow, and the second-largest direct investment and technology inducement country in Korea, second to Japan.

2. Through pressure generated from Section 301, market access issues for cigarettes (May 1988), wine (January 1989), beef (March 1990), insurance (March 1988), advertisement and films (December 1988) were solved. Through super 301, the liberalization of agricultural products and the process of lifting investment restrictions began. Import restrictions based on localization policies were also lifted. Through special 301, negotiations have almost solved telecommunications issues. For the financial market, the financial policy talk is continuing since its start in February 1990.

3. Korea is still a developing country in its agricultural sector. The agricultural sector in Korea accounts for 9.2 percent of GNP and 18.3 percent of total employment. What is more significant is that rural households are heavily dependent on their revenue from rice, about 49.4 percent of their total income on the average.

4. U.S. officials also excluded the possibility of SII-type approaches between Korea

and the United States for the near future. They mentioned at the conference that after the North American FTA, the next most likely countries to make an FTA with the United States would be either South American countries such as Chile or Singapore.

5. TAG is a monthly meeting between Korean government officials and U.S. embassy staff. It aims at the early settlement of trade issues before they can become serious due to overpoliticization.

6. There are many hypotheses on what is policy. The private interest models assert that it is a result of the struggle among competing special interests. If we adopt the public interest models, policy is formulated either by constituencies or market failure. See Peter Narvarro, *The Policy Game: How Special Interests and Ideologues Are Stealing America* (New York: Wiley, 1984), pp 3–10.

Index